Latin American Monographs

Second Series

Emancipation, Sugar, and Federalism

Barbados and the West Indies, 1833–1876

25

Center for Latin American Studies
University of Florida

Emancipation, Sugar, and Federalism:

Barbados and the West Indies, 1833–1876

Claude Levy

A University of Florida Book

UNIVERSITY PRESSES OF FLORIDA
FAMU / FAU / FIU / FSU / UCF / UF / UNF / USF / UWF
Gainesville

Latin American Monographs—Second Series

Library of Congress Cataloging in Publication Data

Levy, Claude, 1924–
    Emancipation, sugar, and federalism.

    (Latin American monographs; 2d ser., 25)
    "A University of Florida book."
    Bibliography: P.
    Includes index.
    1. Slavery in Barbados—History. 2. Slavery
—Emancipation—History. 3. Sugar trade—
Barbados—History. 4. Barbados—Economic
conditions. 5. Barbados—Politics and govern-
ment. I. Title. II. Series: Florida. Univer-
sity, Gainesville. Center for Latin American
Studies. Latin American monographs; 2d ser., 25.
HT1105.B3L48   301.44'93'0972981   79–18084
ISBN 0–8130–0655–4

A University of Florida Book sponsored by the Center for Latin American
Studies

University Presses of Florida is the central agency for scholarly publishing of
the State of Florida's university system. Its offices are located at 15 NW 15th
Street, Gainesville, FL 32603. Works published by University Presses of
Florida are evaluated and selected for publication by a faculty editorial
committee of any one of Florida's nine public universities: Florida A&M
University (Tallahassee), Florida Atlantic University (Boca Raton), Florida
International University (Miami), Florida State University (Tallahassee),
University of Central Florida (Orlando), University of Florida (Gainesville),
University of North Florida (Jacksonville), University of South Florida
(Tampa), University of West Florida (Pensacola).

PRINTED IN U.S.A.

Preface

THE HISTORY of the West Indies is rich in color, especially the narratives of the early explorers and settlers who first made their way into the Caribbean Sea. During succeeding centuries many travelers also recorded impressions of various islands, but only in relatively recent times have serious scholars given attention to the important political, social, and economic realities of the area. Such scholarly studies may appear less exciting than writings of a more romantic character, but these works are necessary to bring into focus a unique way of life and set of conditions in the West Indies. The statistical information enables historians and social scientists to visualize the actual conditions of the region and its inhabitants. With this goal in mind, I have sought out facts pertaining to the volume of the crops, the cost of food, the level of wages, and other topics of practical significance.

This account of Barbados concentrates on conditions and trends from 1833 to 1876. These dates encompass a period during which the planters of Barbados were thought to have attained their greatest prosperity, notwithstanding several major crises that confronted them in the nineteenth century. The Negro masses did not share in the good fortune of the planters; on the contrary, these were times of intense hardships for many blacks.

There were three big problems in the West Indies after 1834: the circumstances of the aftermath of emancipation, the modification of preferential duties on British colonial sugar, and the failure of self-government throughout most of the former slave colonies. Barbados benefitted from an absence of the calamities that arose in the other islands, where many basic habits and institutions were altered as a consequence of the troubled times. Its unique achievements explain why Barbadian leaders opposed all efforts to join the island with its less favored neighbors in the Caribbean Sea. A short time after the federation crisis of 1876, another serious problem appeared, the result of the rise of the sugar beet industry in North America and Europe. The increased supply of sugar caused markedly reduced prices throughout the world, making it increasingly difficult for West Indian growers to compete with the massive quantities of cheap sugar being produced elsewhere. This burden, added to the federation crisis, brought an end to the uncommon prosperity which Barbados had enjoyed after slavery, and the island gradually sank to the economic level of the other struggling British colonies in the Caribbean Sea.

With the completion of this work, I would like to thank several individuals who have supported me in various ways. I am especially indebted to the late Professor Lowell J. Ragatz of Ohio State University, who watched over my endeavors from beginning to end, and I am grateful also to Professor Vincent Todd Harlow, now deceased, who persuaded me many years ago to begin my research at Oxford. A warm expression of appreciation is deserved by H. A. Vaughan, Esq., Barrister-at-Law, for providing a number of interesting materials from Barbados. My friend and colleague Dr. Cary Wintz was kind enough to read several versions of the manuscript. I am greatly indebted to the librarians and staff members of the Bodleian Library (Oxford), British Museum (London), United Society for the Propagation of the Gospel (London), Public Record Office (London), West India Committee (London), Barbados Museum and Historical Society (St. Ann's Garrison), Barbados Public Library (Bridgetown), Library of Congress (Washington), and the Heartman Collection of Texas Southern University (Houston). I am not personally acquainted with Professor Jerome S. Handler of Southern Illinois University, but I am nevertheless thankful to him for the outstanding example he has set as a scholar of Barbadian culture and society. Last, I come to the family members without whose unselfish support and encouragement this work would not have been possible: my mother, Suzanne, played an important part by arranging for the microfilming of numerous materials in London, and my wife, Doreen, was a faithful source of devotion, patience, and wisdom throughout the long task. It is to the late Professor Ragatz and to the love and labor of these two women that I gratefully dedicate my efforts.

Engravings are reproduced from Robert H. Schomburgk, *The History of Barbados* (London: Longman, Brown, Green, and Longmans, 1848). Maps are drawn by Doreen Levy.

Contents

My very chains and I grew friends,
So much a long communion tends
To make us what we are;—even I
Regained my freedom with a sigh.

Lord Byron

1. Prelude to Emancipation in Barbados, 1627–1833

DURING the two centuries between the European settlement of the West Indies and the parliamentary abolition of slavery in 1833, British humanitarians endeavored to improve the status of the black man in the colonies. As early as 1671, when the founder of the Quaker sect, George Fox, came to Barbados in person, he pleaded for leniency toward the Negroes and recommended that their owners let them go free "after a considerable term of years, if they have served them faithfully."[1]* He deeply annoyed local proprietors, who pressed for various laws against the Quakers, including one which fined them for not attending militia drills that contravened their belief in pacifism. After sentencing a Friend to death for blasphemy, an early governor ordered the furnishings of the Quaker meetinghouse thrown out and the doors and windows nailed shut.[2] The local gentry, meanwhile, assured themselves that humanitarians in Great Britain had not necessarily agreed on emancipation as their ultimate goal; as long as plantation products continued to create large profits for British investors, the proprietors believed that they were in a favorable position to ignore antislavery agitation. But even in the most profitable days of slavery, the planters always reacted uneasily when critics in the home country berated the system of labor on which their livelihood depended.

Slavery in Barbados went back to the initial settlement of 1627, when the number of Africans was put at ten or less, though accounts conflicted. It is

* Notes begin on page 161.

1

believed that such Africans were already regarded as slaves, but the full legal definition of slavery was unclear for some time. Records also show thirty-two Indians among the original settlers, but the red man adapted poorly to forced labor and Indian bondage eventually died out.[3]

In its formative stage, Barbados was a typical, raw frontier colony. The majority of its inhabitants understandably came from a class that aspired to improve its economic status and was attracted to Barbados by stories of the land's prodigious ability to grow an almost endless variety of exotic crops. The most accessible parts of the island were soon privately acquired from the various controlling officials, and the colony thus obtained its first generation of estate owners. The land itself had to be cleared of dense rain forest, and most of this work was performed by indentured British laborers, who came in great numbers during the 1630s. Their exact number is obscured by contradictory records.

These early efforts in Barbados were aimed at the growth of tobacco as the main money crop. But growers in Virginia and Maryland had already secured control of the market, and the initial high price of tobacco was sinking. To make matters worse, the Barbadian product was notoriously poor in quality, and the indentured laborers and many of the planters were disinclined to the rigors of tropical agriculture. There was little incentive to work, because the island abounded with wild pigs, fowl, and fruit. No elaborate housing was needed; heavy drinking was universal, and almost everyone was idle. Barbados' failure as a tobacco colony was soon evident.[4]

By 1643, however, many Barbadians were already aware of a salutary change as a result of the adoption of sugar rather than tobacco as the main crop. Dutch entrepreneurs from Brazil had a large part in introducing Barbadians to the technology, capital, labor, and machinery necessary for the large-scale production of sugar. The Dutch had many reasons for concentrating their efforts on Barbados: they feared losing their foothold in Pernambuco to the Portuguese; Barbados was a generation ahead of the other British West Indian colonies in social and economic development, and, once cleared of its original jungle overgrowth, it had arable land; such places as the Leeward Islands were too small for crops that required much land, and Jamaica, though large enough, was still held by the Spanish, who were at war with the Dutch. This was a crucial time to begin cane production—no Caribbean territory provided sugar for Europe, where tea and coffee drinking had made sugar a greater necessity than tobacco in every household.[5]

The need to create in Barbados an economic system capable of meeting the increased demand for sugar impelled several important alterations in local economic institutions. There had to be organized a massive force of unskilled workers capable of sustaining the monotonous drudgery of planting, tending, and cutting fields of cane. A smaller force of trained laborers was also needed, to perform the nonagricultural duties connected with the manufacture of sugar. Dunn has explained why workers in both categories were likely to be Negroes. Barbadian planters already had a reputation for cruelty to white indentured laborers, which made it increasingly difficult after 1640 for them to procure workers in the home country. Moreover, indentured laborers were unwilling to work for their original employers after the expiration of their contracts, but a black slave was the permanent property of his purchaser. He was cheaper to feed and clothe than a white person. In addition, the African Negro was already a farmer, experienced with the hoe and other simple farm tools and acquainted with the needs and use of livestock. He was familiar with the tropical climate and with the food that was customary in such places. But, most important, the Negro, though sometimes rebellious, was more easily subjected to the hardships and indignities of servile labor than was the white man.[6]

The planters of Barbados were the first British proprietors in the West Indies to import slaves on a large scale. By 1660 Dutch slave traders were being excluded from the British colonies, and within a few years Charles II began to charter slave companies in Great Britain, the most famous of which was the Royal Africa Company. Barbados enjoyed an important voice in the company's affairs, because several of its important inhabitants were major shareholders. Following the revolution of 1688 the new monarch, William III, allowed other investors in England and Scotland to share in this traffic, but the arrangements continued to give the planters of Barbados special advantages. By this time a strong demand for slaves had arisen in Jamaica, but British slavers, as in the past, brought their cargoes mainly to Barbados and often refused to travel the additional distance to the western part of the Caribbean Sea. This meant that Barbadian estates had a choice of the most desirable Negroes at the lowest cost.[7]

Monoculture was another feature of the plantation system in Barbados after 1640. Planters began to concentrate almost every shilling, acre, and worker on sugar production. Such a habit made it necessary for the inhabitants to depend on outside suppliers; intermittent food shortages had a harmful effect, particularly on the slaves. When circumstances in world sugar markets changed during the eighteenth and nineteenth centuries, Barbadian planters saw fit from time to time to augment their production of food crops.[8]

The most important characteristic of the West Indian plantation system was its need for large infusions of capital, which British commercial firms selectively loaned to the planters to enable them to purchase slaves and the elaborate machinery required to manufacture sugar from cane juice. As the number of heavily capitalized estates expanded in Barbados, the number of small landholders dwindled. The uncertainty of early records in Barbados makes it difficult to estimate the numerical distribution of landholders or to gauge the size of their holdings. Handler has cited figures showing that the number of small properties declined from more than 11,000 in the 1640s to 2,639 in 1679. As a result, the island's sugar industry was controlled by about 300 wealthy planters, whose holdings amounted to 300 or more acres each. This concentration of economic power was accompanied by a massive exodus of whites, most of them former indentured laborers, who left to seek opportunities in other parts of the Americas. The number of European descendants in Barbados declined from approximately 37,000 in 1640 to little more than 3,500 in 1712, while several authorities suggest that the number of Negroes increased from a few hundred in the 1630s to about 47,000 in 1683.[9]

The dwindling white minority of Barbados, like its counterpart in the Leeward Islands and other neighboring French and Spanish possessions, never forgot that the preponderance of slaves was a constant threat to their lives and property, but the promise of acquiring great wealth from sugar overcame their fears. By 1655 a British visitor commented on the results of introducing cane plants: Barbados was "one of the Riches Spotes of ground in the wordell and fully inhabited.... The Illand is but small; but it maintains more souls than any peese of land of the bignis in the wordell."[10] When Father Jean Labat stopped at Barbados in 1700, he was startled to find large shops stocked with luxuries from Europe and Asia. Goldsmiths, jewelers, and watchmakers enjoyed a prosperous living, Labat wrote, and the principal city, Bridgetown, had an appearance of cleanliness, gentility, and opulence that was unknown elsewhere in the West Indies. A few years later, John Oldmixon concluded that the planters and merchants of Barbados lived in greater splendor than many wealthy noblemen in England.[11]

These accounts eventually caused humanitarians to suspect that slaves in Barbados were being severely exploited, and British leaders visualized the planters' mansions and the Negroes' huts as contrasting symbols of wealth and deprivation. Such generalizations were greatly oversimplified. Undoubtedly, the fitness of the slave quarters varied from one estate to another and from colony to colony. Probably the most elaborate slave dwellings were located in Jamaica, where Matthew Lewis found a number of large cottages, wattled without, plastered within, and with a hermitage-like appearance. But there were also many cottages in Jamaica that were inferior in size and sturdiness to those in Barbados. According to Oldmixon, every Barbadian estate was like a neat "little African City, and the planter's House like the Sovereign's in the midst of it."[12] But the reckless destruction of native timber by the early settlers made it necessary for many slave cottages in Barbados to be constructed of mud and plantain leaves, uncomfortable during the rainy season, and the paucity of land meant that the houses had to be closely grouped. Even the small spaces separating the cottages were filled with poultry, livestock, and vegetable patches, which produced an uneasy sense of tightness that was not seen in the other islands.

As different as planter and slave were in their social and economic circumstances, all Barbadians were joined by common experience with hurricanes, heat, and tropical humidity. Whites and blacks alike suffered from a lack of drinking water, which the planters drew from rusty cisterns and the Negroes and cattle drank from muddy ponds. Both races knew the discomforts caused by ants, flies, and mosquitoes; all were the victims of expatriation, solitude, boredom, and languishing vigor. Following a visit to Barbados in 1803, Daniel McKinnen commented glumly on the meager and sickly appearance of the slaves and the planters, a condition he attributed to the harmful effects of the climate.[13]

In addition to the planters and workers, there was a class of poor whites in Barbados. Popularly referred to as "red-legs," such whites were brought to the island to satisfy the provisions of a local deficiency act of 1697, which required estate owners to provide one white militiaman for every sixty slaves on their properties. The law likewise obliged the planters to equip each militiaman with a house and plot of ground. Because of the scarcity of white females, the planters were unable to supply them with wives of their own race, which prompted the red-legs to take black concubines, some of whom were slaves. Contemporary accounts differed in assessing the usefulness of the white militiamen as a counterweight to the teeming majority of blacks. According to some writers, they served a purpose in thwarting rebellion, but many humanitarians were convinced that they caused much trouble by stealing food from the slaves, scorning blacks as inferiors, and forcing their Negro women to perform more work at home than the planters expected from them in the fields.[14]

British abolitionists had other reasons to complain of the ill treatment of the blacks, but the most notorious example of the planters' harsh policy was the Barbadian act, extensively imitated in the other colonies, exonerating any slaveowner for killing or maiming a wayward Negro. The law imposed a fine of £15 "if any man of wantonness or only of bloody-mindedness kill a negro or other slave," especially if the deed was committed without provocation. Such a penalty failed to deter acts of brutality, however infrequent it was sometimes argued they were. In 1804, Governor Seaforth expressed concern that the killing of blacks was more common than observers had previously thought. In the following year the legislature finally passed an act making the murder of a slave a capital offense, but the law was hedged with so many qualifications that it had little effect. Its provisions were that the slayer had to commit the crime maliciously, wantonly, and without provocation, facts which had to be proven by the testimony of white witnesses only. Occasionally, a planter was accused under these provisions, only to be discharged by the grand jury because of what was ruled to be insufficient evidence. The absence of workable restraints on slaveowners continued to cause concern at the Colonial Office, which finally dispatched a special commissioner in 1822 to investigate the problem throughout the West Indies. The resulting report was disturbing to the officials in London. From every standpoint, the author declared, the Barbadian slaveowner, more than any other proprietor in the sugar colonies, was restricted by no law other than his own conscience. He conceded that "no man or set of men...has [the] power to call him to account for working his slave as much as he pleases; for chaining; for starving him." It was not until 1826 that the first white person accused of beating a Negro to death was convicted in a Barbadian court, and his penalty was only a few weeks in prison.[15]

One of the most pressing needs of the white minority in Barbados was measures to insure their safety in the midst of the blacks. The council and assembly early enacted a number of statutes to restrict the conduct of the workers, but copies of such acts soon disappeared or survived only in fragmentary form. In 1661 the legislature codified existing practices into a comprehensive slave law containing the basic regulations that governed the blacks for many years thereafter. The same measure, with a few exceptions, was reaffirmed by the Barbadian Legislature in 1676 and in 1682. But the general statute of 1688 explained more fully that such special provisions were necessary for Africans, whose "barbarous, wild, and savage nature" required strict supervision to restrain the "Disorder, Rapines, and Inhumanities to which they are naturally prone and inclined."[16] The planters were allowed to exercise such complete authority that a slave could not marry, own property, discipline his children, or attend dances or funerals without his owner's consent. Laws specified that a bondsman could not leave the estate without a written pass, nor could he beat drums, possess firearms, or engage in commerce without permission. The guilt or innocence of blacks accused of violating the regulations was determined exclusively by the owner, who customarily imposed such penalties as whipping, branding, nose-slitting, and castration. More serious crimes—stealing goods valued at more than a shilling, murder, rape, and assaulting the master—were capital offenses, tried by two justices of the peace and three freeholders; conspiracy, the most infamous crime of all, was decided by court-martial. In the event that a slave was executed, the owner usually received compensation from public funds.[17]

As stated, Barbados' slave code was extensively copied in the other British colonies, but because there was a shortage of workers in the Leeward Islands and other places, slaves accused of crimes in these places were treated more leniently. In Antigua and Montserrat, whipping rather than death was the penalty for stealing livestock; if a group of blacks in Jamaica committed a capital offense less than murder, only one member of the gang was hanged as an example.

One would expect that Barbados would be the scene of frequent uprisings, and there were many occasions when such troubles were momentarily awaited. But revolt was difficult: every part of the island was exposed to view, and it was not easy for the rebels to conceal themselves. Nevertheless, in 1675, a female slave reported to her owner that a group of Gold Coast Negroes was planning to murder every white inhabitant and to enthrone an African as their king. A speedy court-martial resulted; six Negroes were burned at the stake and eleven others beheaded. In the end, after executing thirty-five blacks, the authorities granted the female informant a full discharge as her reward. The colony had further alarms in 1683, 1686, 1692, and 1702, but the only event approaching a general uprising in Barbados was the Easter rebellion of 1816. The danger of insurrection was much greater in Jamaica, where rebellious blacks could hide in the jungle hills. Dunn has also observed that such troubles there usually began on the large plantations, where the slaves felt a sense of safety because of their numbers.[18]

The harsh laws of Barbados were not enforced in full measure against the slaves, and the abolitionists in the home country who claimed that the treatment of Negroes was more severe in Barbados than elsewhere were not accurately informed. Probably the most striking example of cruelty on the part of a slaveowner was set in Tortola by Arthur Hodge, who reportedly caused sixty men, women, and children to be flogged to death. He was convicted of murder and sentenced to death in 1811, but a crowd of whites rioted in an attempt to prevent the execution; it was carried out only after the governor proclaimed martial law. Edward Huggins was tried and acquitted of brutality in Nevis for giving a hundred lashes each to two boys suspected of stealing a pair of stockings. In the Bahamas a young female servant was pilloried for fifteen days, followed by a flogging so severe that she died. A court sentenced her owner to five months in prison, where several prominent citizens came to comfort him; a few days after he was released, his friends gave him a public dinner.[19]

Numerous writers who compared slave practices in the European nations of the Western Hemisphere concluded that servitude was mild in the Spanish and Portuguese colonies, where, because of the humanizing influence of the Roman Catholic Church and because of laws and conventions fostered by the metropolitan powers, slaveowners treated their slaves with some degree of leniency. The same religion and similar statutory provisions were found in the French colonies. Many thought that, in general terms, the British West Indies and the United States, where Protestant churches held sway, afforded the worst treatment to the black man, but several scholars have shown that there were numerous exceptions to this theory. Harris has argued convincingly that the presence of the church in Latin America made little difference. Boxer has collected evidence to suggest that Brazil, reputed to be the place where slaves were treated most liberally, was a veritable hell. Hall has indicated that many planters in the French colonies were cruel to their Negroes despite the presence of a powerful church and the close superintending power of the royal government in Paris. It was equally true that generalizations concerning the slaveowners in the British West Indies and the United States were often not valid.[20]

Practically all recent studies of slavery show that there is no basis for characterizing slaveowners of various countries as kind or cruel. Davis has theorized that economic pressures, especially opportunities to make profit, had a greater influence than the planters' benevolent or malevolent tendencies. He shows that during the nineteenth century slavery was harsh in the Deep South because the prevailing high price of cotton induced planters to maximize gains by extracting as much labor as possible from their slaves. Slavery was milder in Virginia and Maryland because the price of tobacco had fallen, and nothing could be gained by adding to the size of the crop.[21] These principles did not necessarily apply in all situations, but they were clearly visible in Barbados following the passage of the Sugar Duties Act by Parliament in 1846, when the profits of the local planters eventually exceeded all others in the British West Indies. Hence, the period 1846–76 was one during which the Barbadian laborers, although no longer in bondage, experienced harsher conditions than they had been accustomed to as slaves.

Undoubtedly, the critics and defenders of slavery were both prone to exaggerate, but, as elsewhere, the chief criticism of servitude in the Caribbean was valid—that the absence of enforceable restraints allowed slaveowners to dictate their own limits to the treatment of Negroes. Most planters preferred to think of themselves as respectable gentlemen who managed their workers humanely, but they were reluctant to punish specific instances of cruelty toward blacks. Even when laws were passed for the protection of the slaves, the proprietors who controlled the legislature, sat on juries, and presided over the courts were loathe to penalize any member of their own race. Such was the main complaint against slavery wherever it was practiced. Mathieson wrote, "we must conclude that actually in Barbados and practically everywhere the slaves in anything short of murder were at the absolute disposal of their owners; and the question of their treatment thus resolves itself into a personal equation depending on the provocation given on the one side and the forebearance exercised on the other." Phillips made a similar assessment: "the slave regime was a curious blend of force and concession, of arbitrary disposal by the master and self-direction by the slave, of tyranny and benevolence, of antipathy and affection."[22]

Living conditions among blacks were undoubtedly harsh during the early history of Barbados. Planters strove to make quick fortunes, then to retire to Great Britain as wealthy squires, aims that prompted them to overwork their slaves while maintaining them as cheaply as possible. The local code of 1661 declared that estates should supply workers with an annual clothing allotment, which included drawers for men and petticoats for women; but the rules did not specify the rations of food, nor did they say much about working conditions. The penalty of five shillings for ignoring the provision concerning clothing was so small that the proprietors frequently elected to pay the fine in lieu of providing the allowances, and it was well known that when wars, crop failures, and depressions gave the estate owners reason to reduce the customary rations of foods, the Negroes suffered from hunger. Overwork and malnutrition accounted for the high death rate among blacks late in the seventeenth century, which in turn explains why some authorities believed that the number of slaves in Barbados actually diminished from 46,602 in 1683 to 46,462 in 1724 despite an influx of about 3,000 new Africans per year. As long as the planters could rely on cheap replacements from abroad, the death rate of the workers did not affect them economically. British humanitarians, therefore, hoped that by cutting off the supply from Africa, they could force the planters to provide better for their slaves.[23]

The economic development of the Caribbean islands acquired by Great Britain from France during the latter half of the eighteenth century meanwhile heightened the demand for slaves, and thereby their value, throughout the British West Indies. This in turn inspired Barbadian slaveowners to aid in the comfort of their Negroes by providing them with Osnaburg breeches, cotton undergarments, and, in some instances, even waistcoats. As a result, the cost of maintaining a slave in Barbados after 1763 rose from an unknown, inconsequential sum to £4 a year, which was equal in value to about two days of labor out of six. In order to supply a better assortment of food to the slaves, many Barbadian estates by 1815 were in the habit of devoting as much as two-thirds of their land to the growth of provisions. By this time it was uniformly agreed that the Negroes of Barbados were among the best fed workers in the West Indies, and it could also be argued that they were better off than some industrial and agricultural workers in Europe.[24]

The nature and amount of work performed by the slaves in Barbados were approximately the same as in the other parts of the British West Indies. A typical arrangement was for the first gang, adults between sixteen and fifty years of age, to do the heavy labor connected with planting, cultivating, and harvesting the crops. Such persons were supervised by a head driver, a slave who goaded them with a whip. Barbadian women, who toiled as strenuously as the men, carried baskets of manure weighing as much as seventy pounds, and when they returned to the cottages at night, they faced additional family duties. The lighter toil of scattering fertilizer was reserved for the second gang, made up of elderly adults and children between twelve and sixteen years of age. Younger persons, under twelve years of age, were formed into the third gang for weeding and cleaning up. There was another group of agricultural workers in Barbados, some 30,000 slaves who were hired out by their owners as "jobbers" to work on other plantations. Such laborers were allowed to keep a part of their earnings, but they were also driven more strenuously by their temporary employers than by their owners. Jobbing had the additional harmful effect of separating workers from their families.[25]

While there was no law in Barbados, as there was in Jamaica, to prohibit the use of slaves before five o'clock in the morning or after seven at night, the workday in Barbados was approximately the same as in Jamaica, beginning at sunrise and ending at sunset, with an interruption of a half hour for breakfast at nine in the morning and two hours for the midday meal. Sunday was a holiday, which the slaves devoted to the cultivation of their gardens and to peddling vegetables and poultry. Other holidays included two days at Christmas and a day on Good Friday. In neighboring colonies, most planters also allowed the slaves to do as they pleased during the twenty-six Saturdays of the out-of-crop season, from the beginning of June through November, but the planters of Barbados gave the slaves only a half day on Saturdays.[26]

The two busiest seasons, as in the other colonies, were planting time, beginning in late November, and the harvest, from March to June. There could be little doubt that the field hands were overworked during such periods, when the planters were in a hurry to cut their canes before the onset of the summer rains. Boilerworkers in the sugar mills regularly were on duty throughout the night. Yet, despite the rigorous work that was required of them, the blacks reportedly were never more exuberant than during the harvest, when many had enough energy after work to engage in a frenzy of dancing and merrymaking. Such high spirits often mystified the humanitarians, but, as somewhat overstated in 1822 by a British traveler, "the improvident negro, far from pining in misery, dances and sleeps, trifles and dreams away life, thoughtless, careless, and happily ignorant of his unprotected condition." According to Sturge and Harvey, the carefree attitude of the masses in Barbados was a tribute to the good care given to them by their owners: "Like good farmers ... [the owners] bestowed the same attention upon them as upon their cattle; and if the Negroes had been animals and not men, their success would have done honour even to their humanity. Their aim was to keep them in the highest working and breeding condition, in which they succeeded; and though ever reputed the severest disciplinarians, yet theirs was the only sugar colony where the population rapidly increased [after the abolition of the slave trade]."[27]

Wherever there was a shortage of labor in the West Indies, expediency dictated that the planters should use the most unfit slaves as household domestics, but in Barbados they customarily choose the most attractive females to serve as cooks and maids. To be thus named was to gain entry into the owner's house, which the Negroes regarded as an oasis of comforts, luxuries, and privileges unknown to slaves who worked in the cane fields. As in other colonies, many females, especially domestics, served to satisfy the sexual desires of their masters. The British Crown expressed an opinion in the seventeenth century that the resulting mulatto offspring, more commonly known as "colored," should enjoy the same status as their fathers. But it soon became the established principle that such children were regarded as slaves, socially inadmissible to the white class. Solicitous still of the needs of their progeny, the planters gave the half-castes reduced work loads, allowed them to serve as assistant overseers, and trained them as skilled workers. Eventually many of these individuals were freed by their fathers. It was more rare for a planter to manumit a slave who was fully black and in no way related to him by blood. These arrangements offered one of the few avenues of social mobility in Barbados, where the "freedmen," as Handler prefers to call such ex-slaves, gained the opportunity to migrate to towns where admission to craft specialization symbolized a higher status than plantation work. For the moment, such persons enjoyed many of the same liberties and privileges as whites. They were allowed to organize associations, hold public meetings, draw up petitions, be tried in ordinary courts, serve in the militia, and acquire any kind or quantity of property. In contrast, the inheritance and ownership rights of the emancipated class in Jamaica were proscribed by law. Eventually, colonial governments everywhere began to discourage slaveowners from discharging their Negroes, and as the number of freedmen increased, they began to limit the planters' right to emancipate blacks. In Demerara, a slave could not be freed without the consent of the court of policy. Elsewhere legislatures imposed fines on individuals desiring to manumit workers, and in 1801 the Barbadian Council and Assembly undertook to keep down the growth of the number of free Negroes by taxing the manumission of females more heavily than that of males. Similar regulations throughout the sugar colonies forbade free colored and free black persons to testify at court, serve as jurors, vote, hold civil or military office, and intermarry with whites.[28]

British humanitarians and religious leaders, who had hoped that planters would voluntarily mitigate the restrictions on freedmen and eventually lessen the hardships of slavery, finally concluded that such reforms could be achieved only by parliamentary intervention. But the influence of the estate owners in the British West Indies was so great that for two centuries they were able to defy public opinion, the imperial government, and the Crown itself. The institutions by which the West Indies were governed, therefore, acquired historical importance which leaders in Great Britain could not ignore.

The Crown did not originally intend for any group of local inhabitants to exercise such a degree of power; and when Charles I assigned the Caribbee Islands in 1627 to the Earl of Carlisle, he left the proprietor with broad residual powers to enable him to appoint all officials, collect taxes, administer justice, provide military protection, and issue decrees without consulting the colonists. The original royal charter vaguely stated that laws should be made with the consent and approbation of the freeholders, but when Carlisle appointed governors to the several islands, he authorized them "to do all ... things ... for the advancement and establishing the public good ... according to the laws and laudable customs of England."[29]

Unable to manage the colony's many problems single-handed, the first governor of Barbados, Sir Charles Wolverston, appointed a council of twenty members. For a few years, he and the upper chamber monopolized the ruling powers and concentrated all the executive, legislative, and judicial functions in their hands. In 1639, however, a new executive officer, Henry Hawley, authorized the island's freeholders to choose an assembly consisting of two burgesses from each of the eleven parishes. For the first two years the new house, or "Hawley's Parliament," as it was called, was only an advisory body, but in 1641 the governor gave it the right to initiate legislation. Thereafter the council and assembly also acted jointly in the selection of local commissioners for defense and for the settlement of disputes among merchants and planters. This was the beginning of a trend in the Barbadian legislature to increase its control by assigning administrative powers to boards and committees consisting of its own members. Within a few years, the council and assembly decided that they were coequal with the Houses of Parliament in Great Britain, and when the Puritans deposed Charles I in 1649 the members of the Barbadian legislature declared their independence from the British Parliament. To submit to a body in which they had no representa-tion, they declared, "would be a slavery far exceeding all that the English nation hath yet suffered."[30]

Cromwell's soldiers forced Barbados to surrender to British control again in 1652, but the terms of the capitulation guaranteed that the colony would be ruled as in the past, with a governor appointed in England, a nominated council, and an elected assembly. The leading member of the upper house, Daniel Searle, explained that Barbados intended "to remain under England's protection, but not to own England's jurisdiction." Many important civil and military powers nevertheless were still combined in the executive, who commanded the militia, enjoyed rights of jetsam and flotsam, issued letters of marque and reprisal, appointed officials, granted pardons, and performed various other functions. The concurrence of the council was needed to summon the assembly, but the governor adjourned, prorogued, and dis-solved the legislature on his own authority.[31] A veto of the governor could not be overridden, but because the legislature supplied the money for his salary it was able to apply considerable pressure on him. In response to the wishes of the planters, many of whom had remained loyal to the Crown during the interlude of the Puritan Commonwealth, Charles II in 1663 extended the powers of the upper house at the expense of the governor by requiring him to seek its assent to create courts, appoint justices, regulate fees, grant land, and establish forts. The only real powers left to the executive were his right to veto legislation and to prorogue and dissolve the legisla-ture. The imperial government ultimately saw that it was a mistake to increase the powers of the council to such a degree; when it endeavored at a later date to transfer some of the powers of the upper chamber back to the governor, local leaders complained vehemently of unconstitutional inter-ference. Following the restoration of Charles II the assembly likewise considered itself to be fully autonomous, with power to create its own rules, elect a speaker, appoint a clerk, discipline its members, decide disputed elections, conduct public hearings, summon witnesses, and impeach public officials. Similarly, it claimed the exclusive right to initiate money bills, which the council could not even amend, and its members often declared that they possessed the same privileges and immunities as the members of the House of Commons in the mother country.[32]

The particular persons who gained control of the government in Bar-bados intended that the political institutions of the colony should be a monopoly which rested with the white race alone. According to a statute of 1772, the legislature prescribed that the right to elect assemblymen was reserved to every free and natural-born subject who was twenty-one years old, a member of the Christian religion, and possessed of ten acres of land or a house valued annually at £10, with the exception of "the descendants of Negroes." The Barbadian Assembly clung so tenaciously to this last restriction that in 1811 it ordered the prosecution of several emancipated persons who appealed for its removal. The council and assembly made a modest concession in 1817 when, as a reward for their loyalty throughout the Easter uprising of the preceding year, the members granted the free colored and free black residents the right to testify in court. A few years later, when leaders from the same class argued anew for the right to vote, which the legislature of Grenada had just conferred, the Barbadian assembly sternly rejected the appeal and hinted that any further agitation would cause it to curtail existing freedoms. The Colonial Office continued to favor a liberalization of the suffrage laws in the West Indies; in 1828, Wellington's government issued an order-in-council abolishing all legal distinctions against free persons of color in the crown colonies of British Guiana and Trinidad. The Barbadian assembly refused to follow the example until 1831, when the sugar planters' need for an imperial loan finally induced Barbados, along with Jamaica, Dominica, and Tobago, to grant freedmen the right to vote.[33]

The administration of justice in the West Indies was another monopoly that was controlled by unsalaried white justices of the peace, the majority of whom were planters and many of whom served simultaneously as members of the legislature. As an anonymous critic said, it was easier to "find more security and more speedy justice in the most distant provinces of the Ottoman dominions" than in Barbados.[34]

In addition to relying on stringent laws, leaders in Barbados eventually came to understand that religion and education were important because of their influence on the conduct of the inhabitants. Whatever support the planters gave the church rested for a long time on the assumption that the effect of religion was moderating on the whites and inflammatory on the blacks, but it was lawless conduct among the early white settlers that prompted the legislature in 1646 to establish the Anglican church officially and to divide the island into eleven parishes, each with a church, rector, and elected vestry. For the first few years there was no supervision from England over the local churches, and the rectors were chosen by the governor, acting with the consent of the legislature and vestry; but in 1661, Charles II placed the clergy in the West Indies under the jurisdiction of the Bishop of London, who then began to designate the ministers in each colony. These arrangements did not appear to produce any improvement in the prelates, the majority of whom continued to be army veterans and bankrupt planters. Such early ministers were paid at the rate of a pound of sugar for each acre of land in the parish, but in 1740 the assembly decided to recompense the clergy with a regular salary of £150 per annum. It also assigned glebe lands to the rectories and authorized the parish vestries to supplement the salaries of prelates from time to time.

Barbados continued to be wanting in outstanding churchmen, and the conduct of many of its ministers was marred by drunkenness, sexual license, and gambling. The comforts that the clergy enjoyed added to the problem by irritating the colonists, who saw too clearly that such clerics were bored with life on a tropical island. Local citizens began to regret their generosity to the church, and ultimately the Barbadian Council and Assembly acted to prevent the vestries from supplementing the ministers' earnings by more than £70 per year. In the words of the assemblymen at Bridgetown, the restriction was needed because "divers clergymen ... have been busy intermeddlers in the election of vestrymen, and, with a design to have their stipends increased out of the parochial assessments, have used undue practices by themselves and their agents to influence such elections, and thereby have occasioned heats and divisions among many of the inhabitants of this Island."[35]

Whatever beneficial effect resident statesmen believed that religion exerted on whites, they continued to fear that it was emotionally unsettling to Negroes. As early as 1676 the legislature passed an act prohibiting all persons from offering religious instruction to blacks. Various individuals nevertheless continued to be interested in converting the slaves to Christianity, and in 1710 Sir Christopher Codrington, the governor-general of the Leeward Islands, bequeathed two estates in Barbados to the Society for the Propagation of the Gospel, the principal missionary organ of the Church of England. The benefactor's will stipulated that both estates should be managed by persons who were under vows of poverty, chastity, and church discipline but who were also able to contribute some practical benefit to the Negroes. A few Anglican catechists eventually came from Great Britain to the two plantations in Barbados, but it was more than a century after Codrington's death before the British government showed an interest in the religious instruction of blacks. As late as 1824 Canning bluntly declared that the established church was intended for the benefit of the white man and was "no more calculated for the negro than for the brute animal that shares its toils."[36]

Several sects in Great Britain displayed an active desire to convert the slaves, and the Quakers appear to have been the earliest to devote their attention to such a purpose in Barbados. The planters, as mentioned, deeply resented such efforts, and as a precaution against the antislavery dictum of

Fox's followers, the Barbadian Legislature in 1676 made it unlawful for any slave to attend a Quaker meeting. In time other missionaries arrived, including the Moravians in 1765 and the Wesleyans, or Methodists, in 1788. Disregarding the planters' objections both groups provided religious training for blacks. Because the Moravians taught that obedience to superiors was a virtue, the planters treated them more amiably than the Methodists, whose radical tenets, according to Schomburgk, found few adherents among whites. Threats of violence intermittently drove the Methodists out of the colony, but they always reappeared, displaying a dogged determination to carry out their mission among the slaves.[37]

The Wesleyan concept of man's equality before God evoked efforts on the part of West Indian as well as British leaders to strengthen the influence of the Anglican religion among the colonists, including the slaves. In 1797 the colony passed a law requiring Anglican ministers to give Negroes the same moral and religious training that was provided by the Moravians, and in 1808 the imperial government decreed that there should be at least one Sunday school in each parish. Gradually, the gentry in Barbados began to think that there should be a place for blacks in the Church of England, and in 1822 the council and assembly supplied funds to erect an auxiliary chapel to accommodate the expected overflow of black worshippers from the cathedral at Bridgetown. For the moment the old regulation continued to set blacks apart from the whites in church.[38] In 1824 Parliament provided for more extensive efforts on the part of the Anglican church among freedmen and slaves by forming two dioceses in the West Indies. One included Barbados with the Windward and Leeward Islands, the other consisted of Jamaica and its dependencies. Colonial Secretary Bathurst explained that it was preferable for the Negroes to be instructed by Anglicans than by nonconformists. The British government agreed also to pay a generous salary of £4,000 per annum to the new bishop in each diocese, and it likewise provided £2,000 a year for each of two archdeacons, as well as annual grants to assist in paying the stipends of other ministers, curates, and catechists. The first bishop of Barbados was William Hart Coleridge, a nephew of the poet Samuel Taylor Coleridge. A tireless worker, Coleridge in 1831 had created six new chapels in Barbados and had started work on a dozen other church buildings.[39]

From the foregoing account, it can be seen that education for blacks in the British West Indies was largely synonymous with religious instruction. At the same time, there were efforts in Barbados to provide a more general type of training for whites, and during the eighteenth century Barbados was known in the neighboring islands for its numerous places of learning, which included a multitude of private academies, a lesser number of parochial establishments, and a few schools of charity. A private academy consisted of a teacher, who tutored pupils for a fee, often in his own home; a parochial establishment was ordinarily located in a public building and was supported partly by parish funds and partly by student fees. The teachers in both instances were mainly the descendants of clergymen and merchants. Because of the planters' traditional reluctance to encourage the education of Negroes, few schools of any description were open to nonwhite children, even if they were not slaves. Whether it was specifically unlawful to teach the slaves to read in Barbados is unclear, but Handler states that the children of freedmen were excluded from private academies attended by whites and from the parochial establishments.[40] It was also apparent that most charitable institutions in Barbados were reserved for the benefit of whites. The most famous of these was Harrison's Free School, which a local merchant founded in 1735 for the education of twenty-four indigent white boys annually. In 1819 a group of civic-minded planters also established a Central School in Bridgetown to accommodate an unspecified number of poor males and females, but blacks were ineligible. In 1826 the same group formed a separate counterpart for white girls. Private funds, donations from the parish vestries, and annual supplements by the council and assembly collectively supported both institutions until 1859, when the legislature assumed full responsibility.[41]

The Moravians and Methodists were the first persons in Barbados to offer any form of organized education to the slaves, and the two sects began at an early date to teach reading and writing. As seen, the efforts of the Methodists in particular annoyed local proprietors, but the thought that the classroom might be used to impress the masses with the merits of docile behavior eventually convinced the council and assembly that every Anglican minister should offer instruction to the slaves, who, somehow, should not be made literate in the process. Not all of the clergy's teaching met with complete approval; in 1827 a group of planters in St. Lucy Parish denounced their rector, W. M. Harte, for undermining the racial distinctions considered necessary to their safety, "by inculcating [in the blacks] doctrines of equality inconsistent with their obedience to their masters and the policy of the island." The unpopular man was promptly indicted, found guilty of a misdemeanor, and sentenced to pay a fine of one shilling, whereupon Harte appealed to George IV, who granted a pardon.[42]

However retarded the cause of Negro education, efforts to educate the children of freedmen were not altogether lacking in Barbados. Throughout

Drawn on Stone by W L Walton from a Sketch by Hedges

Hullmandel & Walton Lithographers

CODRINGTON COLLEGE

most of the period of slavery, a few ex-slaves were able to save sufficient money to hire teachers for their offspring. Both white and black teachers were employed for the purpose. It was not until 1818 that the first public school, the Colonial Charity School, was created for the education of nonwhite children exclusively. This establishment, the first of its kind in the West Indies, was supported entirely by voluntary contributions from the freedman class and from a few white benefactors. In 1819, the first year of its operation, the institution provided regular daily instruction to fifty-seven young freedmen and to thirty-two slave children.[43]

Other important strides in public education were made after 1825 by the new bishop, who eventually founded many church schools throughout Barbados and the Windward Islands. Such institutions operated on weekdays, at night, and on Sundays, but for a time there were separate locations for the instruction of whites and blacks. By 1829 Coleridge had created eleven day schools in Barbados for free blacks and slaves, and he had also established four places to teach poor whites. It is interesting that at first, reading, writing, and arithmetic were taught in all institutions attended by whites, but the bishop did not allow such subjects to be offered to the Negroes until 1830. Meanwhile, in 1827 the trustees of Lady Mico's Charity in Great Britain decided to apply £120,000 to the advancement of mass education in the West Indies, and as a result, Barbados gained five additional free schools.[44]

Apart from the church's efforts to provide public education in Barbados, an attempt was also made to establish a college of higher learning in the island. The idea grew out of Codrington's will, which stipulated that the income from his estates was to be used partly for the support of an unspecified number of professors and scholars to "study and practise [sic] physic and chirurgery, as well as Divinity." With these purposes in mind, the trustees began to erect several buildings in 1716, but a shortage of funds delayed completion until 1745. Even then, the results were disappointing. As Bennett observed two centuries later, Codrington College was the most costly and ambitious undertaking to be made in British West Indian education during the eighteenth century, but it failed completely to accomplish its purpose. Bennett attributed the disappointing results to a conflict of ideas. Some of the trustees envisioned a college as a classical academy to prepare young men for admission to Oxford and Cambridge; others believed that the institution should concentrate on educating the poor. In an effort to serve both purposes, Codrington College therefore functioned for a time as a cheap place for the pre-university training of whites and as a free primary school for the poor. This dual role ended in 1834, when Coleridge converted the college exclusively into a typical British grammar school and seminary.

A shortage of money hampered the college for many years, and had it not been for the financial support of private benefactors in the home country it would have closed.[45]

Despite the fact that the planters in the West Indies were so firmly in control of their political and social institutions that any suggestion of interference from Great Britain was likely to be resented, British intellectual and religious leaders began to argue more vigorously after 1800 that the home country should establish some controls on slavery. The first overt act by Parliament in this direction was the abolition of the slave trade in 1807, but one of the unintended effects of the reform was to heighten the demand for laborers in the Western Hemisphere and therefore to contribute to an illicit trade in Negroes between the West Indies and the United States. Because the traffic was carried on largely by foreign vessels, the commanders of British warships on patrol in the Caribbean Sea hesitated to interfere. Eventually public opinion demanded stricter measures, and orders went out from London authorizing British ships to search suspected vessels. As a further precaution to prevent slaveowners from shipping their Negroes abroad, William Wilberforce, the renowned humanitarian leader in the House of Commons, introduced a bill in 1815 requiring each slave's name and description to be recorded in an official register kept by the governor, who then would have the means of detecting the disappearance of a Negro. The registry bill, however, was ill conceived. Assigning to the governor the embarrassing duties of inspector made him appear as the planters' adversary, and, as the Barbados agent in London warned, local leaders in the West Indies immediately branded the measure as an unconstitutional intrusion in the affairs of self-governing colonies.[46]

The planters in Barbados wildly exaggerated Wilberforce's proposal and printed distorted versions of the debate in Parliament, suggesting that slavery itself would end on January 1, 1816. Their intention was to unify whites against the registry bill, but the rumor also excited the Negroes, many of whom seriously expected to be freed. When the awaited deliverance did not occur, the slaves became restless, and on Easter Sunday, April 14, a group of blacks in St. Philip Parish rioted and set fire to the cane fields. Within a few hours, the trouble had spread to several neighboring parishes. British soldiers crushed the uprising the next day, but not before numerous plantations had suffered extensive damage. Only one white person had been killed, but scores of Negroes were hanged and the planters seized on the occasion to argue that further British meddling was certain to cause recurrences of the disorder. The House of Commons was unimpressed, and many members now pledged their support to Wilberforce's bill, unless the colonies voluntarily agreed to register the slaves. Fearing the possibility of imperial intervention, the Barbadian legislature passed a registry act in January 1817.[47]

British humanitarians steadily continued to agitate against the abuses of slavery, and in 1823 their new leader in Parliament, Thomas Fowell Buxton, charged that the harsh treatment given the Negroes in the West Indies was contrary to the Christian religion. It was England's duty, he said, to abolish servitude promptly. The House of Commons was not convinced that the time had come to free the slaves, but it unanimously adopted three resolutions promising an amelioration of the hardships of bondage as soon as possible. Colonial Secretary Bathurst immediately urged the legislative colonies in the West Indies to adopt a list of reforms recently established in Trinidad by order-in-council. Accordingly each colony was to appoint a "protector" to safeguard the slaves from cruel treatment, and the blacks should have the right to testify against their owners. Overseers and drivers should no longer use the whip, especially on females, and a precise record should be kept of all punishments administered on the estates. Fees formerly charged for the manumission of slaves ought to be abolished, and all Negroes should have the right to purchase their freedom and to be permitted to acquire property. Savings banks should be created to foster thrift and industry, and Sunday markets ought to be abolished to encourage better family and religious habits. Provisions likewise should be adopted to protect Negroes from being sold and separated from their wives and children. Such conditions already prevailed in the Spanish West Indies, and Bathurst warned that if any British colony failed to enact equivalent regulations, Parliament was ready to adopt them at once.[48]

The results of these efforts were disappointing. In Demerara a slave revolt ensued and was suppressed at a cost of more than a hundred Negro lives, and the Methodist missionary accused of inciting the revolt died in prison while awaiting execution. In Jamaica eleven Negroes were hanged for conspiracy, and in Trinidad, St. Lucia, and Dominica fears of insurrection also swept over the inhabitants. In Barbados, where the scene was somewhat calmer, the upper house passed a resolution denouncing the colonial secretary's views on slavery, which "bore no more resemblance to the actual state of things in this country than a caricature commonly does to the object which it is meant to ridicule." The Bathurst plan was a mere catalogue of indulgences to the blacks, it added, and the governor, Sir Henry Warde, openly supported the residents' claim that amelioration was unnecessary and dangerous. The cheerful disposition of the Barbadian Negroes, Warde believed, was proof of the lenient habits of the owners. Finding itself in the advantageous position of having the support of the executive against his superiors in London, the legislature flatly rejected the demands of the Colonial Office. As it explained in a memorial to the imperial government: "If ... [unreasonable] expectations are entertained by those under whose control we are placed—if nothing less than implicit conformity is required ... if, in short, a plan has already been organized for our destruction; if it is determined that we shall be the victims of fanaticism, prejudice, and injustice, we must submit; but neither threats nor persuasion will ever induce us to put the finishing hand to our political, perhaps natural existence."[49]

The whites of Barbados were still flushed with anger when a new Methodist minister, William Shrewsbury, arrived at Bridgetown in the summer of 1823. When he began to criticize abuses committed by the planters against the Negroes, local leaders determined to rid themselves of the nuisance. Crowds of indignant citizens assailed the cleric in the streets, and bands of armed intruders broke up the Methodist Sunday worship. Warde's refusal to provide legal protection to the unpopular minister encouraged the turmoil, and in October a mob of angry citizens gleefully demolished the Methodist chapel. The agitators explained in an anonymous handbill:

> The inhabitants of this island are respectfully informed that in consequence of the unmerited and unprovoked attacks ... repeatedly made upon this community by Methodist missionaries ... a party of respectable gentlemen formed the resolution of closing the Methodist concern altogether; with this view they commenced their labours on Sunday evening, and they have the greatest satisfaction in announcing that by twelve o'clock last night, they effected the total destruction of the chapel.
>
> To this information they have to add, that the missionary Shrewsbury made his escape yesterday afternoon in a small vessell.... It is hoped that as this information will be circulated throughout the different islands ... all persons who consider themselves true lovers of religion will follow the laudable example of the Barbadians, in putting an end to Methodism and Methodist chapels throughout the West Indies.[50]

Expressing astonishment at the violent deed, Warde offered £100 for information likely to lead to the arrest of the responsible persons, when a second handbill appeared threatening would-be informers with the "punishment which their crimes will justly deserve."[51]

Antislavery leaders in Great Britain lavishly condemned Warde for having wronged the Methodists, and the House of Commons also warned the influential class in Barbados against any further "scandalous and daring violation of the Law." When the Methodists in Barbados were again threatened with riots in 1824, the governor did not hesitate to call out the troops to prevent a recurrence of the trouble.[52]

Had the government in London taken advantage of the unfavorable light which the Shrewsbury incident threw on the planters instead of quailing in fear of public criticism, it might have effected some improvement in the legal status of the blacks in Barbados, where residents grimly awaited forceful action from London. British public opinion, however, was divided, and Cobbett was convinced that "the West Indians [were] men as gentle, as generous and as good as ever breathed," while he thought the Methodists were "impudent Vagabonds ... [who] richly merited the pulling down of their den." Wilberforce feared that the amelioration policy was moving too quickly, and Buxton was dismayed that many members of Parliament were tiring of the slavery issue and becoming hostile toward the humanitarians. "The degree, I will not call it opposition, but virulence against me is quite surprising," he wrote.[53]

But political leaders in Barbados, who suspected that the attack on the Methodist chapel would inevitably produce a strong reaction against them in the home country, decided that token compliance with the recommendations of the Colonial Office was expedient. The strategy of the legislature would be to gauge what measures would satisfy the imperial government without actually impairing the slaveowners' control of their Negroes. In 1824 the speaker of the Barbadian Assembly introduced a bill "to consolidate and improve" the existing slave laws of Barbados. Such a measure, he explained to the planters, would not only render the governing of the blacks more efficient but would also discredit "the diabolical and infamous aspersions of a few interested and designing hypocrits [in the home country] who are ... keenly and immovably bent on your destruction."[54]

The bill offered by the speaker conceded the right of the slaves to give legal testimony and to acquire property. It diminished the fees required for manumission and provided for the appointment of a slave protector. But it likewise stated that every Negro who was unable to prove his liberty would be presumed to be unfree, that death should be imposed on any bondsman who threatened to strike his master, and that any white person who killed a mutinous slave should be, as in the past, excused from prosecution. The legislature debated the mild changes in existing practices for more than a year, and when finally approved in 1825 the Consolidated Slave Law was disallowed by the imperial government on the ground that it varied too much from Bathurst's recommendations.[55]

Reviewing the results of their labors, antislavery leaders in Great Britain noted in 1826 that the flogging of females was still prevalent throughout the West Indies. Nowhere were savings banks established for the blacks, nor had any provision been made for the slaves to purchase their freedom. Only a few colonies had forbidden the separation of workers from their families. The Anti-Slavery Society therefore concluded that since amelioration had failed, Parliament should no longer hesitate to end servitude. The British government was not ready for such a drastic step; as Canning explained in the House of Commons, because Great Britain itself had profited by

Table 1.1. Recommended Legislation in Barbados and Other British West India Colonies, 1823–26

Recommended Laws	Colonies Passing	Colonies Not Passing
Admission of slave evidence	Barbados, Bahamas, Dominica, Grenada, St. Vincent, Tobago	Antigua, Jamaica, St. Kitts
Legalization of slave-owned property	Barbados, Bahamas, Dominica, Grenada, Jamaica, St. Vincent, Tobago	Antigua, St. Kitts
Reduction of manumission fees	Barbados, Bahamas, Grenada, Jamaica, St. Vincent	Antigua, Dominica, St. Kitts, Tobago
Prevention of the separation of slave families	Barbados, Grenada	Antigua, Bahamas, Dominica, Jamaica, St. Kitts, St. Vincent, Tobago
Provision for the appointment of a protector of slaves	Barbados, Bahamas, Grenada, St. Vincent, Tobago	Antigua, Dominica, Jamaica, St. Kitts

SOURCE: Hansard, 1826, 14:968–82, 15:1284–1366.

establishing slavery in the West Indies, it could not rightfully turn on the planters and suddenly place the entire burden of emancipation on them alone.[56] The parliamentary under secretary for colonies, Horton, admitted that many of the reforms lately adopted in the slave colonies were disappointing, but he believed that several provisions nevertheless improved the status of the Negroes. The Barbados Consolidated Slave Law, while falling short of Bathurst's expectations, contained more provisions to reduce the hardships of the Negroes than the laws of any other British colony, except those of Grenada (table 1.1).

The Barbadian legislature subsequently amended the Consolidated Slave Law again and removed the immunity formerly given to a white person who killed a rebellious slave. At the same time, several important political changes took place in Great Britain. Canning died four months after he succeeded Liverpool as prime minister in 1827 and in turn was succeeded by Lord Goderich. In the shuffle the Colonial Office was assigned to Huskisson, who was more leniently inclined toward the planters than Bathurst had been. The new colonial secretary confirmed the Barbados law in the hope that the legislature would accept several additional modifications in existing slave practices. Huskisson noted that the protector of slaves in Barbados was a slaveowner and was incapable of being altogether impartial toward blacks. The appearance of a slave in court was hampered by many petty restrictions, and planters were legally entitled to disqualify the testimony of their own Negroes. The use of the whip in the field, which St. Vincent and Grenada recently prohibited, was not abolished, and the flogging of females was also allowed to continue in Barbados. No limit was placed on the time a person might be kept in stocks, and apart from the general rule that owners convicted of cruelty were subject to a small fine there was no regulation of the planters' power to punish the workers. Only if convicted twice of cruelty to the same Negro was the owner required to free the abused person. Barbados continued to deny the slaves the right to purchase their freedom. Huskisson believed that the criminal penalties imposed on the blacks in Barbados were too severe. Such outmoded punishments as slitting of the nose and branding were recently abolished, he observed, but death was still required for intimidating the master, killing livestock, or invoking supernatural powers, and quarreling, swearing, lighting fireworks, or driving a horse faster than a gentle trot carried a sentence of thirty-nine lashes. Other laws prevented slaves from having funerals after dark, engaging in amusements after nine o'clock at night, or holding dances without a justice's permit. The enumeration of so many restrictions, Huskisson feared, was likely to provoke the Negroes into acts of defiance.[57]

Whatever hope Huskisson may have had to correct these defects in Barbados was largely unwarranted. The legislature refused to repeal the punishments that it considered necessary in a slave society. It would not give the workers the opportunity to purchase their freedom, which it feared would convert every plantation into a poorhouse by allowing able-bodied Negroes to gain their liberty while requiring the planters to support all blacks who were physically unfit to render profitable service.[58]

The course of British politics soon turned to the planters' disadvantage. The issue of Roman Catholic emancipation split the Tories in 1829, and in 1830 the Whigs, traditionally pledged to reform, came to power with Henry Brougham, the abolitionist, as lord chancellor. Goderich, in his new position as colonial secretary, immediately enjoined the legislative colonies in the

West Indies to adopt the same measures as the imperial government had
introduced to regulate slave labor in the crown colonies of British Guiana
and Trinidad. The provisions were to be adopted in their precise language
and exact extent, the colonial secretary advised; otherwise Parliament would
exercise its overriding authority and enact the regulations without the
concurrence of the local legislatures. Unmoved by this threat, the Barbadian
Assembly was intransigent. It regarded Goderich's demands as "evil ten-
dency" and refused to entertain "any Bill for the adoption of the said Order, as
required by His Majesty's Government." As a further sign of defiance,
Barbados invited the neighboring islands in the West Indies to issue a joint
remonstrance against the high duties collected on colonial produce in the
home country.[59]

The Colonial Office diligently continued to seek ways of forcing the
self-governing possessions in the Caribbean Sea to ameliorate slavery more
fully, and in April 1831 the imperial government threatened to increase the
duty on West Indian sugar and rum unless the colonies adopted additional
measures. The result was an outcry from the West India Merchants and the
West India Planters and Merchants, the two principal sugar lobbies in
London, who reminded the prime minister that a similar effort to dictate to
the American colonies had caused a revolution. Even the threat of raising the
duty on colonial produce would precipitate "such a convulsion" as to
compel the West Indies to separate from Great Britain.[60]

The force of circumstances continued to run contrary to the planters'
interests. In August 1831 a violent hurricane laid waste to St. Lucia, St.
Vincent, and Barbados. Nearly £2 million worth of damage was done and
hundreds of victims were killed or injured. The imperial government
responded by providing £500,000 in loans for the restoration of the damaged property; but in its generosity was implied colonial dependence on the
imperial power.[61] Henceforth the Whig government in London would press
for the abolition of slavery as soon as possible.

Prime Minister Grey, meanwhile, was having other problems; when the
Whigs saw that their slim majority in the House of Commons was too
fragile to guarantee the passage of their reform measures, he diffidently
advised William IV to call a fresh election in the summer of 1831. The
situation gave leaders in the West Indies a hope that the menacing reform
party might be ousted and replaced by men more favorably disposed to the
sugar colonies. The planters' friends in Great Britain waged an active
campaign against Grey's candidates, but by this time such groups as the West
India Merchants had indicated their readiness to yield to public opinion. The
lobby informed the voters that it was no longer opposed to the abolition of

Negro bondage: "The only difference of feelings ... relates ... to the time and manner of terminating slavery."[62]

When the elections of 1831 resulted in the Whigs' return to power with a clear majority in the lower house, the planters in the sugar colonies realized that the end of forced labor was close at hand. They could only wonder under what conditions they would operate their estates in the future.

2. Barbados and the Abolition of Slavery, 1833–1834

THE LIBERAL trend that arose in Great Britain during the 1820s and produced such social, economic, and political changes as the enactment of a more humane criminal code, the lessening of the corn duties, and the enfranchisement of the Catholics eventually led the Whigs in the 1830s to a succession of reforms that were even more striking. Of these, the Reform Act of 1832 was the most serious blow to the British West Indies, because it eliminated the pocket borough seats in the House of Commons formerly purchased by the sugar interests, thereby removing one of the principal ways by which the colonies had restrained Parliament from undertaking the abolition of slavery. Even before the Reform Act went into effect, such celebrated foreign liberals as the Marquis de Lafayette pressed British statesmen to emancipate the blacks,[1] and the Colonial Office began to draft a bill to end slavery.

The new Whig government was aware that such a measure was repugnant to the planters, and in order to strengthen the emancipation policy in the West Indies, it loosely joined Barbados and the Windward Islands under a common governor-general in 1833. As a means of safeguarding him from local pressure, the British government also decided that the new official's salary should be defrayed entirely from imperial rather than colonial funds. Leaders in the Windward Islands were glad to be rid of the expense, but the planters of Barbados preferred that the executive be dependent on them for his livelihood.[2]

28

The magnitude and unpopularity of the great change that the imperial government sought to introduce in the slave colonies made it important for the administrative officers to be politically astute and tactful. The new governor-general of Barbados and the Windward Islands, Sir Lionel Smith, lacked these necessary qualities. A retired lieutenant general, Smith was unbending, impatient, and too vigilant of the dignity of his office. Even his redeeming traits—a high will, perseverance, and industry—provoked resentment. To make matters worse, Smith's arrival at Bridgetown in 1833 coincided with strong feelings of racial hostility resulting from the trial of a Negro accused of raping a white woman. Believing it to be his duty to inveigh against the many abuses of slavery, Smith openly declared himself to be an abolitionist, and his actions were such that many Negroes came to believe that he intended to give them their freedom at once, without waiting for Parliament to act.[3]

While the Colonial Office hoped to persuade the planters that emancipation did not necessarily mean economic ruin, Smith, unlike the genial and high-spirited governor of Jamaica, Lord Sligo, treated local leaders with scorn and condescension. In his opening address to the Barbadian legislature in May 1833, he "congratulated" the members on being recently relieved of paying his salary. The sum provided by the imperial government, Smith said, would not enable him to live in the same degree of splendor as his predecessors, who had benefited largely from the assembly's "imprudent generosity," but this would not prevent him from being attentive to the interests of the people of both races. The governor also noted that a more impartial enforcement of the laws was needed and that the existing untrained justices of the peace, who were incapable of administering the laws equally to the whites and blacks, should be replaced by professional jurists. Moreover, a regular police establishment was lacking in Barbados, where there was now an increasing need to prevent the races from harming each other. Three weeks later in its reply to the brusque message, the assembly retorted, "your short experience in this colony and want of instructions ... have not enabled you to submit to our consideration anything of a new or interesting nature." In June, Smith advised the new colonial secretary E. G. Stanley (the future fourteenth Lord Derby) that there appeared to be an "unaccountable soreness" in the legislature.[4]

If local leaders were dissatisfied because he had shown himself, in Smith's words, to be "warmly interested" in the welfare of the slaves, he believed they were even more deeply offended because of his concern for the freedmen, "this much injured people." In several ways, the governor advised, freedom had imposed heavier burdens on them than had slavery, since they could no longer rely on the estates for their support. Furthermore, as long as there was a surplus of servile laborers in Barbados, the proprietors would not employ free blacks. It was possible, Smith also feared, that they would elect to rid themselves of the excessive number of elderly and infirm workmen by giving them their liberty before Parliament could act to abolish slavery. Then the swollen number of freedmen would be compelled to compete for jobs with laborers still in bondage. Otherwise, many discharged persons would have no means of support; as it was, the proprietors were complaining that the free Negroes were stealing food from the slaves.[5]

Whatever handicaps stood in the way of the ex-slaves, however, did not deter them from efforts in their own behalf. From the end of the seventeenth century, when it became more common for planters to manumit slaves, free black women busied themselves peddling homemade pickles and jams, while the men worked as butchers, cabinetmakers, carpenters, masons, and tailors. Others earned wages as clerks, and a small number of accountants, surveyors, and solicitors also appeared. Commenting in the 1830s on the progress of some of the free Negroes and their descendants in Barbados, Thome and Kimball observed: "One of the wealthiest merchants in Bridgetown is a colored gentlemen [i.e., freed half-caste]. He has his mercantile agents in England, English clerks in his employ, a branch in the city [of London], and superintends the concerns of an extensive and complicated business with distinguished ability and success. A large portion ... of the merchants of Bridgetown are colored. Some of the most popular instructors are colored men and ladies, and one of these ranks high as a teacher of ancient and modern languages. The most efficient and enterprising mechanics of the city are colored and black men. There is scarcely any line of business which is not either shared or engrossed by colored persons, if we except that of *barber. The only barber in Bridgetown is a white man.*"[6]

Such a view of the freedman's achievements was somewhat exaggerated. While there was an impressive number of such persons whose toil and ingenuity produced a comfortable living, few attained wealth, and for many there was a darker and more sordid side to their lives. Because the island was a British military station, many female ex-slaves were able to earn a livelihood as prostitutes, an occupation which was more common at Bridgetown than in any other city in the British West Indies. Moreover, William A. Green has shown that in Barbados, which was the only place in the sugar colonies where the whites outnumbered the free Negroes, the local prejudice against skin color was more pronounced than in any other of Great Britain's Caribbean possessions. The whites kept themselves apart from emancipated persons of mixed blood, while the latter segregated themselves from free blacks, who in turn kept themselves at arm's length from the slaves. The social and economic distinctions that resulted from gradations according to the degree of color were also more conspicuous in Barbados than elsewhere.

As a consequence, with a few interesting exceptions, the principal business and professional undertakings in Bridgetown were controlled by whites, while freedmen were largely confined to huckstering. Even when a colored or black person managed to acquire wealth, of whom London Bourne was an example, such an individual continued to be a victim of discrimination and prejudice. Thus Bourne, who was the owner of the building where the Bridgetown Merchants Exchange met, was refused membership in the organization because he was not white.[7]

Whether the ex-slaves of other sugar colonies in the British West Indies were better off than those of Barbados is not known. Many freedmen in Jamaica earned a good living as craftsmen, and some were able to amass sizable fortunes as dry goods merchants in Kingston. Jamaican pimiento production was also largely controlled by ex-slaves. In Dominica, the same class not only monopolized the cultivation of coffee but reportedly owned 22 percent of the slaves. Handler indicates that a significant number of freedmen in Barbados possessed slaves, but the actual figures are uncertain.[8]

It is not difficult to understand that Smith expected the freedmen to play an important part in local affairs. The imperial government insisted that emancipated blacks uniformly should be entitled to the same civil and political rights as the whites, and, as shown, Barbados legislated in 1830 to remove the legal distinctions formerly imposed on ex-slaves. The new suffrage qualifications were such, however, that only seventy-five freedmen were able to meet the requirements. Similarly, the law discriminated in favor of whites, by stipulating that new voters (mainly colored and black) were to possess freeholds valued annually at £30, while registered voters (mainly white) continued, as in the past, to vote with £10 freeholds. A second measure passed in 1833 restricted Negroes from serving in the militia by disqualifying persons "who may hereafter become free," unless they were possessed of two acres of land or a house with a yearly value of £10. Complaining of the discriminatory practices, a group of free colored and black persons headed by Samuel J. Prescod, the colored person soon to become the publisher of The Liberal newspaper, pressed Smith for relief. The governor promptly pledged his support and added, "you are ... not only fully entitled ... to be raised also to confidential civil employments, but I consider it very desirable, at this moment, that you should be appointed Magistrates in particular. The energies, rectitude, and integrity found among you should ensure benefits to the public in the discharge of those duties." Smith explained that the council of Barbados was the only local body in the West Indies that had a constitutional right to refuse an appointment made by the executive, but he promised that he would seek authority from London to override the opposition.[9]

Hearing of the governor's reply to the petitioners, the council angrily complained that he had not even spoken to it concerning the rights of the freedmen. And his inopportune remarks placed the upper house in a position where it could only "incur the obloquy of unpopular measures but cannot share in the grace of concession." What was worse was that Smith had excited mistrust and suspicion among a class that should be conciliated instead. Hurriedly the governor wrote to his superiors in London. Knowing the blind bigotry with which the council had resisted every practical relief to the free colored and black residents, he had no hope of gaining anything from it by persuasion. Moreover, he was convinced that freedmen generally were better suited to hold public office than many whites, who "have nothing but old rights and prejudices to maintain their illiberal position." In contrast, the balance of refinement, morals, education, and energy was chiefly in favor of the ex-slaves and their descendants. Therefore, Smith hoped that the imperial government would amend the royal instructions and allow him to make appointments from any class without having to seek the council's concurrence.[10]

The Colonial Office did not fully sympathize with the governor. Although its noted legal adviser, Sir James Stephen, was strongly opposed to a policy of appeasing the island legislatures, he feared that such an attempt to curtail the powers of the Barbadian Council would cause so much resentment that the outcome of emancipation would be jeopardized. The colonial secretary also disapproved of any change in the royal instructions at the moment and likewise ordered the governor not to make any further pledges to the Negroes which could heighten the planters' hostility toward the mother country.[11]

Stanley introduced the long-awaited emancipation bill in the House of Commons in May 1833, explaining that such a drastic step was required because the West Indian governments had failed to mitigate the cruelties of slavery. The words of the colonial secretary were harsh: the voice of warning had spoken in vain, he declared; the tongue of honest and affectionate counsel was not heeded; the legislative colonies in the West Indies had evaded the efforts of the imperial government to ameliorate the hardships endured by the blacks. As a result, Parliament had no choice but to end slavery. Therefore, on 1 August 1834 all slaves under six years of age would be freed outright; those over that age would be required to work for their former owners as apprentices for a period of twelve years. Except for additional labor performed by the apprentices in their own free time, no wages were to be paid to them. The planters, however, were expected to supply the necessary food, clothing, shelter, and medical care. At the same time, in order to safeguard the Negroes from being overworked or otherwise abused, all questions and disputes arising between them and the estate holders would be settled by special justices, or stipendiary magistrates, appointed and salaried by the Crown. And because the British government recognized that the end of slave labor necessarily required a major adjustment on the part of the planters, Parliament was prepared to offer them £15 million in loans.[12]

After consulting with the Barbados agent in London, the local proprietors concluded that it was futile for them to oppose the imperial government's decision to abolish slavery. But, having suffered heavy losses from a recent hurricane and from a decline in sugar prices, they continued to hope for better terms from Great Britain. The Barbadian gentry therefore urgently informed the House of Commons that Stanley's proposal gave the planter no choice but to "disobey the law, or consent to defraud his creditors [in Great Britain], ruin his family, and convert a peaceful and contented peasantry into hordes of banditti." Provided, however, that the slaveowners were given fair compensation, the legislature recognized Parliament's right to abolish slavery throughout the British empire. The members of the assembly therefore candidly petitioned Parliament in July 1833:

> Does the Barbadian Legislature mean to say that England, repenting ... of the part she has had in establishing and cherishing a system which she now thinks criminal, shall not have the power to terminate it? Far from it! Only let the course be straight forward, honest, and constitutional. As England is avowedly the author and was for a long time the chief gainer ... let her bear her share of the penalty of expiation.... Let a fair and just indemnity be first secured to the owner of the property which is to be put to risk ... and then the Colonists will cooperate in accomplishing a real and effective emancipation of the slaves. All wise and well intentioned emancipationists will hail this alliance, conscious that without the cooperation and instrumentality of the resident Colonists, their object can only be attained through rapine violence and bloodshed, destroying all the elements of civilisation and ending in anarchy.[13]

Confronted with similar appeals from the other West Indian legislatures, Stanley modified his proposal to give the planters a cash indemnity of £20 million instead of a loan. Among other new provisions included to satisfy British humanitarians, the apprenticeship period was reduced to six years for praedials (field workers) and to four years for nonpraedials (artisans and household servants). The Colonial Office gave this advantage to the latter because the nature of their duties in the boilerhouse and at the owners' home often required them to toil for unlimited lengths of time on command, whereas, according to the revised bill, field hands were not to be employed more than forty-five hours a week or in excess of nine hours a day. An

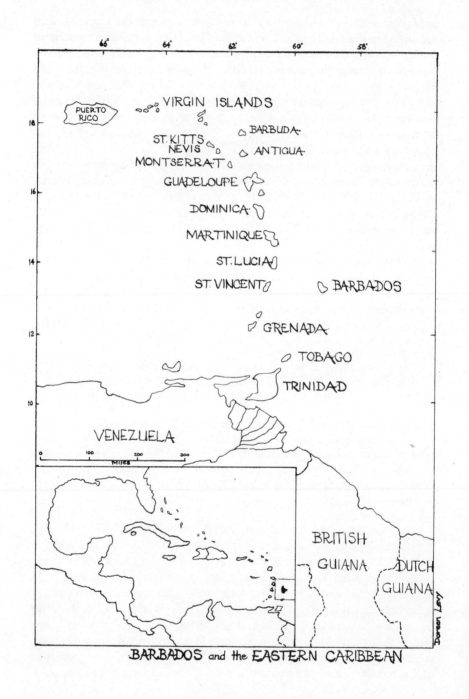

BARBADOS and the EASTERN CARIBBEAN

apprentice could be freed at any time by his master, but he could also obtain a discharge by purchasing it at an appraised value. Other details pertaining to the working routine and laborers' allowances would be decided by the colonial legislatures in order to meet the peculiar conditions of each locality, but in no colony were the planters to receive compensation until the governor had certified that the local regulations conformed fully to the general intentions of the British government.[14]

Acting on the urgent advice of the sugar lobbyists in London, the Barbadian legislature approved the principles contained in Parliament's revised emancipation bill. But it objected to the method of computing the amount of compensation per Negro, which varied from colony to colony according to the local market value of each slave. This meant that the proprietors of Barbados would receive an average of £20 per slave and those of British Guiana £50. For obvious reasons Barbadian planters preferred a uniform indemnity throughout the West Indies.[15]

The slaveowners of Barbados were eager to augment their share of the £20 million voted by Parliament, and were prepared to forgo their right to apprenticed labor altogether in return for a larger per capita payment. But the imperial government was unwilling to make any new concessions, because it believed that the island already enjoyed an advantage over the other colonies as a result of its redundant labor supply. Moreover, Stanley favored the idea of apprenticeship as an intervening period during which the Negroes would be prepared for their final freedom by undergoing a series of social and economic improvements.[16]

It was now up to the colonies to pass their own laws for local regulation of the apprenticeship system. Antigua and Bermuda took the bold step of giving the blacks full freedom in 1834. The Barbadian legislature was slow to act in any way, and in October 1833 Governor Smith "mildly invited" the council and assembly to do their duty.[17] Another month passed, and Smith reminded the legislature in November that the payment of compensation to the slaveowners awaited the passage of appropriate local measures. Quoting at length from Stanley's dispatches, Smith emphasized that the self-governing colonies in the West Indies were free to determine many of the subordinate details of apprenticeship. As an indication of what was expected, Stanley had forwarded the copy of an order-in-council regulating the new system in the crown colonies of Trinidad and British Guiana. The colonial secretary explained that the order was not supplied for servile imitation but as a guide to assist local legislatures. Nevertheless the imperial government would not tolerate any long delays, and each locality was expected to adopt such laws as "bear upon the face of them a real and sincere desire to act up to the spirit and intention of the British Parliament and people."[18]

In contrast, in December 1833 Jamaica responded obligingly to the Colonial Office's advice. Ignoring Stephen's warning that several imprecise provisions in the colonial law would result in future disagreement, Stanley confirmed the measure in the belief that it was an example of promptness that could serve as a model for other islands in the British West Indies. He expected that whatever problems existed in the Jamaican statute would be voluntarily corrected by the legislature, in order to allow the slaveowners, who needed funds, to receive their compensation as early as possible. The colonial secretary thus did not foresee the extent of Kingston's opposition, which eventually became so heated that the imperial goverment was forced to threaten the suspension of the colony's constitution in 1838.[19]

Meanwhile, it was several more months before the legislature at Bridgetown finally passed a bill, in April 1834, providing for the governing and maintenance of the apprentices after August 1. The Colonial Office thought that the measure was defective in numerous details, but it confirmed the act on the understanding that the slaveowners would receive no compensation until the council and assembly had adopted several necessary amendments. At the same time, Stanley was eager to secure an orderly transition from slavery to freedom in the West Indies, and he ordered the governors to ready all of the troops at their disposal. Such forces included the militia and police, but the colonial secretary cautioned that they were not to be used to intimidate the Negroes.[20]

Smith agreed that there was a real danger of disorder in Barbados, but he preferred to rely exclusively on British soldiers rather than the local militia, which he feared was prone to acts of brutality toward the blacks. Apart from a few white constables who had been engaged from time to time by the justices of the peace, there was no police force whatever on the island. The governor therefore urgently advised the legislature to create an unarmed body of policemen, who would be "firm and determined in the execution of their duties but ... refrain from violence and conduct themselves with civility to all." Similarly, the governor continued to press the council and assembly for permission to replace the local justices, "a most ignorant and corrupt set of men," with trained police magistrates responsible to him alone. Otherwise, Smith warned, he would be helpless to prevent whites and blacks from colliding.[21]

The Barbadian legislature had a different view of what was needed to preserve order, and it doubted that an unarmed group of policemen would have much effect on thousands of Negroes just released from servitude. Nor was the council ready to authorize the governor to appoint magistrates without its approval. The members delayed acting on Smith's recommendations for another half year, until July 1834. With less than a month before emancipation, the legislature created two separate police establishments, one for Bridgetown and the other for the rural parishes. Hastily perusing the two measures, Smith saw that nowhere in the island were the police under his control. The St. Michael Parish vestry was the managing body of the Bridgetown police, and the rural police were to be administered by a board consisting of members of the council and assembly. Because of the high frequency of crime in the densely populated area of Bridgetown, the legislature agreed that the governor should appoint three police magistrates to the town, but such appointments required the confirmation of the upper chamber. Commenting on the provisions, Smith observed that the legislature had effectively concentrated control of the police in the hands of the planters, who had a direct interest in using their power to coerce the Negroes. In Smith's words, the recent measures were "the most cruel and sanguinary that ever disgraced a British legislature."[22] But August 1 was close at hand, and the governor felt he had no choice but to yield or to leave Barbados' large population without protection. On July 28, three days before the end of slavery, the governor confided his worst fears to the Colonial Office. Apprehensions appeared to seize the proprietors at every turn, he declared, and such a frenzied feeling in itself could provoke acts of violence. "My own opinion," he wrote, "is that our greatest danger is the unbending spirit of the planters and the tenacity with which they cling to arbitrary power over the negroes, and hence I by no means think that the first burst of ... modified freedom will be half so trying as the disappointment likely to arise from the practical operation of the laws of the Colonial Legislatures."[23]

Anticipating that a large number of blacks would congregate at Bridgetown on emancipation day, Smith concentrated several detachments of British regulars at the capital. He also issued a proclamation warning Negroes that "the law is strong and the law will punish you if you do not work." The governor, meanwhile, hoped to mark the beginning of the new age by setting aside the first day of August as a thanksgiving holiday, but the legislature refused to grant the request.[24]

Despite serious misgivings on the part of the whites, bondage terminated in Barbados without a sign of trouble. Smith noted with satisfaction that the local apprentices were busily occupied with their duties. "The Island was never more tranquil," he wrote on August 5 to Thomas Spring-Rice, the new colonial secretary. But problems accompanied the end of the old system in some of the other colonies. In Trinidad, where many Negroes objected to apprenticeship, a large number of workers rioted at Port-of-Spain. There was also a threat of disorder in the Essequibo district of British Guiana, and in St. Kitts and Montserrat military action was necessary to induce runaway apprentices to return to the estates.[25]

3. Negro Apprenticeship in Barbados, 1834–1838

W HEN THE imperial government confirmed the Barbados emancipation law in June 1834, it expected that the legislature would agree to amend
the measure in several respects. The legislature had expressed its willingness
to cooperate with Parliament. But the hostility that arose between Governor
Smith and island leaders over several petty issues delayed the settlement of
more important matters, and such key personalities at the Colonial Office as
Sir James Stephen foresaw a danger that the local council and assembly
would secretly undermine the goals that Great Britain was seeking for the
emancipated class.[1]

The task of explaining what modifications were needed in the West Indian
emancipation acts fell to Stanley's successor, Thomas Spring-Rice. The
measure adopted in Barbados was defective in several particulars, the
colonial secretary advised. Such artisans as boilerworkers, carpenters, and
masons were required to serve as apprentices until 1840 and thus were not to
be discharged with the other nonpraedials in 1838. The planters had the right
to confine apprentices in plantation prisons, which created another opportunity for them to coerce their former slaves. Watchmen and tenders of cattle
could be worked in excess of the forty-five-hour weekly limit that the
imperial government intended to apply to all laborers in the fields. Planters
had the authority to transfer disorderly household servants to agricultural
duties, which entailed a change in classification from the nonpraedial to the
praedial class and thereby prolonged the apprenticeship of the former

domestics by two years. Compared with the rations of food and clothing provided apprentices in British Guiana and Trinidad, the Barbadian scale of allowances was inadequate. Spring-Rice observed that in Barbados the apprentices were supplied with one pound of fish per week instead of two, children under twelve years of age were given half rations, clothing allowances were generally inferior to those of British Guiana and Trinidad, and the apprentices were not provided with blankets.[2]

A similar set of complaints concerning the defects of the Jamaica act produced a strong reaction in Great Britain's largest Caribbean colony, where the assembly complained that Spring-Rice had exhibited "an equal ignorance of our institutions and disregard of our public and private rights."[3] In contrast, the Barbadian legislature reacted mildly, and in November 1834 it amended the local emancipation act. The changes did not coincide altogether with the wishes of the Colonial Office, but the council and assembly nevertheless hoped that the new measure removed the principal objections against the original bill. The altered version restricted the use of watchmen and tenders of cattle to forty-five hours per week, even if it meant that the estates had to "leave the cattle and crops in the fields at the mercy of the apprentices."[4] While the island's leaders believed that the planters should continue to use private prisons, the new act specified that all places of confinement were to be inspected by the special justices appointed by the Crown. The former slaveowners would retain the right to transfer troublesome household servants to the fields, but such workers remained in the nonpraedial classification and therefore would be discharged in 1838 instead of 1840. The planters would also be required to supply each apprentice with an additional set of outer garments per year.[5]

The Barbadian legislature was convinced that Spring-Rice would not demand any further modifications. Its members therefore continued to believe that the planters rightfully deserved the services of boilerworkers and other artisans until 1840, because such laborers were more important to the production of sugar than were the field hands. Similarly, they considered that the mild temperatures in the West Indies obviated the need for blankets, that two pounds of fish per week were not essential to the health of the apprentices, and that full rations were not required by children under twelve years of age.[6]

With the exception of the new clothing allowance, which was somewhat more than the Negroes were assigned as slaves, the rations called for in the amended emancipation act were equal to those given to the blacks during slavery. The food, consisting of four pounds of plantains, potatoes, yams, or eddoes, was admittedly unbalanced and monotonous. But these were defects which the planters believed were off-set by the addition of green vegetables, poultry, pork, and mutton, which the apprentices were able to produce in their free time. Humanitarians in the home country heatedly argued that half rations were insufficient for growing children, and despite the fact that foreign visitors often remarked that Barbadian workers appeared healthier and better fed than those of the neighboring islands, officials in London considered that the allowances provided there were inferior to those supplied elsewhere in the West Indies. The Colonial Office therefore continued to insist on two pounds of fish for every apprentice and full rations for children of all ages.[7]

The Barbadian proprietors glumly maintained that many of them could not afford to supply even a single pound of fish per week. The item was a costly import, and if the mother country imposed such a heavy burden, the former slaveowners would ultimately be forced to withdraw the customary indulgences that they had given to the Negroes as slaves. Otherwise, they planned to continue supplying daily quotas of rum and sweetened water, as well as holiday rations of salted meat. In addition, the local proprietors were in the habit of excusing aged Negroes from heavy labor and allowing them instead to attend the work gangs as cooks and water-carriers, concessions that the planters of Jamaica had lately withdrawn.[8]

Although British functionaries regarded the changes in the Barbados emancipation act as a hopeful sign, in 1835 the new colonial secretary, Lord Glenelg, adamantly required stricter compliance with the expectations outlined by Spring-Rice. He therefore directed that all artisans, whether connected with the production of sugar or not, should be treated as non-praedials and discharged in 1838, and because household servants were not accustomed to the rigors of agricultural work they should not be punished by being transferred to the fields. Glenelg understood that a few planters were financially unable to provide the apprentices with the allowances recommended by London. But in such an event, whether the omitted item was fish or any other article, the estates should give the workers whatever free time was necessary for them to grow their own food. The colonial secretary even envisioned an extreme situation in which the entire forty-five hours per week reserved to the planter might be needed by the worker to supply his own necessities. In such a situation, Glenelg thought that the estate owner had no claim whatever on apprenticed labor. He therefore spelled out what the Barbadian legislature did not wish to hear—that apprenticeship was an unequal bargain in which the principal obligation was owed by the planters to the former slaves.[9]

The blunt message did not win many additional concessions for the Negroes, except in British Guiana and Trinidad, where the Crown controlled nominated legislatures. Even British Guiana balked at the imperial government's demand requiring the repeal of a local restriction which prevented the apprentices from leaving the estates without the owners' consent. Pessimistically noting that the ruling class in the West Indies was seldom willing to yield to the advice of the Colonial Office, Glenelg concluded that the majority of local councils and assemblies would do nothing voluntarily for the blacks. As explained by Robert B. Clarke, the Barbadian solicitor general and leading member of the assembly, "His Lordship... thought of all the Colonial Legislatures in terms of the most unmeasured reprobation."[10]

At the same time that the Colonial Office was struggling to improve the status of the former slaves, a local survey in Barbados revealed that 83,150 Negroes had been freed on 1 August 1834, which meant that there were more former slaves per square mile in Barbados than in any other sugar colony. Of the individuals thus liberated, 52,193 were classified as praedials and 14,732 as nonpraedials. The rest were free children under six years of age and persons too old or diseased to perform profitable labor. The planters logically considered that such a large concentration of workers in an area as small as Barbados (166 square miles) was the best guarantee that the estates would continue to benefit from an abundance of laborers. But with a population of more than five hundred ex-slaves per square mile, the island was "ever tremblingly alive to the dangers of insurrection," in the words of a past governor. Even Smith feared that the greatest danger of disorder arose "from the unfitness of the slaves themselves to bear the great transition from slavery to civil rights." The legislature agreed, and despite the ill humor which it bore toward the governor, it provided him liberally with the military supplies that were required to preserve order. In another gesture of cooperation, it passed an act officially empowering the special justices appointed by the Crown to rule in all matters arising between the planters and their apprentices.[11]

The monthly reports of the special justices provide the most reliable source of information concerning the actual operation of apprenticeship. Subject only to the restriction that field hands were not to be used more than forty-five hours per week, the planters in the West Indies were free to allocate total working time as they saw fit. The special justices, however, revealed that the working routine in Barbados did not vary much from one district to another, with the exception of Bridgetown, where the majority of laborers were servants and craftsmen (nonpraedials). Because of the great surplus of such apprentices in Bridgetown in relation to the small number of former owners, the latter continued to send workers into the country to search for employment, a habit which, as noted, was unsettling to the Negroes. Blacks in the rural districts, on the other hand, were subjected to a more systematic routine from Monday through Friday, with Saturday and Sunday left for them to work in their gardens or to do as they pleased. On most of the local estates, the nine-hour workday preferred by the planters began at six in the morning and continued until the same hour in the evening, with an interruption of an hour at breakfast and two hours at lunch, which, it will be recalled, was approximately the same arrangement as had existed during slavery.[12]

With only minor variations, the daily routine was very similar throughout the West Indies. But in Jamaica there was an important difference: because of the great surplus of unoccupied land the proprietors elected to provide the apprentices with large garden plots in lieu of allowances, and in order to give the laborers an opportunity to cultivate their own food, they also agreed to a reduction of the workweek from forty-five hours to forty and a half hours. At the same time the planters divided what was left of the weekly working period as nearly as possible into five eight-hour workdays from Monday through Friday. Many laborers saw that it was to their advantage to have a nine-hour workday from Monday through Thursday, with only four-and-a-half hours of duty on Friday morning, which would give them an additional half day to devote to their own interests on Friday afternoon. Because the provision grounds in Jamaica were usually located at a distance from the workers' cottages, the arrangement also gave them time to reach their gardens by Friday night, rather than spending Saturday morning in the long walk. But many of the planters in Jamaica refused to allow the additional half day off on Friday, thus causing much dissatisfaction among the apprentices.[13]

Likewise, there were numerous causes for discord between proprietors and workers in Barbados. The main complaints of the Barbadian planters were that the apprentices were insolent, idle, negligent, disobedient, and thieving. Such objections to the behavior of the former slaves were general throughout the West Indies. Even in Antigua, where the planters renounced the right to apprenticed labor and gave the Negroes full liberty in 1834, the complaints were the same, suggesting that apprenticeship provided no more causes for discord than did freedom.[14]

The reports of the special justices in Barbados also indicated that there were relatively few complaints from the large plantations, where the owners obtained good results from the apprentices by exhibiting a spirit of leniency and generosity. But on the smaller estates, the planters practiced miserly habits, drove the apprentices from dawn until dusk, tricked the Negroes into working beyond the legally authorized number of hours, refused to allow rest periods, cheated the blacks of their proper rations, withheld the customary indulgences, and frequently assaulted the workers.

Another source of irritation in Barbados after 1834 arose from the reluctance of the ex-slaves to perform additional tasks for wages during the planting and harvest seasons. Figures supplied by the special justices during the first two years of apprenticeship indicated that it was possible for a Barbadian laborer to earn as much as 1s.3d. for Saturday work, yet they did not show much interest in performing additional duties during their free time. Mathieson pointed out that many free workers in Antigua were not inclined to do additional labor; other writers observed that the apprentices of St. Lucia and Dominica likewise spurned a share of the planter's crop in return for performing additional duties.[15] On the other hand, in 1834 the special justices of Jamaica reported that the number of Negroes currently engaged to toil in their own time exceeded all expectations, and the figures of the following year showed that extra labor was being performed on nearly 70 percent of the Jamaican estates. Approximately half of the apprentices of Trinidad were likewise engaged in supplementary work on Saturdays, and many former slaves were available for additional duties in British Guiana. But even the high pay currently offered in the last three places mentioned was not enough to prevent the workers from abandoning the estates to settle on unoccupied land.[16]

One of the aims of the Colonial Office was to encourage Caribbean laborers to seek their freedom before the end of the apprenticeship period. The worker could accomplish this in several ways: by prevailing on the proprietor to give a free discharge, by agreeing with him on a suitable price, or by obtaining a judicial appraisement enabling the ex-slave to purchase his freedom without the planter's approval. In addition, the special justices had the authority to discharge any apprentice who had been treated with undue cruelty.

While the records in Barbados frequently are unclear, they nevertheless supply some interesting insights. They show that 907 apprentices were discharged in Barbados between 1 August 1834 and 1 August 1835. Of these, two were for cruelty, 865 were free and voluntary, and 40 were by appraisement, all of the last being granted in Bridgetown. The larger number of voluntary discharges (661) likewise occurred in Bridgetown, while only 246 discharges were effected in the ten rural parishes. The same records also indicate that of the total number of apprentices voluntarily released, 578 were nonpraedials, 285 were praedials, and two were unclassified. From the information in the reports of the special justices, it can be seen that more than 70 percent of the discharged apprentices were from Bridgetown, that the number of nonpraedials discharged exceeded the number of praedials, and that the majority of these appeared to be female house servants.[17]

It was also apparent that few discharges were effected by purchase. The explanation lies in the fact that in Barbados, as in the other former slave colonies, the judicial boards established to assess the value of an apprentice's discharge consisted of two local justices of the peace and one special justice. As the latter was the only member likely to give a low assessment, the price of securing a discharge was often more than the Negro could afford. Blacks understandably regarded the appraisement system as so much trickery, and a few apprentices resorted to their own cunning to obtain low appraisements. Thome and Kimball told of an amusing incident in which a Negro overseer wished to purchase his freedom. Recognizing that his owner valued him highly, the worker tied a bandage around his head, gave his face a wrinkled and haggard appearance, and allowed his clothes to become tattered and soiled. In a few weeks, the black man seemed to become old and feeble, and when he hobbled with the aid of a cane to the district station house to apply for a discharge he was appraised at £10. The forlorn man paid the sum and emerged shortly afterwards in full vigor as the manager of a small estate.[18]

Freedom, by whatever means attained, did not always lead to a life of ease. After obtaining their discharges, many blacks shunned plantation work, which bore the stigma of servitude, and multitudes of former apprentices roamed over the island in a futile search for jobs as footmen, valets, butlers, and coachmen. They soon learned that such duties were performed by Negroes who were still under the obligation of apprenticeship or by persons who had secured their freedom in former times and who were more hostile toward recently discharged blacks than were whites. The dissolution of a few lesser estates near Bridgetown made it possible for a number of discharged blacks to acquire small plots of ground, but the quality of the land was generally so poor that the occupants were forced to supplement their earnings as porters and boatmen in the town. In contrast, by 1835 the workers of Jamaica had an abundance of cheap land at their disposal, and, as noted, many squatters were able to obtain it free of all costs.[19]

From a material standpoint, the most destitute people in Barbados after 1834 were the 14,000 free black children under six years of age. Under the provisions of the local emancipation law, the estates were not required to support such persons unless they were voluntarily apprenticed to them by the parents. A few charitable planters supplied the children with food and clothing, but with only two free days in the week (Saturday and Sunday), the Negroes were unable to give their offspring the care they required. At the same time, a number of estate owners and overseers, annoyed by the adults' refusal to apprentice the children, evicted several hundred young blacks from their homes, which, in turn, resulted in an undetermined number of deaths. Such results, Special Justice George Kennedy believed, could be blamed largely on absentee landlords, who left their estates "to the guidance of men who have no ultimate character to gain, and who wish to screw as much labour as they possibly can from the apprentices, which necessarily enriches them, and the absentee planter receives his rent without knowing how his Negroes are abused."[20]

It was one of the dilemmas of emancipation that planters and Negroes were both responsible for the neglect suffered by the young blacks. Whereas slavery weakened the Negro family by transferring the parental role to the planters, emancipation abruptly ended the estates' obligation to support the children without providing any practical measures to assure that the parents would assume the responsibility. Thomas Parry, the archdeacon and future bishop of Barbados, later estimated that during the course of a single summer, over five hundred children died from lack of support. One of the chief goals of moral and religious leaders in the West Indies, therefore, was to strengthen the black family structure, with the mothers and fathers fulfilling the traditional roles of providers and protectors of their offspring. As Parry pointed out in 1841, their efforts did not meet with much success.[21]

Determined to rescue the infant Negroes from abandonment, Smith relied on the embarrassment of public exposure to induce overseers and planters to restore the young blacks to their homes, and he accordingly published the names of the guilty persons. In a few days, the children were back with their parents, but the governor nevertheless pressed the legislature to pass an act giving mothers additional free time to care for the young. The legislature irately refused on the ground that as long as the Negroes had the opportunity to secure the offspring's support by apprenticing them to the estates, any relief to the workers in the form of additional free time was unnecessary and would only foster greater indolence among the adults. According to Smith, the parents continued to spurn the alternative given to them by law, and he believed that very few children, if any, were being apprenticed to the estates.[22] The mothers reportedly threatened to poison their offspring in preference to apprenticing them, and some Negroes even sent their young from their homes because they feared that their presence on the estate might give the planter a claim to their services. Stressing that every mother had a natural right to put aside her occupational duties in order to care for her progeny, Glenelg ordered Smith to prosecute any planter who interfered with such a right. Even if it was not possible to convict a planter, the colonial secretary hoped that the unfavorable publicity could once more be relied on to prevent other persons from committing the same offense.[23]

Bishop Coleridge believed that religion and education could be relied on to strengthen the ability of the workers to look after family matters. His religious efforts suffered a temporary setback as a result of the destructive hurricane of 1831, which wrecked many of the churches built at Barbados since 1824. But by 1839 the energetic bishop had created twenty-three new chapels in the colony, in addition to dozens of places of worship in the Windward and Leeward islands. In fact, the prelate worked so quickly that the parish rectors were unable to keep up the pace, and Coleridge was forced to assign several of the new chapels in Barbados to curates, or assistant ministers, some of whom were not adequately trained for the work. There was an increase in the number of Anglican clergymen in Barbados, the Windward Islands, and the Leeward Islands (table 3.1).

Table 3.1. Anglican Clergy in Barbados and Other Colonies of the Barbadian Diocese, Selected Years

Colony	1812	1825	1834
Antigua	6	8	12
Barbados	14	15	29
British Guiana	1	7	10
Dominica	1	1	2
Grenada	2	2	4
Montserrat	1	1	2
Nevis	3	3	3
St. Kitts	5	5	7
St. Lucia	0	1	1
St. Vincent	1	2	3
Tobago	1	1	1
Trinidad	0	2	2
Virgin Islands	1	1	2

SOURCES: William H. Coleridge, "Statement of Churches, Schools, and Chapels in Barbados," with MacGregor to Russell, 5 December 1839, CO 28/129. See also Coleridge's "Summary of the Number and Cost of Churches, Schools, and Chapels in Barbados to 1837," CO 28/159. Information on the number of such institutions in Barbados after emancipation is also found in the *Barbados Blue Books,* 1830–65, CO 33/42–75 and Schomburgk, *Barbados,* p. 99.

Coleridge wrote that the increase in the number of churches and the clergy had an elevating effect on the workers, and he noted that in the course of a few years the majority of blacks in the diocese had given up such African practices as bringing food to the graves of the dead. Yet, foreign visitors often noted that the masses of Barbados were less concerned with religion than were the inhabitants of the neighboring colonies, where nonconformist missionaries aroused a lively interest in church activities. In contrast, Barbadian laborers attended church infrequently, and many blacks did not even partake in baptismal and marriage ceremonies. "There is no great disposition amongst them to attend religious instruction," John Davy wrote a few years after Coleridge's retirement, and many who participated in church services did not bother to dress up for the occasion. In comparison Sunday worship was a special event in the other British West Indian colonies, where the blacks appeared for church in fancy waistcoats and silk hats and many wore expensive jewelry. In Jamaica the laborers were willing to spend more money for their funerals than for medical care.[24]

From a humanitarian point of view, the efforts to promote the Anglican religion in Barbados produced disappointing results. Admittedly the Church of England could claim a larger membership than any other denomination, but the British form of worship was too formal and restrained to have much appeal to the former slaves, who preferred an animated type of ritual. Furthermore, as several critics rightly noted, the insistence of the bishop on separate pews for whites and blacks was a clear indication that the Anglicans were unwilling to accept former slaves as spiritual equals.[25]

The nonconformists had a different attitude toward the black race, but the workers of Barbados were as indifferent toward them as toward the Anglicans. As a Methodist minister admitted, "even the Negroes themselves [in Barbados] were prejudiced against us." During the ten years following emancipation, there were only a few Methodists and apparently no Baptists in Barbados, whereas in Jamaica there were numerous Methodists and thousands of Baptists. Dissenting clergymen in Jamaica willingly incorporated into traditional Christian practices such African ritual forms as spirit-possession, magic, and divination, and they likewise played an active role by assisting in the creation of free villages and by offering plans for the Negroes' political, social, and economic advancement. Neither Anglicans nor non-Anglicans in Barbados were ready to offer such concessions or to assume such a role in behalf of the workers. In Trinidad, where the Roman Catholic clergy had a strong influence, the pre-Lenten celebration of the carnival provided what Donald Wood has portrayed as a healthful opportunity for the blacks to rid themselves of emotions kept in check the rest of the year.[26] But in Barbados, the planters continued to stress that the aim of religion was to restrain rather than to excite the masses.

As shown, Coleridge had an equal interest in education and religion, and under his guidance, the Anglican church rapidly increased its schools in Barbados from eight in 1825 to 155 in 1834. The number of such facilities in Barbados was unmatched anywhere in the British West Indies (table 3.2).

In 1834 the imperial government decided to allocate £25,000 a year to support the church's educational activities in the former slave colonies; two years later, when it increased the figure to £30,000, it appointed an official inspector, Charles Latrobe, to report on the progress of education in the West Indies. The resulting investigation disclosed that there were 213 schools of all descriptions in Barbados, which meant that the island had more places of instruction per square mile than any other British Caribbean colony. But Latrobe added disapprovingly that as yet only two or three parochial schools were admitting blacks: "In no island has the distinction of color been kept up with regard to education to the degree observable in Barbados," he wrote. Of the 13,869 pupils in Barbados, only 2,439 were children of apprentices; of these, the majority were enrolled in Sunday schools for religious training only. The remainder of the schoolchildren were the offspring of freedmen and of whites.[27]

Table 3.2. Numbers of Church Schools in Barbados and Other Colonies of the Barbadian Diocese, Selected Years

Colony	1812	1825	1834
Antigua	0	8	32
Barbados	2	8	155
British Guiana	0	2	37
Dominica	0	0	4
Grenada	0	1	18
Montserrat	0	0	19
Nevis	0	6	19
St. Kitts	0	6	64
St. Lucia	0	0	3
St. Vincent	0	1	14
Tobago	0	0	13
Trinidad	0	2	4
Virgin Islands	0	0	6

SOURCE: Schomburgk, *Barbados*, p. 99.

Following the publication of the Latrobe report, Coleridge redoubled his efforts to provide some form of daily instruction to Negro children. The number of day schools, night classes, and Sunday schools was greatly increased during the next decade, but as W. G. Sewell observed, "all schools [in Barbados] are under church influence and are necessarily imbued with church prejudices."[28]

A steady rise in the number of criminal convictions following the end of slavery persuaded many leaders in Barbados that religion and education were not enough to control the unruly behavior of the inhabitants and that strict laws were needed as well. Crowded into shabby tenements in the

towns and enticed into grog houses and brothels, many discharged apprentices squandered their earnings on cards and dice and soon found themselves
in jail, charged with vagrancy, fighting, or stealing. "We have the misfor-
tune," the Barbadian chief justice complained in 1836, "of being dependent
on a peasantry so wholly demoralized, that the contemplation of this fact
fills us with alarm." A member of the assembly described the conduct of the
Negroes at Speightstown as being nearly savage:

> Sir, if there was a place which required the strong arm of the Law to
> keep in subjection the idle, the dissolute, and the licentious, it is
> Speight's Town.... Sir, were I blessed with the descriptive powers of
> Shakespeare, or did I have at command the extraordinary pencil of
> Hogarth, still I should feel myself at a loss to describe or represent the
> scenes of debauchery and libertinism which are daily and nightly
> exhibited in the streets and lanes of Speight's Town. Sir, the most
> profligate character that ever figured at Billingsgate would feel herself
> at a loss to manufacture such oaths and such obscene and blasphemous
> expressions as are minutely uttered in the streets and lanes.... Sir, the
> females of that part of the town which is contiguous to the Bay, are
> entirely deprived of any view of that quarter by the constant walking
> to and fro of naked men upon the open Beach.... Gaming is carried on
> in the public lanes by moonlight, and the losing party, it is more than
> probable, from the number of robberies which are committed, draws
> off to pay by theft what he has lost by gambling.... The calls of nature
> are relieved within the view of respectable characters; and the virtuous
> female is actually afraid of walking through the streets....[29]

In 1834 the members of the legislature speedily passed an act enlarging the
list of capital offenses to include attempted murder, arson, sodomy, robbery,
blackmail, riotous destruction of property, abortion, and breaking into a
church or chapel (table 3.3). Other new provisions called for long periods of
banishment from Barbados for involuntary manslaughter, killing or injuring cattle, and assaulting a policeman. For such petty offenses as flying kites,
indecent exposure, trespass, and "other indecorous behavior," the council
and assembly imposed milder penalties of imprisonment and fines. A
further provision also stated that any time lost by an apprentice while
imprisoned was to be made up following his release by requiring him to
work for his employer during his free time on Saturdays. Such a regulation
produced an additional burden on the laborer and was especially unjust to an
individual who was acquitted after being required to wait in jail for trial. But
in an indirect way, the rule operated to the benefit of the ex-slaves by giving
the planters an interest in safeguarding them from injury while they were in
prison.[30]

Because most of the foregoing legislation was copied from laws which the Colonial Office had already approved in Antigua, leaders in the Barbadian legislature did not expect the imperial government to question the need for the same provisions in Barbados. In fact there were many more examples of harsh laws in the British West Indies. The Jamaican vagrancy act imposed heavy fines and imprisonment on persons for merely threatening to leave their families unsupported; residents of St. Kitts who were convicted of

Table 3.3. Penalties Imposed in Barbados, 1834

Murder	death
Attempted murder	death
Arson	death
Rape	death
Sodomy	death
Abortion	death
Robbery of chattels, money, or valuable property	death
Obtaining money by threatening to accuse another person of an infamous crime	death
Breaking and entering a church or chapel	death
Riotous destruction of property	death
Exhibiting false signals to ships	death
Armed burglary	death
Involuntary manslaughter	7 years transportation
Stealing goods valued at £5 or more	7 years transportation
Killing or injuring cattle	4 years transportation
Assaulting a policeman	2 years transportation
Taking fish from a pond	2 months in prison
Killing pigeons	1 month in prison
Using profane language	1 month in prison
Quarreling	1 month in prison
Failing to keep the Sabbath	1 month in prison
Firing guns	1 month in prison

SOURCES: "An Act for the Prevention and Punishment of Malicious Injuries to Property," 6 September 1834, "An Act for the Prevention and Punishment of Offenses against the Person," 6 September 1834, "An Act for the Punishment and Prevention of Larceny," 6 September 1834, all in *Barbados Acts,* CO 30/21.

spreading seditious rumors were given sixty lashes; in Dominica, making any noise whatever in the street was punishable by a jail sentence.[31]

Colonial Office personnel, who uniformly suspected that the Caribbean planters would seize any excuse to deprive apprentices of their freedom, conceded that strict laws were required to prevent the spread of disorder among the former slaves. Stephen cited Barbados as an example where stern measures were probably needed, because "the prevalence of crime in Barbados is unequalled in any other British colony except New South Wales."[32] On the other hand, statistics provided by the Barbados jail reports suggest that the great majority of criminal offenses were of minor rather than major magnitude and that the friends of the Negroes in the West Indies and in Great Britain were inclined to see the literal threat of the local law rather than its psychological effect of discouraging misconduct (table 3.4). It could also be argued that many British criminal laws were as harsh as those of Barbados, but Glenelg believed that such regulations in the home country were enforced with more judicial restraint than in Barbados. There, according to Smith, hordes of arrested blacks at the Bridgetown jail formed a scene of "poverty, nakedness, and disease," and police used the whip with equal force against males and females. Nothing would be gained by seeking indictments against the police for committing acts of brutality, Smith wrote, because "no jury could be found to convict any member of that frightful oligarchy."[33]

Table 3.4. Confinements in Barbados Town Hall Jail, 20 June–5 November 1835

Debt, 13	Disobedience, 101
Murder, 2	Insolence, 54
Bestiality, 1	Idleness or neglect, 34
Burglary, 19	Desertion of work, 95
Larceny, 15	Injury to property, 14
Perjury, 1	Nuisance, 1
Sheep stealing over value of 25s., 10	Assault, 31
Stealing under value of 25s., 34	Vagrancy, 7
Arson, 1	Selling without license, 4
Petty theft, 156	Stealing manure, 1
Stealing poultry, 7	Exciting sedition, 1
Stealing roots, trash, fuel, etc., 41	Rape, 1
Trespass, 3	

SOURCES: "Barbados Gaol Report," 20 June–5 November 1835, with Smith to Glenelg, 13 April 1836, CO 28/117.

As had been seen several months earlier, the Colonial Office was reluctant to antagonize the Barbadian legislature by interfering excessively in local matters, but by 1835 it concluded that it was important to bring many harsh laws in Barbados under the governor's control. Among such measures that were passed shortly after emancipation, the most suspicious in the eyes of the London officials was the law entrusting the administration of the rural police to a board consisting entirely of local councillors and assemblymen, the majority of whom were also planters having a direct interest in exercising power over laborers. The imperial government saw that such an arrangement impaired the effect of emancipation by restoring the Negroes to the absolute control of their former owners, and it disallowed the questionable measure in the hope that the legislature would pass a new bill assigning the body to the exclusive control of the governor. As an additional guarantee that the laws of Barbados would be fairly enforced, the Colonial Office, responding finally to Smith's appeals, authorized the governor to appoint all police magistrates and justices without the concurrence of the council. Smarting at this defeat, the upper house angrily objected and the assembly petitioned the colonial secretary to recall Smith. But at the same time the legislature decided to yield to the demands of the imperial government and to pass an act temporarily placing the police under the authority of the executive for a period of six months.[34]

Smith did not expect the legislature to go further toward removing the imperial government's final objections to the Barbados emancipation law, and unless the composition of the council was altered he believed that it was useless to seek the cooperation of its members. In the spring of 1835, however, an unexpected vacancy in the upper chamber gave the governor an opportunity to appoint a new member of his own choosing. He promptly named Henry Sharpe, the Barbados attorney general. Sharpe was already widely disliked by the planters because of his liberal attitude toward Negroes, and, as Smith expected, the members of the council objected that Sharpe, an officer of the Crown, was ineligible to serve in the upper chamber. Unless the nomination was withdrawn, at least six of the most influential members announced their intention to resign. The leading opponent of the governor in the council, Renn Hamden, headed a group that Smith characterized as disloyal to the imperial government. In desperation, the governor appealed to the Colonial Office to replace the "six violent men" with persons on whose support he could rely. Should the authorities refuse to grant his request, he believed there was no choice but for him to resign.[35] There was also strong opposition to the governor in the assembly, where Clarke was described by Smith as an active instrument of the council. Meanwhile, Smith's responsibilities as governor-general of the Windward Islands also contributed to his difficulties. "If your Lordship could only see [me]," he added wryly in a dispatch to Glenelg, "you would be reminded of the willing jackass whose master went on loading him ... until he sank and died."[36]

Although Smith was eager to undertake every practical step to advance the Negroes' cause, he failed to recognize that in a small society such as Barbados, where membership in either house of the legislature was an important social symbol, it was expecting too much to assume that the council and assembly would blindly ratify every recommendation exactly as dictated from London. The members of such bodies everywhere in the West Indies undoubtedly preferred the imperial government to impose its own measures, without relying on them to act on policies that were unpopular with influential inhabitants. The authorities in the home country fully realized that the legislatures in the Caribbean colonies were reluctant to adopt voluntarily laws that were detrimental to planters' interests. Even the dour Glenelg admitted that, considering the circumstances, the council and assembly at Bridgetown had conducted their business in a dignified and statesmanlike manner. He could not say the same of the Jamaican legislature, which gave early approval to emancipation but subsequently withheld money votes in a desperate effort to thwart London's attempt to implement the necessary details.[37]

Sir Henry Taylor, head of the West India Department at the Colonial Office, continued to regard Smith as a conscientious executive, but Stephen feared that the removal of six council members "by wholesale" would cause an irreparable rift between the home government and leaders in Barbados. Glenelg, however, was also unwilling for the governor to relinquish his office and ordered Smith to refuse the resignations from the upper chamber and to withdraw Sharpe's nomination.[38]

The time was approaching for the imperial government to apportion the £20 million voted by Parliament to the former slaveowners, and in August 1835 the legislature at Bridgetown passed several bills removing most of the imperial government's objections to the local emancipation act. The new provisions gave the apprentices the desired quantity of fish per week, provided for blankets every two years, abolished the use of plantation prisons, and permanently assigned the police to the supervision of the executive. The legislature did not specify that boilerworkers and other artisans should be discharged as nonpraedials in 1838, but the imperial government overlooked the omission. Taking advantage of the new mood of cooperation in Barbados, Smith addressed the legislature amicably. The governor promised henceforth to give serious consideration to the council's opinion in all important matters affecting the colony, and he also pledged to serve the interests of both races equally.[39]

A few weeks later Glenelg officially certified that the planters of Barbados were eligible to receive their share of the slavery compensation fund created by Parliament. The dispatch which carried the good news to Bridgetown contained no hint of the struggle that had been waged with the local legislature since 1833. Glenelg effusively declared: "On perusing the various addresses from ... the Barbadian Legislature it is impossible not to be deeply and favourably impressed by the tone in which, under circumstances of the most trying nature, the discussion on their part had invariably been conducted. They have not only adhered inflexibly to the calm and courteous style befitting all public intercourse between the different branches of the Legislature [i.e., the governor] without yielding to feelings which might have rendered some departure from it natural and venial; but with a candour which I acknowledge with respect and gratitude, they have rendered full justice to the arguments and motives of the Ministers of the Crown, even when those Ministers were compelled to oppose their wishes and controvert their opinions."[40]

Having finally created a harmonious relationship with the legislature, Smith soon alienated the workers by insisting on punishing those who neglected their duties. The apprentices should be orderly and industrious, he instructed the special justices, and they should fulfill their obligations honestly for their former owners, who had agreed to provide them with better care than was known by many workers in other parts of the world. "For all besides," the governor added, "they [the former slaves of Barbados] are dependent on their employers' favour and kindness." Eager to give the Negroes an idea of what was expected of them, Smith appointed three planters to create a scale indicating the quantity and type of work to be performed by an apprentice on a single day. By giving the estates the option of adopting daily work quotas, Smith hoped not only to satisfy the needs of the estates but to encourage the workers to complete their assigned tasks early, which would enable them to devote the remainder of the day to their own affairs. He also intended to use the quotas prescribed in the work scale as a standard for punishing indolence, and he ordered the special justices to nail the code to their walls in public view. Smith was convinced that every task listed could be completed by two o'clock in the afternoon, but many British humanitarians feared that the prescribed duties would strain even the strongest workers. To make matters worse, the elaborate code was unduly complicated and capable of aggravating already troublesome misunderstandings between planters and apprentices.[41]

The proprietors and overseers generally suspected that the workers would botch their assigned tasks in order to finish early in the day. The majority of estates consequently were reluctant to experiment with the plan, and on some properties where the system was tried the apprentices refused to turn out because they suspected the governor had decreed that their appearance at work would make them slaves again. "This they credited to me," Smith complained in disbelief, "who they well knew had encountered every odium and insult in establishing their right to be treated like human beings." Within a few days, however, the owners of the troubled estates disavowed the cumbersome arrangement, and the wary Negroes returned to work.[42]

By 1836 most of the major problems associated with the launching of apprenticeship in Barbados appeared to be settled. A few planters continued to complain that the average compensation paid per slave in Barbados was less than half that paid in British Guiana and Trinidad, and such persons hoped that Great Britain would find other ways of indemnifying them.

Table 3.5. Compensation for Emancipation of Slaves in British West Indies

Colony	Number of Slaves	Total Compensation (£)	Average Compensation per Slave (£. s. d.)
Jamaica	311,070	6,149,955	19.15. 1
British Guiana	82,824	4,295,989	51.17. 1
Barbados	83,150	1,719,980	20.13. 8
Trinidad	20,657	1,033,992	51. 1. 1
Grenada	23,638	616,255	26. 1. 4
St. Vincent	22,266	550,777	26.10. 7
Antigua	29,121	425,547	14.12. 3
St. Lucia	13,291	334,495	25. 3. 2
St. Kitts	19,780	329,393	16.13. 0
Dominica	14,175	275,547	19. 8. 9
Tobago	11,589	233,875	23. 7. 0
Nevis	8,815	151,006	17. 2. 7
Bahamas	10,086	128,296	12.14. 4
Montserrat	6,401	103,556	16. 3. 3
British Honduras	1,901	101,399	53. 6. 9
Virgin Islands	5,135	72,638	14. 1.10
Bermuda	4,026	50,409	12.10. 5

SOURCE: *PP,* 1837–38, 44:154.

There is evidence that the planters of Barbados had no genuine cause for complaint: the average compensation per slave in Barbados was higher than in Antigua, the Bahamas, Bermuda, Dominica, Jamaica, Montserrat, Nevis, St. Kitts, and the Virgin Islands (table 3.5), and the total amount remitted by the imperial government to Barbadian slaveowners was £1,719,980, the third largest sum paid in the West Indies. Likewise, Barbados had an advantage over the neighboring colonies in numbers of apprentices available to work on the estates (table 3.6).

The first two years of the apprenticeship system in Barbados resulted in numerous complaints that were brought to the special justices; these were cause for concern in London. By 1835, though, many planters began to feel that emancipation had not brought any great harm. Unlike the sugar proprietors in Jamaica, the former slaveowners of Barbados were soon convinced that wage laborers were as suitable to their needs as slaves had been in former times, and when Smith left to assume the governorship of Jamaica in 1836 the council openly apologized for the trouble it had caused him. "The present flourishing condition of the island," it declared in a

Table 3.6. Apprentices per Square Mile in British West Indies, 1843

Colony	Area in Square Miles	No. Apprentices per Square Mile
Jamaica	4,411	71.7
British Guiana	89,480	.9
Barbados	166	501.0
Trinidad	1,863	11.9
Grenada	133	196.9
St. Vincent	150	167.4
Antigua and dependencies	171	269.6
St. Lucia	238	57.0
St. Kitts	65	290.0
Dominica	305	48.8
Tobago	116	102.0
Nevis	36	176.0
Bahamas	4,404	2.3
Montserrat	32	194.0
British Honduras	8,867	.2
Virgin Islands	59	89.0
Bermuda	21	212.0

SOURCE: Deerr, *History of Sugar*, 2:306.

farewell address, "and the happiness of the inhabitants cannot be ascribed to adventitious circumstances—they are chiefly the result of your Excellency's laborious zeal and judicious administration."[43]

The events that Smith witnessed at his new post form the basis of some interesting comparisons with Barbados. On his arrival at Kingston, the governor was startled by the lack of activity on the estates, which he thought could be remedied by adopting the same work quota plan he had proposed in Barbados. But such a system, which sought to impose equivalent work quotas on all apprentices, was even less suited to Jamaica than to Barbados, because variations in the Jamaican climate and soil produced radical differences in working conditions from one locale to another. Failing to inspire confidence in the planters, Smith was soon embroiled in a succession of bitter conflicts with the assembly, involving such questions as the food and clothing allowances due the workers, powers of the special justices, the state of the prisons, the vagrancy law, and voting requirements. He despaired that the legislature would ever "correct the evils I exposed to them" and candidly advised the Colonial Office that the abuses practiced against the Negroes were "the worst of all the late slave colonies." [44]

The problems experienced by Smith in Kingston worsened to such a degree that in 1839 the legislature was able to force his recall by refusing to vote the money required to carry on the government. This in turn triggered a complicated chain of events in Great Britain, where Lord Melbourne introduced a bill in Parliament to suspend the Jamaican constitution. When the measure came to a vote, several Whigs, traditionally reluctant to interfere with constitutional self-rule in the colonies, voted with the opposition, thereby reducing the government's majority and forcing its resignation. Melbourne returned to power a few weeks later, but an important change was taking place in the imperial government's policy toward the West Indies. Thereafter, the Colonial Office would appoint conciliatory governors, of whom Smith's successor in Barbados, Sir Evan Murray MacGregor, former governor-general of the Leeward Islands, and Sir Charles Metcalf in Jamaica were good examples. In a final summation of Smith's career a few years later, Schomburgk explained the principle reason for his lack of success in the West Indies: "His administration was just and even-handed, and though it has been observed that his inflexible temper and conduct would have rendered him more fitted to execute the laws of an arbitrary government than those of a free country, the important measures and changes of those days which were forced upon the colonists afford perhaps the best excuse for the style he adopted in his messages to the Legislature and the conduct which he followed in his intercourse with those over whom he presided."[45]

If material prosperity was the main measure of progress, the start of the apprenticeship system in Barbados under Smith was not as disappointing as some planters had feared; under MacGregor more propitious results were achieved than many persons had thought possible. The island prospered from an abundance of labor, favorable weather, and high sugar prices. The records of such large estates as Easy Hall indicate an increase in the cost of producing sugar, from £4.1s.4½d. per hogshead of 15 cwt. in 1832 to £5 in 1835. At the same time, the island experienced a rise in production, from 18,757 hogsheads (13,325 tons) in 1832 to 27,318 hogsheads (19,728 tons) in

1834, which more than offset the effects of the increased costs.[46] In 1838 the sugar crop amounted to 31,786 hogsheads (23,679 tons), and the value of the total exports reached £960,368, the highest to that point in Barbados' history (table 3.7).

During the first months of apprenticeship, the success of Barbadian planters in maintaining the level of sugar production was momentarily matched by several neighboring colonies. The lieutenant governor of Grenada reported that order and tranquillity among the apprentices had resulted in a good crop yield. The administering officer of Tobago noted equally satisfactory results, and Governor Sligo of Jamaica wrote that the size of the crop was somewhat diminished but the quality had improved.[47] It was only a short time, however, before more disturbing news was heard

Table 3.7. Exports from Barbados, 1832–38

Year	No. of Hogsheads[a] of Sugar Exported	Total Value of All Exports (£)
1832	18,757 (13,325)	408,363
1833	27,022 (19,349)	553,628
1834	27,318 (19,728)	736,006
1835	24,189 (17,234)	b
1836	24,815 (18,621)	749,193
1837	31,220 (22,286)	897,990
1838	31,786 (23,679)	960,368

SOURCES: *Barbados Blue Books*, 1832–38, CO 33/44–49; Deerr, *History of Sugar*, 1:194.
a. Figures in parentheses represent the number of tons estimated by Deerr.
b. Not available.

from several of the former slave colonies. The officers administering Trinidad, Dominica, and Montserrat reported that the apprentices were unwilling to work; the governor-general of the Leeward Islands complained that the laborers of St. Kitts were on the verge of revolt because they had not been given their full freedom, as had those in nearby Antigua. Troops had to be used to restore order in British Guiana, and in Jamaica some recalcitrant Negroes were flogged.[48] By 1836 Barbados was the only former slave colony that was able to keep enough workers in the fields to sustain a high level of production; output was declining in all of the British West Indian colonies except Barbados and British Guiana (table 3.8).

The governors in the West Indies attributed this widespread decline in production to the apprentices' desertion of the estates, the unwillingness of free Negroes to work for wages, and the reluctance of creditors in Great

Britain to extend sufficient funds to the planters. But the main problem was shortage of labor. As Sligo and Smith explained from Jamaica, planters could not expect apprentices to be as willing to do as much work in an eight- or nine-hour day as they had done in twelve, eighteen, or twenty hours as slaves.[49] Clearly, the abundant supply of laborers in Barbados gave reasons for optimism that were lacking in the other colonies.

Another long-range trend was showing up in Barbados, and it would have unfavorable effects on planters and workers alike. Since 1800, the estates usually grew enough sweet potatoes, yams, eddoes, guinea corn, and hay to satisfy the needs of the inhabitants and livestock. But soon after the end of slavery in 1834, the growth of cane in Barbados was so greatly

Table 3.8. Volume Changes in Sugar Production in British West Indies, 1831–34, 1835–38

Colony[a]	Percentage of Increase or Decrease	Colony	Percentage of Increase or Decrease
Barbados	+24	Jamaica	−15
British Guiana	+ 9	Grenada	−20
St. Vincent	− 5	Dominica	−33
Trinidad	− 7	Tobago	−36
St. Lucia	−12	Nevis	−40
St. Kitts	−13	Montserrat	−50

SOURCE: Burn, *Emancipation and Apprenticeship*, p. 367.
a. The figure for Antigua is not given in the source.

extended and the cultivation of food so diminished that it became necessary to import cereals, meat, fish, and fodder. Thus, while the island's exports in 1838 exceeded those of the previous year by £62,378, its imports in 1838 surpassed those of 1837 by £124,177, resulting in a net setback of £61,799. At the same time, the refusal of American provisioners to accept sugar as payment had the additional harmful effect of depriving Barbados of the small coins that were needed to pay the laborers' wages.[50]

———————

Despite numerous problems that persisted in the British West Indies after 1836, by the time of MacGregor's arrival at Bridgetown the Colonial Office's attitude toward the results of apprenticeship in Barbados was one of guarded satisfaction. The power to settle disputes between the estate owners and apprentices had been assigned to special justices; a limit had been set on the amount of work required of the field laborers; the planters were learning to be more efficient in the management of their estates; miscegenation, which the authorities in London considered harmful, was decreasing. On the other hand, the imperial government continued to express dissatisfaction over some issues. There were no legal provisions in the Caribbean colonies for the support of free black children; the penalty for assaulting an apprentice (£5 in Barbados) was too small; prisons and jails were managed by local officials; numerous arguments between workers and employers kept alive hostility between the races. But the Colonial Office rightfully understood that the most serious defect was that the former slaves were not free to sell their labor to employers of their own choice. Glenelg saw clearly

Table 3.9. Apprentices' Scale of Allowances and Commutations in Barbados

Allowances	Commutations
30 lbs. of roots per week or 10 pints of guinea corn to all apprentices above 10 years of age; to all under 10, half the quantity	To all apprentices above 16 years of age, ½ acre of land for raising provisions; to all under 16, ¼ acre of land
2 lbs. of fish per week to all apprentices	£1.5s. a year or 17 days free of work
1 jacket or penistone 2 shirts or shifts 2 petticoats or trousers 1 cap or kerchief 6 skeins of thread	In money for each full-grown man or woman, 2 dollars 8 bits; for a second size man or woman, 2 dollars; for an apprentice 10–16 years of age, 17½ bits; for apprentices from 10 years of age down, 15 bits
1 blanket every 2 years	1 dollar

SOURCE: "Scale of Allowances and Commutations," with Smith to Glenelg, 8 December 1835, CO 28/116.

that many of the failings of apprenticeship were difficult to correct, yet he believed that two glaring defects in the West Indies needed immediate remedy: the planters should be prevented from defrauding the Negroes of their allowances, and the apprentices should be given better safeguards from physical assault.[51]

As in the other colonies, the law in Barbados spelled out in considerable detail the quantities of food and clothing to be supplied the workers. It also specified that the planters were entitled to substitute other rations, money, time or land in lieu of some or all of the specified allowances (table 3.9). From the beginning of apprenticeship, many economy-minded planters in Barbados elected to alternate such costly imported items as fish with one of the commutations authorized by the local law. But the Barbadian scale of allowances was complicated and confusing, especially for the apprentice, who did not understand whether the choice of substitutes belonged to him or to his employer. It had to be expected that such a complicated body of rules would increase the likelihood of disagreement.

It was, however, a suspicion that the Negroes were still suffering from punishment by the whip that attracted the attention of British humanitarians. As countless reports arrived in London of unwarranted assaults on West Indian workers by estate owners and overseers, a movement arose to cut short the remaining period of apprenticeship. Smith's denunciation of the planters in Jamaica has already been noted, but Sligo had also castigated the proprietors for cruelty toward blacks. In his words, "persons who have been used to the diplomacy of the lash . . . [were not] acquainted with the best methods of influencing human minds by persuasion." On another occasion he informed Glenelg, "you thought that they [the planters] would not so soon forget the munificent gift of the British nation nor their compact . . . of remedying the defects of their Abolition law."[52]

As early as 1835, Thomas Buxton moved in the House of Commons for an inquiry to determine whether the conditions under which Parliament had granted £20 million to former slaveowners had been met. He acknowledged that the end of slavery had taken place with less trouble than had been expected, a result which he believed could be attributed to the patience of the workers rather than the wisdom of the planters. But if it could be shown that the former slaveowners were brutally oppressing the blacks, he believed that Parliament should demand a refund of the money that it had given them.[53] The members of the West India Planters and Merchants in London were sufficiently troubled by Buxton's motion to send a deputation to speak with Melbourne, who promised to oppose any attempt to deprive the proprietors of their compensation. The motion did not pass, but the House of Commons did appoint a select committee to report on the condition of the African population in the West Indies. Its findings resulted in recommendations that heavy fines be imposed on persons who assaulted an apprentice, effective regulations be adopted to protect former slaves from being maltreated in prison, and flogging, of females in particular, be outlawed.[54]

Responding to pressure from the British press, Glenelg sent a questionnaire to the governors of the West India colonies demanding detailed information about the actual working conditions, diet, medical care, and lodgings of their laborers. He was especially eager to know what circumstances existed in the prisons. Meanwhile, a delegation of humanitarians, including Joseph Sturge, Thomas Harvey, and John Scoble, sailed from the home country to inspect the Caribbean colonies. Their account depicted "cruelties unheard of, unthought of, in the worst days of slavery."[55] The treatment of apprentices on the estates was harsh, but the worst abuses were being committed in the local prisons, which consisted of small unventilated chambers where multitudes of workers were confined for months at a time. Many unconvicted persons awaiting trial were kept in chains, and the guards not only assaulted the prisoners at will but routinely tortured them on the treadmills. Describing the treatment of female inmates on such a device at the town hall jail in Bridgetown, one of the visiting humanitarians reconstructed a lurid scene:

> Such a sight I never saw before.... The[ir] heads [were] shaved quite close, with a handkerchief tied round them.... No difference whatever was made between them as to the amount of punishment. When we arrived ... the brutal driver was flogging them with the cat with as much severity as he had previously flogged the men; he cut them wherever he listed, and as often as he pleased.... On the mill there was a mulatto woman, perhaps about thirty, dreadfully exhausted—indeed, she could not step any more.... The driver flogged her repeatedly, and she as often made the attempt to tread the mill, but nature was worn out. She was literally suspended by the bend of the elbow of one arm, a negro [guard] holding down the wrist at the top of the mill for some minutes; and her poor legs knocking against the revolving steps of the mill until her blood marked them. There she hung, groaning, and ... [frequently] received a cut from the driver, to which she appeared almost indifferent.... But she was not the only one who suffered; a black girl, apparently about eighteen, was equally exhausted. When we arrived she was moaning piteously. Her moans were answered by the cut of the whip. She endeavoured again and again to tread the mill, but was utterly unable. She had lost all power, and hung, in the same helpless way with the mulatto woman, suspended by the left arm, held on by the wrist by the negro [guard].... It was most affecting to hear her appeals to the driver, "Sweet massa, do pity me—do, sweet massa, pity me—my arm is broke." Her entreaties to be relieved were answered by cuts from the whip....[56]

Leaders in Barbados, such as Solicitor General Clarke, treated the visiting humanitarians with scrupulous respect; they were aware of the damaging effect any unfavorable publicity in Great Britain could have on them since several members of Parliament continued to demand punitive steps against the planters. Commenting frankly on the state of the prison at Bridgetown in 1836, the Barbadian jail commissioners admitted, "Hitherto our goal has been so wholly inadequate to our wants, and has been so neglected, that only the worst results could have been expected from such a vicious system." But the local commissioners believed that the prisons of Barbados were no worse than those of other colonies, where flogging of females was part of the daily routine and treadmills were introduced at the governors' suggestion. Thome and Kimball wrote in 1837 that most local jails were uniformly dirty, badly ventilated, and "unfit to keep beasts in." In Jamaica the majority of prisoners were shackled by the neck and worked in chains, and according to official reports eleven convicts had died in a single workhouse. In Dominica the cells used for solitary confinement were so small that the inmates did not have sufficient room to stand.[57]

The members of the Barbadian legislature likewise argued that, on the whole, the island's apprentices were worked less than those of any other British colony in the West Indies and that they were treated more leniently and generously than the peasants in Great Britain and Europe. By way of contrast, they said that during the harvest in Jamaica boilerworkers were kept on duty throughout the day and night, and on some Jamaican estates the mill hands were worked from Monday morning until the following Sunday morning. Only during occasional interruptions, when the mills were being resupplied with fresh canes, were the boilerworkers able to doze for a few minutes. In contrast such laborers in Barbados were seldom kept on duty more than twelve hours a day.[58]

Eager to avert British interference in local affairs, the council and assembly in 1837 adopted a new set of prison regulations: the treadmill was removed, females were no longer subject to corporal punishment, males would be flogged only on orders from the governor, and every cell would be cleaned daily.[59] These modifications did not come in time to prevent the imperial government from sending J. W. Pringle to inspect the West Indian prisons. Submitting his findings a few months later, the investigator confirmed that the Bridgetown jail consisted of a single room beneath the ground floor of the town hall, the same building in which the legislature met. The prison chamber measured a mere thirty by thirty-five feet, and in this small space more than three hundred inmates were often herded. The walls were dirty and in need of painting; the air smelled of urine; confined persons were mixed indiscriminately, regardless of age, sex, or crime; females were separated from males only at night. The inadequate diet consisted of vegetables and water, and the prisoners were not attended by a physician. Officially the establishment was under the supervision of the governor, but its actual management was in the hands of a jailer, who, according to Pringle, was so ill paid that "no fit person will long continue in the situation." However, there was no evidence that the convicts were being physically abused at that time, and the treadmill, which had attracted the wrath of the humanitarians the previous year, was no longer in use. Reporting separately on the state of the rural prisons in the parishes, Pringle considered them to be among the worst in the West Indies. The buildings were without windows and toilets, and, in his opinion, the stench was the worst he had ever experienced.[60]

While members of Parliament discussed the Pringle report, the Barbadian legislature passed an act providing for the conversion of the entire town hall into a prison, thereby making it necessary for the council and assembly to meet elsewhere. The improved facilities included several large cells, a hospital, water pumps for washing, and a chapel. New regulations also stipulated that the confined persons should be supplied with hammocks instead of being required to sleep on the floor; an adequate sewage system was to be built and kept in good repair; the walls should be whitewashed monthly; debtors should be separated from criminals. Commenting a few months after the completion of the new jail, a royal engineer observed that the building compared favorably in spaciousness, ventilation, and sanitation with any prison in Great Britain and that in general convicts in Barbados were now better fed, better lodged, and less worked than most soldiers sentenced by court-martial anywhere in the British Empire. "Bearing in mind the labour expected of the field Negroes [in Barbados]," he insisted, "it appears to me that the most numerous class of prisoners, when under confinement, have nothing but the temporary loss of freedom to regret." Meanwhile the Barbadian legislature decided that conditions in rural prisons were too bad for them to be repaired; henceforth such places would be used only in emergencies or when there were too many prisoners to be properly housed at the Bridgetown jail. As a final measure to assure British humanitarians that the apprentices would not be abused on the estates, the council and assembly passed a bill increasing the fine for assaulting a worker from £5 to £10.[61]

The enforcement of many other regulations intended for the protection of the apprentices was in the hands of the special justices, whose efficiency and integrity were questioned by antislavery leaders. Commenting on the behavior of these officials Thome and Kimball wrote disapprovingly, "they associate with the planters, dine with the planters, lounge on the planters' sofas, and marry the planters' daughters." Undoubtedly there were many who served conscientiously and in return suffered from low pay, overwork, and insults from whites and blacks alike. But there were also enough examples of drunkenness and misconduct among them to suggest that they were no better suited to serve as arbiters between apprentices and masters than many of the local justices of the peace. Furthermore, the special justices were entrusted with the purpose of administering apprenticeship in such a way as to prepare the blacks for the civic and moral obligations to be imposed on them as free citizens; as explained by Burn a century later, they failed in this because most of them were men of coarse character. In some places the majority were individuals whose temperament was hardened in military services or on plantations and who naturally thought that the solution to most problems was punishment of the Negroes. Such persons, Burn feared, discharged their duties with greater mechanical aptitude than with conscience, and they frequently tended to favor a quick decision rather than a considered one. Many of the special justices ignored matters that were likely to cause them difficulty or unpopularity, and they valued their own convenience and comfort more than they did the success of the apprenticeship system.[62]

Brushing aside reports of the recent improvements at the Bridgetown jail, scores of British humanitarians in 1837 petitioned the Colonial Office for the termination of apprenticeship as soon as possible. Accounts purporting an increase in the infant mortality rate of Barbados meanwhile caused antislavery leaders in London to think that such a trend in itself would eventually force parents to apprentice children to estates in order to secure their proper support. If the Negroes refused thus to obligate their offspring, the humanitarians suspected that the Barbadian legislature would put the children to work without the parents' consent. To prove this supposition, Buxton quoted a speech in which Clarke urged the assembly to "rescue ... the children from the curse of idleness and ... enable them to provide for themselves at a future date by honest and profitable industry."[63] The local leader denied having any ulterior motives, but the *Birmingham Philanthropist* in Great Britain charged that

> In Barbados, the combination amongst the planters is such, that it would require a degree of moral courage not to be expected ... for one of their number to adopt a liberal and enlightened course.... Besides the mortality occasioned by the present system to the free children, the disgust of field labour which it keeps alive in the minds of the parent[s] greatly increases their reluctance to having them put to any kind of agricultural work and the masters generally are able to throw obstacles in the way of their getting any kind of efficient instruction till the end of apprenticeship, so that there is ground to fear many of them will imbibe idle habits that will not easily be removed.... Speaking of the state of the free children ... the planters had settled it in their own minds, after 1834, to have the children apprenticed, and when the parents unanimously refused, in a fit of disappointment, many turned them out upon the public roads, and refused to allow the mothers any time to attend them, or any of their usual indulgences. They [the planters] told them "See what your friends in England have done for your children."[64]

Eager to deter the imperial government from abolishing apprenticeship earlier than originally intended by Parliament, the Barbadian legislature acted on MacGregor's recommendation and passed an act making it unlawful for parents to apprentice their offspring to estates. Colonial Secretary Glenelg confirmed the measure at once.[65] The governor meanwhile impatiently rebuked the humanitarians for publishing distorted accounts of the estate owners' misdeeds toward blacks, and he summoned a meeting of the special justices to determine whether the new system of work in Barbados had imposed any undue hardships on laborers. The justices replied that the majority of Negroes had been treated fairly by the planters; if there appeared to be numerous complaints, it was because the attempted arrangements were governed by so many vague regulations that neither worker nor proprietor fully understood his rights and obligations. Rules concerning allowances were particularly complicated, and even the provision giving a discharge to an apprentice who was twice assaulted by his master was a source of trouble because it encouraged a worker to provoke a second assault. But the special justices believed that the worst irritations in the West Indies were caused by the humanitarians themselves, who had introduced "to the heated imagination of the apprentices an overwrought picture of the oppression." It would be wise, MacGregor added in a dispatch to the colonial secretary, if critics in Great Britain waited for proof before accusing the proprietors in Barbados of every cruel deed committed by the former slaveowners of other Caribbean colonies.[66]

Buxton admitted that he had unknowingly exaggerated Clarke's motives toward black children, but other British leaders continued to press in 1838 for an end to all forms of unpaid labor. They argued that termination of the nonpraedials' services, scheduled to take place in 1838, would antagonize the praedials, who were required to wait until 1840.[67] As a matter of principle, Glenelg opposed an official act by Parliament shortening the apprenticeship period, because the imperial government had promised the planters in 1833 that the labor of field hands would be available to them until 1840 unless it was willingly abridged by the colonial governments themselves. Meanwhile he strongly urged the British West Indian legislatures to abolish apprenticeship voluntarily in 1838. In the event that local councils and assemblies were not agreeable, the colonial secretary introduced a bill designed to bring laborers under the supervision and protection of the imperial government by giving governors the power to inspect estates, regulate working conditions, and discharge any Negro who was grievously mistreated. Such a measure was necessary, Glenelg explained to Parliament, because "the evil feelings generated by a long course of wickedness still rankled in the breasts of the oppressors," who now had recourse to worse instruments of torture than had ever been employed "in the heights of their most licentious barbarity."[68]

Glenelg's bill was enacted into law in April 1838, to go into effect two months later wherever apprenticeship was still practiced. Commenting on the colonial secretary's intemperate reference to the sugar proprietors, MacGregor also protested that such a drastic law was not needed in Barbados, where he believed that the planters had acted liberally toward blacks. Glenelg refused adamantly to excuse the colony from the provisions of his act, and he warned MacGregor that public feelings in Great Britain were so deeply aroused that the refusal of any West Indian legislature to abolish all forced labor in 1838 would probably be followed by more drastic demands from London.[69]

Throughout the spring of 1838 MacGregor urged the island's leaders to act promptly on Glenelg's admonition, because he was also convinced that Barbados had nothing to fear from a system of labor based on wages. Local proprietors had freely admitted the same on numerous occasions, but the assembly argued that any reduction of the apprenticeship period should be accompanied by a parliamentary act providing additional indemnity to the planters. Following a heated debate in the lower house, Clarke appealed to the members to give workers their freedom. He argued that the law recently adopted in Great Britain for the future management of apprenticeship would make the relationship between the estate owners and the Negroes intolerable. He advised the lower chamber, "I say ... the ... labourers deserve this boon at our hands. I say they are fit for freedom—that they deserve it ... as a reward for their good behaviour. The time has come to acknowledge this—the day has happily arrived when they should be released from the last link in the chain of slavery, when by a vote of this House, a cheerful and obedient population will be converted into a happy and contented, and a grateful community of free men."[70]

Bishop Coleridge quickly endorsed these remarks, and in May the council and assembly passed an act abolishing apprenticeship in August, three months hence. The members expressed hope that the large sums of money spent by the imperial government on educational and religious training would have a moderating influence on the Negroes when they attained their liberty. Compliance with the Colonial Office's desires did not mean that the planters were fully reconciled—on the contrary, they were greatly annoyed. As the assembly explained in a memorial to the home government, "We who have been voluntary parties to ... the extinction of slavery are entitled to expect that the odium which has so long rested on the whole of the Upper Classes of Colonial Society because of the delinquencies of a few of its disreputable Members will now be removed; that the distrust with which

every thing emanating from them has been uniformly viewed, will at length
cease to operate to their prejudice; that the philanthropy which has so
actively been displayed in rescuing the working Classes from Slavery, will
not persevere after its extinction in attempts to injure the characters of the
Gentlemen of this Country, who were no parties to its creation."[71]

The legislative bodies of Montserrat, Nevis, Tortola, St. Kitts, St. Vincent,
Tobago, Grenada, and the Bahamas also gave prompt approval to ending all
servile labor in 1838 instead of 1840. But news that the leaders in Bridgetown
had surrendered to pressure from London caused consternation in British
Guiana, Trinidad, and Jamaica, where the proprietors had vowed their
opposition to any change in the existing system. The court of policy in
British Guiana and the council of Trinidad withheld their consent for several
months before yielding. It was in Jamaica that the most stubborn opposition
was offered and where Smith had already warned that the assembly "would
delight in getting up an Insurrection for the pleasure of destroying the
Negroes."[72] Yet even at Kingston, where the irate leaders' conduct bordered
on open defiance to Great Britain, the legislature eventually passed the
unpopular act that was thrust on them from London.

Even these measures in the Caribbean colonies did not end the concern in
Great Britain for the former slaves. As yet Barbados was the only colony
that had improved prison conditions, while the assembly in Jamaica was
unwilling to sanction such reforms. It also refused to end corporal punishment. The imperial government continued to object to the harsh treatment
of convicts generally in the West Indies, and in July 1838 Parliament passed
the West India Prisons Act, depriving the local legislatures of the right to
administer all places where persons were confined against their wishes.
Henceforth such establishments would be controlled by the governors
alone. The Jamaican legislature denounced the parliamentary act so vehemently that many persons in Great Britain regarded the event as the cause of
the final breakdown between Jamaica and the Melbourne government,
already mentioned.[73]

MacGregor again reminded the Colonial Office of the improvements that
Barbados had voluntarily undertaken at the town hall jail in Bridgetown,
and he appealed to the imperial government to excuse the island from the
provisions of the new prison law. Failure to do so, he feared, would only
further inflame the planters against the home government. The colonial
secretary's refusal to comply with MacGregor's urgent request led the
governor to sound a warning. The imperial government, he wrote, had
repeatedly failed to realize that uniform policies throughout the colonies
were not always suitable, and unless officials in London were willing to
guarantee that Barbados would not continue to be punished for deeds

committed in other places, local opposition to imperial policy in the future would be justified on the grounds that it was impossible to satisfy the authorities in London.[74]

———————

Because Barbados had exceeded the other colonies in the Caribbean Sea in opposing amelioration in the 1820s, the Colonial Office assumed that it would do the same when emancipation was proposed at a future date. But the island's informed residents who read metropolitan newspapers and studied the debates of the House of Commons understood by 1833 that the full force of British public opinion was unalterably in favor of abolition of slavery. They did not aim to prevent the end of Negro servitude but to salvage a few vestiges of their control over the workers—for example, by assigning administration of the police to a body consisting mainly of themselves. Glenelg's firm refusal to sanction the attempt was to be taken for granted, as was his concern for the treatment of the free black children. Such matters were of a magnitude that the Barbadian legislature itself was eventually persuaded to enact suitable remedies, and very few planters seriously thought that the young blacks should be allowed to starve. But Glenelg's strict insistence on compliance with numerous arbitrary details dictated from London caused much ill will among Barbados' influential inhabitants. He failed to take into account that it was more important to seek the support of such persons than to provide each apprentice with three pounds of fish every week. At the same time many problems were magnified unnecessarily by Smith, whose exaggerated humanitarian zeal greatly diminished his effectiveness as an impartial arbiter in the former slave colony. As a consequence, Barbados was virtually the last place in the British West Indies to adopt the important recommendations deemed essential to the success of emancipation.

Many varying opinions were expressed concerning the success or failure of apprenticeship. Judging from the disapproval expressed in Bridgetown when the system was terminated in 1838 instead of 1840 as originally intended, the planters of Barbados must have regarded apprenticed workers as an asset, and, notwithstanding the abundance and consequent cheapness of labor in the island, they contemplated the approach of a new system of wages with much apprehension.

It is difficult to gauge the extent to which apprenticeship improved the Negroes' status from what it had been under slavery. It was a step in the direction of freedom; several British statesmen, including Glenelg and Stephen, regarded it as a necessary intermediate stage during which clergymen and teachers would have the opportunity to transform the blacks into a virtuous peasantry similar to the yeomanry in Great Britain. The period that intervened before complete freedom was permitted would also allow time for colonial legislatures to adopt laws and institutions suited to free persons rather than slaves. Such were the idealistic expectations that individuals in the home country clung to for a time. But it was presuming too much to think that Negroes would regard apprenticeship as anything but another form of servitude. It was probably true that the peasantry of Barbados was more inclined to industry than workers elsewhere in the former slave colonies, but their disappointment in the arrangements adopted in 1833 was expressed in destructive conduct: allowing a piece of machinery to be damaged, abusing a cow or horse, neglecting to weed a patch of land, or feigning illness. Similarly, it was unrealistic to expect the estate holders and overseers, accustomed to obedience, not to respond under the pressure of frustration by committing violence against uncooperative workers, and the presence of special justices did not prevent such misconduct.

The expediency and justice of ending apprenticeship in 1838 instead of 1840 could also be questioned. It prejudiced the proprietary body in the colonies against the superintending role of Great Britain, and the colonial secretary's efforts to coerce the local legislatures encouraged the false impression that the imperial government was always ready to intervene on behalf of the Negroes. Beyond this, the unscheduled termination of the arrangements approved by Parliament in 1833 discriminated against many workers who had purchased their discharges during the succeeding five years.

It is also important to ask about the effects of abolishing apprenticeship. In Barbados and St. Kitts, where there was a dense, immobile black population, there was no apparent impact. A century later Mathieson noted that there were other places in the Leeward Islands where working conditions were identical with what they had been during slavery. The results were different in Jamaica, British Guiana, and Trinidad, where numerous Negroes abandoned the estates and acquired land of their own. There was another important outcome of ending apprenticeship in such places. As Burn declared, it shook the planters and laborers from their mental lethargy and compelled them to seek new alternatives to the inflexible system of compulsory labor.[75] Such was the outcome in many Caribbean colonies. But in Barbados, much of the old system and ideas continued unchanged.

4. The Advent of Free Labor, 1838–1846

DURING THE summer of 1838 Barbadians of both races tensely awaited the end of apprenticeship on August 1. The blacks doubted that they would receive the same freedom as the whites, the planters feared that the Negroes would not work, and the governor expected that confusion would follow on all sides. The estate owners did not know what wages to pay, and the blacks were equally unfamiliar with the responsibilities of hired laborers. Such doubts arose from the inhabitants' mistrust of each other and from their lack of experience with a system of work based on negotiation instead of compulsion. Many annoying questions consequently remained to be settled between the Negroes and their former owners.

The proprietors of Barbados continued to complain of the hastened end of apprenticeship. Their annoyance was apparent when, in response to an offer by the home secretary to supply Barbados with white laborers from British juvenile prisons, Clarke declared in the assembly that "as a burnt child dreads the fire," the landowners had no desire to give the mother country any further cause for complaint against another system of forced labor. The legislature likewise rejected Glenelg's offer to provide Africans liberated from foreign slave ships by British cruisers, on the excuse that lawless savages might endanger the tranquillity of the country. Nor did the planters of Barbados feel that their circumstances warranted the admission of Asiatic coolies or any other form of emigrant labor whose employment would place the estates under regulations framed in London.[1] Yet, despite their

71

obvious ill humor, the Barbadian sugar producers recognized the advantages they possessed in an abundant supply of workers and reliable sources of credit in Great Britain, which in turn caused them to hope that good results might yet be achieved from their altered circumstances. Of all the proprietors in the British West Indies, the estate owners of Barbados continued to earn their reputation as the most enterprising and systematic in the management of their affairs, and they were also prudent in their relations with the imperial government. They did not imitate the caustic attitude c Jamaican leaders toward Great Britain.

The former slaveowners in Barbados aimed to guarantee the profitable cultivation of sugar by hired laborers. Eager to mollify the workers, many planters voluntarily discharged the bulk of their apprentices during the spring and summer of 1838, thereby anticipating the official end of apprenticeship by several weeks. Wages ranged as high as 10d. per day, depending on the skill and experience of the worker.[2] Meanwhile, in order to strengthen the employers' control, the council and assembly enacted a contract law. As in Jamaica, Grenada, St. Vincent, and St. Kitts, the provisions were copied from the Antigua contract law of 1834, which stipulated that five days of continuous labor on the part of a field hand constituted a "general hiring" for a year. The arrangement could be terminated by either party on a month's notice, in which instance the Negro was required to vacate his cottage and grounds. In the event of dismissal by the employer the worker was entitled to be reimbursed for any growing crop left behind, the value of which was to be determined by a local justice of the peace. But if the hired person gave notice, he received no such indemnity. Beyond this, the law provided that any worker who neglected his duty or was insubordinate was subject to eviction, loss of all wages, and up to a year in prison. At the same time, the legislature also passed an act to discourage vagrancy, which it loosely defined as idleness, wandering about, or lodging in any place other than a legally recognized domicile. Other regulations punished the desertion of children by their parents, strengthened the existing penalties against swearing, shouting, gambling, and fighting, and penalized illegal assemblies with three years in prison. Eager to preserve order on the estates, the legislature also empowered proprietors to employ private constables, the majority of whom would be blacks, who were expected to be more effective in controlling the workers than white policemen. Such a system had been tried in Antigua with apparent success.[3]

Although Glenelg understood that there was a need for strong measures to govern former slave societies, he believed that many laws in the colonies were still being enacted in the spirit of slave codes, and he was unwilling to concede that special provisions should be enacted to control the blacks because he feared that such measures gave employers an opportunity to coerce the Negroes.[4] Admittedly, there was a greater need for controlling vagrancy in the West Indies than in Great Britain, and the Barbados act on the subject did not differ radically from the law in the mother country. Nevertheless, the colonial secretary was convinced that such vague provisions would be enforced unfairly against workers in the colonies. Similarly, he disapproved of recent contract laws in the islands, because they provided for protection of employers without giving any corresponding safeguards to workers. He observed that the acts levied harsh penalties on the laborers for trivial misdeeds but that the small fines imposed on the proprietors for assaulting the workers were ineffectual. Glenelg did not consider that a few days of work on the part of the Negro should automatically be construed as a contract for a year or that the planters should have the power to employ constables, whose presence on the estates was a form of intimidation to Negroes. Colonial Office leaders admitted that Antigua had been permitted to pass similar laws, but the colony's offer in 1834 to forgo the right to apprenticed labor had induced the imperial government to accept the measures, with suitable amendments to lessen the severity of some of the provisions. Furthermore, the policy of the home government in 1838 was to oppose all laws that discriminated openly against blacks; therefore the acts recently passed in Barbados to regulate contracts, punish vagrancy, and allow for the appointment of estate constables were disallowed. Other measures that were adopted to discourage workers from deserting their families, gambling, and committing acts of violence were confirmed but in the hope that some of the harsh punishments would be moderated. To insure impartial enforcement of the laws, Glenelg urged the legislative bodies in the West Indies to entrust enforcement exclusively to the special justices who had been present in the islands since the beginning of apprenticeship. The arrangement would be optional in each colony, Glenelg advised, but the imperial government was willing to pay the salaries of such officials wherever their services were continued.[5]

MacGregor opposed the use of special justices after 1838 because he was convinced that local justices would be more influential with workers and planters than would outsiders, whose interference the colonial gentry particularly resented. As he explained, the imperial government still needed local support to make emancipation a success.[6] The legislature passed a strongly worded memorial summarizing its objections to the presence in Barbados of officials subject to orders from London; then it adopted a compromise allowing the island justices to preside in all cases but making their decisions subject to review by an "assistant court of appeals" consisting of three special justices appointed by the governor. Stephen disliked the

Drawn on Stone by W.L.Walton from a Sketch by Hodges

Hullmandel & Walton Lithographers

ST PHILIP'S CHURCH AND MONCREIFFE IN BARBADOS

initial scheme because of the complicated procedures facing a laborer who wished to make an appeal. But the Barbadian legislature simplified the process, and the Colonial Office not only approved the arrangement but recommended its adoption by the other former slave colonies. The plan did not gain general acceptance in the West Indies. The Jamaican Assembly preferred instead to modify its existing judicial machinery by retaining a combination of ordinary and special justices and allowing appeals from both to the Jamaican courts of quarter session. In the Windward Islands, the lieutenant governors, who ruled on behalf of the governor-general in Bridgetown, strongly opposed the Barbadian arrangement; they feared that, unless the special justices were in total control and not likely to controvert local authorities, the few resident planters and estate managers would establish complete control over the Negroes.[7]

During the summer of 1838, as the end of apprenticeship drew near and tension between whites and blacks appeared to increase, MacGregor stationed troops at several strategic locations. Glenelg also requisitioned military reinforcements for Bridgetown, which he regarded as the stronghold that would protect all colonies in the eastern part of the Caribbean Sea from rebellion. But the Canadian revolution of 1837 diverted a large part of the requisitioned forces to Halifax, and the commanding general in Barbados, Sir Sanford Whittingham, was left with a skeleton army, insufficient to suppress a general outbreak even on a single island.[8] On July 27—the end of apprenticeship only four days away—a crowd of several hundred Negroes began to congregate in St. Philip Parish to demand free land and money from their former owners. The governor was sufficiently troubled to ride out to the site and, ignoring personal risk, to address the Negroes. He was convinced, he said, that the workers of Barbados already enjoyed standards of food and clothing unknown to many workers in Great Britain, and the Negroes should also remember that their early release from apprenticeship was achieved with the cooperation of the local legislature and planters. "I ... exhort you constantly," he said, "to bear in mind, that your interests and those of the proprietors are identical, that the cultivation of the soil is absolutely requisite for your support as well as theirs; that you are mutually dependent on each other." Uncertain of the effect of his remarks to the workers, MacGregor warned Glenelg, "Upon these occasions in the West Indian Colonies, it is impossible to be too cautious, because the usages of the negro population, unfortunately debased for ages by the degrading yoke of slavery, are so different from those of freemen, that it is not easy to divine in what light passing events may strike them, and equally uncertain that no people possess in greater perfection the art of concealing their designs." As the final hours of apprenticeship approached, the legislature nervously agreed on August 1 as a day of thanksgiving and prayer. In a last attempt to avert disorder, MacGregor authorized the parish church rectors to act as auxiliary justices, with the power to use the police wherever needed.[9]

The frenzied feelings in Barbados arose from memories of some planters of the Easter uprising of 1816. On August 1, the governor, in full military regalia and accompanied by the commanding general and numerous uniformed aides, paraded into the cathedral at Bridgetown to hear an appropriate sermon by the bishop. Hundreds of blacks listened in awed reverence. A similar spectacle took place on a smaller scale in the rural parishes, where the Negroes filled to capacity the churches and chapels. The Barbadian newspapers described the day's events with satisfaction, and the local inspector of police declared that "not a single breach of the peace, of good order or decorum was known to occur, a fact that would scarcely be credited by persons not witnesses to the same."[10]

Despite this tranquil beginning of freedom for the Negroes, succeeding weeks produced some serious disagreements between planters and workers. The estate owners were willing to pay wages of 10d. per day, which the majority of workers considered too little. Neither party to the system of hired labor had learned how to resolve such questions by discussion and compromise. Suspicious of the provisions of recent local laws and fearful that several days of work in succession would somehow make them slaves again, Negroes refused to serve more than a day at a time and some not more than a day a week. Ten days after the end of apprenticeship, William Sharpe, a local estate manager, complained that there was not a single Negro on duty at any of the twenty properties under his supervision, despite his offer of 1s.3d. per day. Several planters offered even higher wages, thus compounding the confusion; it seemed to the advantage of the laborers not to bind themselves to one estate because the next day would probably bring a better offer from another. Convinced that they had no choice, proprietors threatened recalcitrant blacks with eviction, but the Negroes believed that the Queen had made them a gift of their cottages and refused to leave. In Sharpe's words, the laborers seemed to "breathe an air of defiance ... and as this feeling of insubordination is not confined to ... [a single] estate, some serious mischief might be the result."[11]

If there was any place where the planters were capable of overcoming such problems, it was Barbados. The density of the working population and lack of unoccupied land for the Negroes to settle on were the main guarantees that the former slaves would not refuse estate work. Recognizing the advantage enjoyed by the estate owners, MacGregor encouraged them to be patient, but he also believed that force was justified if the masses continued to be idle. In order to familiarize blacks with the provisions of the contract law (he was as yet unaware of its disallowance), MacGregor issued a proclamation explaining that five days of continuous labor was to be regarded as a verbal contract for a year but that a worker nevertheless was entitled to terminate the agreement by giving a month's notice. If an individual refused to work for the estate where he was domiciled, he forfeited his cottage and land allotment. No Barbadian should have reason to fear or misunderstand such a simple arrangement, MacGregor asserted, but he was convinced that a few local radicals were encouraging the former apprentices to suspect that a new system of compulsory labor was about to be forced on them by their past owners.[12]

Responding in the columns of *The Liberal*, Prescod charged that Mac-Gregor was clandestinely plotting with the planters to restore slavery, an attempt which the people could defeat by withholding their labor until their rights and obligations were fully clarified by London. "The crisis is truly alarming," a proprietor wrote on August 29, and he expected that the "next steps will be revolt and acts of violence." Sensing the need for decisive action, the governor sent troops to arrest several idle black leaders. The jailed Negroes were soon released, on the understanding that they would return to their duties or quit their cottages peaceably.[13]

Seeking to mitigate the tension and to quell suspicions that he was in league with the planters, the governor appointed a commission—the archdeacon, a British military officer, and a recently appointed colored police magistrate, Joseph Garraway—to tour the island in an effort to allay workers' fears. Garraway, the most active member of the commission, explained to the Negroes that their own interests required them to cooperate with the planters, who could not pay adequate wages if they did not prosper.[14]

The former apprentices had been back at work for about a week when, early in October, the dispatch arrived from London disallowing the local contract law and thereby plunging the inhabitants into renewed confusion. Glenelg realized that this action would greatly vex estate owners but that such a step was necessary to prevent what another colonial secretary, Lord Aberdeen, had referred to in 1835 as "the silent growth of a new code depressing below the common level of society" thousands of blacks who had just emerged from slavery. Glenelg admitted that Barbados was not the only colony that had acted to subordinate the former slaves to the proprietors' needs, and he soon announced that the West Indian legislatures generally would be required to modify much recent legislation pertaining to hired labor.[15]

The disallowance of the contract law left Barbados without any regulations for hiring laborers. The masses again refused to work, but MacGregor once more acted promptly, sending out magistrates to persuade them to enter unofficial wage agreements with the planters. Such agreements would not be legally binding but would help to clarify what employers and workers expected of each other. Within two weeks the Negroes gradually returned to their duties, and by the end of a month the judges of the assistant court of appeals reported that most estates were functioning satisfactorily. Thus the transition from apprenticeship to freedom occurred in Barbados without the fearful results anticipated by many of the inhabitants. Several other colonies experienced an equally untroubled end of apprenticeship, but Jamaican planters who were unable to reach wage agreements with their laborers were forcibly evicting the blacks, unroofing the cottages, and turning out the Negroes' cattle.[16]

The workers of Barbados meanwhile continued to be thought of as the most industrious people in the West Indies. The energy with which many blacks applied themselves to a variety of money-making activities surprised critics, who thought that laziness was an inherent characteristic of the African race; in 1838–39, the peasantry harvested 300,000 pounds of sugar on land alloted to them by their employers.[17] A rise in living costs after 1838 drove the masses to produce their own food crops, particularly meat, which was a shilling a pound more expensive in Bridgetown than in London. But the diligent blacks were soon confronted with other problems. Their pigs, chickens, and other livestock frequently trespassed on the proprietors' fields, where they were killed by watchmen, and the planters were also irritated because laborers who cultivated their gardens were often reluctant to give the estates more than four days of work a week. In an effort to obtain five days, many plantations adopted an adjustable rent scale on Negroes' cottages. If the occupant was on duty throughout the needed time, the rent was lowered; if he was absent, it was raised. But as shrewd as the estate owners considered this scheme to be, it did not produce the desired results because it proved to be virtually impossible to collect the increased charge from the workers. Meanwhile, task work, which was used more extensively in other places such as Trinidad, continued to be unpopular with Barbadian planters.[18]

A few planters still feared a labor shortage; this fear led to the enactment of a new contract law in 1840. In contrast with the 1838 statute, which obligated workers to serve for a year, the new act reduced the contract to a month; a second bill lessened the maximum penalty for vagrancy from a year's imprisonment to six months'. The practices that arose in Barbados following the adoption of these measures were important because they formed the basis of the work-rent system that was extensively imitated throughout the British West Indies. According to the general rule, rent was charged to each able-bodied cottage dweller, for which a reduction of one-sixth in wages was made as payment to the planter. This meant that the nonresident worker was paid at a slightly higher rate than persons who were domiciled on the estate. The average pay for a resident laborer in Barbados in 1840 was 10d. per day; nonresidents received a shilling. As long as the former recognized that their labor was reserved exclusively to the plantations where they lived, they were entitled to a low-rent cottage and adjoining garden plot; should they fail to appear for work or otherwise give unsatisfactory service, the owner of the property was authorized to give notice of eviction within a month. Any person who refused to leave when evicted was subject to arrest.[19]

The proprietors defended these arrangements on the grounds that they seldom evicted a worker, yet it was undeniable that such power gave them opportunities to coerce blacks. Workers also complained that many estate owners provided three instead of five days of paid employment a week, which frequently left them short of cash. Many enterprising young males preferred to move from one estate to another in search of lighter tasks and better pay; even in British Guiana, where resident workers were paid high wages, bands of Negroes were often seen wandering from one place to another. The Colonial Office continued to disapprove of itinerant labor because it weakened family ties and because the Negroes' refusal to work for the estates where their women and children were housed gave the planters reason to evict the families or to charge exorbitant rents.[20]

This did not mean that blacks should continue to serve their former owners, who were now their landlords. On the contrary, leaders in London saw that it was expedient for the blacks to sell their labor to the highest bidders, and they could, with cash wages, be free to rent their cottages without being obligated to their landlords. Such a tenancy system was gradually taking shape in Antigua, and in several places in the British West Indies workers were acquiring plots of ground and building their own houses. In Jamaica land could be purchased for as little as £2 per acre; in British Guiana and Trinidad it was being occupied freely by squatters; but in Barbados prices ranged as high as £500 per acre. Glenelg's successor, Lord Normanby, urged blacks to acquire plots at any cost, even if high prices meant that only small areas could be procured.[21] Lord John Russell also believed that even a small garden could fulfill a family's needs, but he regarded this fact with mixed feelings because it suggested that laborers would abandon their work on estates. Statistical accounts reveal that the proportion of nonwhite landowners in Barbados was significantly less than in the other British Caribbean colonies. There were vague indications that a few workers were obtaining land near Bridgetown, where a few estates were being broken up, but, according to Davy, in 1840 there were only 818 holders of less than 10 acres on the entire island. In contrast there were already nearly 8,000 such landholders in Jamaica.[22]

General conditions in the former slave colonies indicated that laborers could benefit from emigrating to places where wages were higher than in their own country. As early as 1836 the planters of Demerara in British Guiana had shown an interest in obtaining workers from nearby islands by purchasing their discharges as apprentices and then shipping them to the mainland as free laborers. Smith opposed the practice because he feared that the Negroes were likely to be overworked in a place where Dutch proprietors had established a tradition of harsh treatment of blacks. The Barbadian legislature responded by passing a law to discourage "divers [sic] persons ... [from] tempting able-bodied labourers and skilful artificers ... to desert their homes and families ... whereby the parishes of this Island are likely to be overwhelmed with impotent families and helpless infants." The provisions therefore required all intending emigrants to apply to the parish churchwardens for tickets-of-leave, which were refused if any dependents were left behind.[23]

When apprenticeship ended in 1838 and workers were presumably free to move from one British possession to another, the court of policy in British Guiana voted £400,000 for bounties to attract workers from other colonies in the West Indies. Barbados' planters, faced with a threat to their labor supply, complained that the indemnity per slave in the former Dutch colony was three times the amount paid them, and they denounced the effort to tempt the unsuspecting peasantry of Barbados into a new system of slavery in order "to swell the already gorged purses" of the Demerara proprietors. The legislature at Bridgetown resolved that the anti-emigration act of 1836 would be strictly enforced, and it imposed a fine of £50 on any individual who attempted to "decoy, or entice away ... any child under sixteen years of age."[24]

A few days later the chief emigration agent from British Guiana, Thomas Day, arrived. Seeking out several colored leaders to hire as his subagents, he offered to pay £10 for each emigrant enlisted, a sum equal to a local worker's yearly income. He also advertised in the newspapers that the average daily wage in his country was 1s.8d., compared to 10d. in Barbados. Persons on the mainland reportedly were able to complete their daily duties in two or three hours, which mean that they received a full day's pay for less than half a day's effort. In addition, Demerara was said to offer an abundance of cheap land, free medical service, friendly places of worship, and shops stocked with the necessities and comforts of a civilized community. But apart from a desire to enlist workers, Day professed that his real purpose was to raise the level of wages in the West Indies.[25]

MacGregor acted quickly to curb the excitement among the masses, and his secretary issued a proclamation declaring that the Queen's representative was "too sincere a friend of the Labouring Population willingly to consent to their being disturbed in their present friendly relations with the Proprietary Body." Because the governor feared, in the secretary's words, that the "Machinations of such a theorist as Mr. Day ... might ... endanger the Public Peace," he had directed the police to guard "the deserving Peasantry of this Island against any imposition that might be attempted ... against them." MacGregor then drew up a list of regulations to protect emigrants during the voyage to British Guiana. The commanders of the vessels employed were to demonstrate that their ships were safe and adequately stocked with pork, beef, bread, rice, peas, coffee, water, and drugs; one indignant captain complained that the supplies required for the short trip to the mainland were sufficient to support an entire shipload of passengers to Europe. At no time during the history of slavery had the planters been expected to furnish their workers with such lavish provisions. MacGregor denied that the regulations were intended to interfere with the Negroes' right to emigrate.[26] Expressing his disapproval in a local newspaper, Day declared: "It is really wonderful to note the extreme pains taken by the high authorities of this Island ... to exhibit themselves in the light of enemies and myself in the light of an advocate of ... improvement in the condition of the labourer, thereby playing into my hands as an Emigration Agent, by exciting in the minds of the emancipated class distrust in them, and confidence in me."[27]

Despite the obvious efforts to deter emigration, hundreds of young males sailed from Bridgetown in 1839. The local legislature therefore redoubled its attempt to persuade the Negroes that Barbados, with its superior climate and purportedly lenient treatment, was a better homeland than British Guiana, where descendants of Dutch planters were harsh and inconsiderate to workers. In order to impress blacks with the rigors of life in the mainland colony, the assembly conducted a series of public hearings where persons claiming to be returning emigrants testified that workers in British Guiana were being swallowed up in the marshes. Many were covered with sores from having stood in muddy water for several days, others were dying of fever, and hundreds of sick Negroes who were unable to work were starving.[28] However exaggerated these claims were, there are indications that the allegations were not altogether unfounded. For many years the swampy environment in British Guiana coincided with a high mortality rate; Adamson's *Sugar without Slaves* (pp. 59–60) quotes a source to the effect that large areas were "so completely under water, that the corpses of those who died (and the deaths were pretty frequent) were placed on bateaux for removal, there being not a foot of dry land in the village."

Because the unfavorable publicity given these conditions in Bridgetown did not deter the blacks from contemplating emigration, the legislature passed an act in 1840 altogether forbidding agents of other colonial governments from enlisting workers in Barbados. Prescod, who was now one of Day's subagents, remonstrated: "The enemies of Right—the real enemies of the Country—those who are disturbing its peace, and troubling it day by day with evil practices, have at length, in the madness of their lust, been hurried into making an open and direct attempt to enslave us!... One of the rights of free men ... is that of going withersoever they please.... Now that the people are free, some of them ... to escape the evils of their condition here ... are leaving the island of their own free will and are emigrating to Demerara. In vain have planter Magistrates and planter Church Wardens lovingly mingled entreaty with the harsher restraint of the laws, to prevent the people from injuring themselves by emigration; in vain have the planter-paid preachers preached, and writers written on the many immense evils they are about to bring on themselves by emigration; the people will go!... Entreaty and abuse, preaching and writing, having thus failed, the Legislature,—our *virtuous* Governor, his *wise* Council, and the *liberal* Assembly—have passed a law to prevent this emigration."[29]

The concern of Barbados' planters over emigration was based on a fear that a reduction of the labor supply would inevitably lead to an increase in wages. But the Colonial Office believed that British Guiana was not entitled to use public funds to obtain workers from neighboring islands because such a policy could foster disagreement among the colonies. Therefore the imperial government disallowed the act providing bounties to emigrants procured in the West Indies. This was followed in 1840 by a attempt on the part of British Guiana's estate owners to organize a Volunteer Immigration Society to supply workers in proportion to the amount of capital contributed by each planter-member. Although most of the persons brought to the colony in 1840–41 were transported under the auspices of this organization, the cost of procuring a small number of emigrants made the experiment an expensive undertaking. By this time almost everyone at the Colonial Office was convinced that the use of emigrant labor in the West Indies should be halted because of the possibility of fraud and deception. But Stephen argued that the imperial government had no right to interfere with a private body of employers, who were entitled to search for workers wherever they could be found.[30] Nor did the colonial secretary, Russell, consider it proper for Governor MacGregor to interfere with the movement of passengers from one colony to another. Yet neither did he believe that emigration should be altogether uncontrolled. The right to impose such controls, Russell advised, belonged to the local council and assembly, whose acts, if imprudent or illegal, were subject to disallowance from London. Hence the law recently adopted in Bridgetown outlawing the activities of colonial agents in Barbados, although controversial in some respects, would be confirmed, but private efforts by planters to obtain workers should not be interrupted.[31]

Commenting on these decisions, Stephen doubted that laws (or a lack thereof) would have much effect on deterring or encouraging emigration in the West Indies. Nor should the responsibility of exercising a choice be denied to any free person. He explained: "Liberty, according to the English understanding ... is the right of every person of sound mind, to do what pleases him, whether for his good or for his hurt, so long as his conduct does not infringe the rights ... secured to his neighbours.... But, as we are convinced, that in the long run, temperance, frugality, and such like virtues thrive best in England without Parliamentary props, so I believe that, in Barbados, the Assembly could contribute nothing to the real advancement of prudence amongst the negroes in selecting their place of residence, without producing greater evil in some other direction. These People must, I apprehend, like the rest of the World, pay the price of Social and Political freedom, and a heavy price it is;—though on the whole, it is a good bargain."[32]

Despite the restrictions against emigration agents in Barbados, by January 1841 some two thousand persons had managed to leave for British Guiana. The number then dropped off because a fall in sugar prices forced the Demerara proprietors to lower wages to 1s.4d. per day and to require more labor from the masses. According to revised regulations, Negroes were required to be on duty at seven o'clock in the morning; those who were not at work by eight were considered absent for the day; no pay was given for completing part of a task; the planters no longer provided free medical care, cottages, land, or daily allowances of rum. Admittedly, wages in British Guiana were still higher than in the other West India colonies, but the new conditions were so unattractive that the exodus of blacks from Barbados had ceased by August 1841.[33]

The heated feelings generated by the emigration controversy did not cool for some time. Prescod, supported by many colored merchants and tradesmen in Bridgetown, resolved that an inter-island association should be formed to protect the interests of their race throughout the former slave colonies. The same persons were in the process of organizing a local chapter of the Anti-Slavery Society when John Scoble arrived from Great Britain to support the movement. Prescod then toured several of the neighboring islands in the Windwards to promote the formation of a "Colonial Union of the Coloured Class." In Prescod's words the main purpose was to "watch the framing of laws in the several colonies ... to assist with advice and money ... and with its whole influence, the injured and oppressed of their race ... to endeavour ... to effect the passing of just and equal laws ... to collect and distribute statistical and other useful information, and to establish if possible a newspaper in each colony, in connection with the association.... The Government of Britain ... will always find it to their interest to conciliate the dominant and influential party [the white minority in the West Indies] unless we break their rest with powerful agitation."[34]

Referring nervously to the proposed colored union in the British West Indies, MacGregor denounced Prescod and Scoble as "unhappy imitators of their illustrious predecessors in the Mother Country, anxious to swell their importance ... by finding more ready outlets in the Colonies for the diffusion of their revolutionary poison." The Barbadian legislature continued to complain of British intruders, whose exaggerated views preyed on the minds of the laborers and retarded the development of confidence between the races in the West Indies. Stephen agreed that many British critics had caused more harm than good; in his opinion, Prescod's employment as a newspaper publisher was in itself "*prima facie* evidence that he has forfeited his claim to benefit society," while *The Liberal* had been used as "a handle for agitation by unscrupulous and selfish ... Writers and other Demagogues."[35] The presence of such agitating influences, he feared, made it necessary for the imperial government to watch over the colonies attentively. Yet Stephen doubted that the Colonial Office's influence was capable of preventing an inevitable Negro triumph over whites. Commenting on the black leaders' demands for a more liberal voting law in Barbados, he predicted: "My own impression on the Subject is that...the so called Rulers of the world [the imperial powers], must submit to be themselves governed by the force of Circumstances, & acquiesce in Measures which would be unwise if the great Mass of Mankind had but the sense to perceive their real Interest. But what are you to do with the bitter, jealous feelings which will be rankling in the Minds of the brown People during the long period of their political inferiority?... [To] remind them that political Authority justly waits upon superior intellectual Culture, is but to throw oil upon the Flame.... [The] breach thus created between the two Races, will not be healed but rather exasperated.... Then will come to the brown, the day of Retaliation; and then will be enacted some kind of test which will virtually exclude the vanquished Rivals. I look to the assertion of an absolute supremacy by the People of Colour, as an inevitable and not very distant Event. The Policy of the Government shd. I think be directed to the object of divesting their success, when at length obtained, of the character of a triumph with its attendant Persecutions."[36]

The attempt to organize a political union of nonwhites in the British West Indies failed because many former slaves were reluctant to put much trust in their own leaders, particularly in Barbados, where the majority of Negroes were more concerned with immediate day-to-day affairs than with politics. While Prescod continued to play an active role in public affairs, he was not equal in influence to such leaders in Jamaica as Edward Jordan or Charles Lake, who, in combination with Jewish merchants, formed the important Town Party. Nor were there any black leaders in Barbados to be compared in energy and ambition to George W. Gordon, who was ultimately hanged for his suspected part in the Jamaican uprising of 1865.[37]

———

When the news reached London of the proposed union of colored peoples in the former slave colonies, Russell observed that there was little likelihood of such an organization having much effect as long as the masses suffered no grievances serious enough to unite them across the sea. Nevertheless, imperial authorities believed that obvious injustices that antagonized blacks should be removed. In particular, they noted that the Barbadian police were commanded almost exclusively by white officers; while the remainder of the force consisted largely of Negroes, many policemen carried swords and other offensive arms, which gave them the opportunity to commit acts of brutality against people of their own race. Other sources of irritation were the high property requirements that excluded the masses from the suffrage and from serving in the militia and the fact that there were few black officeholders in the West Indies.[38]

Complaining anew of the ill-founded concern in the home country, MacGregor placed the local police under new regulations that subjected them to courts-martial and harsh disciplinary penalties, and he persuaded the council and assembly to lower the freehold voting qualification from an annual value of £30 to £20.[39] The latter measure did not increase the Barbadian electorate, except at the capital, where a few blacks possessed the requisite amount of property. But by increasing the membership of the lower house to twenty-four, it allowed Bridgetown to have two assembly-men of its own, and in the election that followed, Negro voters succeeded in capturing a seat for Prescod. Meanwhile, the governor also designated new blacks to the judiciary and to such minor positions as assistant harbormaster and registrar of records.[40] In a more noteworthy effort to give the masses experience in settling civil disputes among themselves, MacGregor induced the legislature to create several "courts of reconciliation" composed entirely of Negro jurors. The arrangement proved to be so useful in resolving family and other minor controversies that Russell recommended the introduction of such courts throughout the British West Indies.[41]

The Colonial Office had been trying unsuccessfully since the 1820s to induce local legislatures to lower the property qualifications for service in the militia, and in 1838 Glenelg recommended the abolition of the local forces altogether. MacGregor argued that the militia was a necessary safeguard against internal disorder, but Stephen believed that military parades and exercises were useful only in relieving the monotonous lives of persons living in the tropics. When the Barbadian legislature refused to abolish the militia in 1839, MacGregor was forced by orders from London to disband the military establishment. Local leaders objected indignantly and hoped that "no further ... agitation will be resorted to by the Home Country, as it is well-known that suggestions from the Colonial Office ... contribute to keep alive the doctrine ... that our laws are still enacted in the spirit of slavery although they have the name of freedom."[42]

MacGregor, wearied by ill health, died in June 1841. His death was regarded as a great loss by the whites of Barbados but was scarcely noticed by the blacks. In assessing his administration, it can be said that MacGregor, by his conciliatory manner, had succeeded in reducing the tension between whites and blacks to the extent that they were now able to work together in reasonable harmony. The appointment of a few educated Negroes to serve as magistrates and the creation of the courts of reconciliation had similar salutary effects. But it would not be realistic to claim that MacGregor was a strong or even willing advocate of the rights of the masses. He felt that much had already been done for the former slaves and that whatever additional benefits they might expect should be attained gradually and as a result of their own efforts. Hence, the majority of colored and black persons appointed to office by the governor were assigned to routine duties, from which he believed that they should work their way to higher positions by proving themselves capable of the responsibility.[43] During the 1830s, the Colonial Office had often expressed a wish to extend the right of officeholding to the former slaves, but it soon changed its mind and was no longer eager to hasten the time when blacks would come to power.

One of MacGregor's most important accomplishments was to restore friendly relations between the executive and the leading citizens of Barbados, whose support was still vital to the success of imperial policy. Among the local figures whose respect and approbation MacGregor won was Clarke, whom MacGregor praised as being incapable of undertaking any act or policy that would operate oppressively on the working population. "On Mr. Clarke's professional ability and zeal," the governor declared, "I entertain toward him sentiments of personal regard, and have been frequently indebted to him for the manner in which he has exerted himself, in the transaction of public business." Only a few years earlier, Smith had castigated Clarke as a troublemaker, but under MacGregor, Clarke contributed to the enactment of numerous useful measures, for which Queen Victoria eventually knighted him.[44]

Although racial tension and misunderstanding continued to mar relations between whites and blacks, the numerous irritations that threatened to erupt into violence in the years after 1833 abated noticeably after 1841. To a great extent MacGregor's successors had to concern themselves less with racial tension than with the more practical problems arising from free trade and competition with foreign sugar.

After MacGregor's death there was a period of undramatic events under the new governor, Sir Charles Grey, who was a trained civil administrator and attorney, not a soldier. His reserved manner created an impression of aloofness, which did not attract enthusiastic local support, but his background—a member of the British House of Commons, chief justice of Bengal, and investigator of the causes of Canadian discontent in the 1830s—gave him a breadth of experience that was useful to his career as a colonial governor in the West Indies. If Grey's administration was not universally popular, it was systematic, business-like, and impartial.

The modest agricultural attainments under Grey (discussed elsewhere) did not signify a decline in the status of the Negroes. On the contrary: later export figures appear dazzling compared with those of 1842–46, but Grey's term in Barbados was noteworthy because there was less want and greater comfort among the masses than there was during many succeeding governorships, when the productivity of the estates was dramatically higher. Admittedly, cheap land was more available in other colonies and wages were higher in such places as Jamaica, but living costs in Barbados were lower than in some of the other colonies and Barbadian workers appeared to be as well fed and adequately clothed as any blacks in the West Indies. The story was very different in 1848, when food costs in Barbados were rising and wages shrank to 7d. per day.[45]

Grey summarized the achievements during the first year of his administration: "The island has not for several years borne so flourishing an appearance as it does at this time ... Your Lordship will remark with pleasure, that the reports of the state of the people continue to be, in the main, favourable. All the opportunities which I have had of personal observation lead me to think that there is not a body of labourers in the world less oppressed than those of Barbados are at the present. Their energy, considering that it is exerted within the tropics, is to me surprising, and they have tastes for enjoyment which are likely to ensure an increasing desire for the money which is obtained by labour." Stanley, once again at the Colonial Office in 1842, commented that emancipation had succeeded beyond his greatest hopes. Stephen observed: "The abolition of slavery has yielded better fruits and earlier than even the authors of that measure dared to anticipate.... The countervailing disadvantages are incomparably less than it seemed reasonable to expect.... Society is on the whole in a healthful and improving state.... The falling off in the profits of capital, though a great evil is largely compensated by an increase in the material comforts ... of the people."[46]

Among the other hopeful signs was a decrease in the number of serious crimes in Barbados after apprenticeship ended in 1838, and the Barbadian legislature abolished the death penalty for such offenses as armed burglary and willful property destruction.[47] This in itself reflected a new feeling of confidence in the masses and suggested that the planters in the legislature were capable of liberal legislation.

Yet, it would be misleading to assume that the employers and workers had no causes for complaint. The majority of Negroes, seeing no advantage in tying themselves to a single estate, continued to prefer day-to-day work. This preference caused proprietors to grumble over the irregular availability of labor, especially during the harvest, when constant work was necessary to gather crops before the onset of the rainy season. When offers of additional pay failed to induce Negroes to work after dark, the planters accused them of indolence. And despite the fact that Governor Grey was satisfied with the decrease in serious misconduct among the masses, there was no corresponding reduction in petty offenses. A police magistrate described the manner in which blacks assaulted one another as "more of savage life than may be expected under our state of prosperity." In fighting, he wrote, "they commonly make use of their teeth, and it is no rare occurrence for a party to a fight to come off deficient an ear, nose, or lip."[48] Much of the unruly behavior resulted from drunkenness, which in turn could be blamed partly on the planters. The habit of giving workers free rum was dying out; but in 1845 the planters of six Barbadian parishes still provided their laborers with spirits, and that year the inhabitants of Barbados consumed not only the entire local supply but also numerous barrels imported from neighboring islands. Other bad behavior resulted from the Negro practice of pilfering, which reportedly deprived the planters of a tenth of their crops; but large-scale stealing was more commonplace in Jamaica, where magistrates complained that bands of marauders carried away quantities of produce every night. Friends of the Negroes in Great Britain rationalized these practices: planters had allowed slaves to take home sugarcanes for their own use, and after the end of apprenticeship those workers could not understand why they were subject to imprisonment for taking a few stalks.[49]

Despite the legislature's recent liberalization of the criminal laws, many whites in Barbados still mistrusted the laborers. When a fire of mysterious origin broke out in Bridgetown in 1845, many people assumed that rebel arsonists had set the blaze; anti-Negro feelings ran so high that the governor was forced to summon British soldiers to protect the workers. Grey observed that "the changes in the ranks and relations which are going on with visible and tangible progress, produce in many persons, and more especially in the young of the European race, dissatisfaction and irritation, and for some years to come, a steady and firm control will be required to prevent the crowd in Barbados from becoming angry with each other."[50]

The imperial government's unwillingness to exercise such control in overseas territories was already clear, however, and by 1840 the Colonial Office was eager to rid itself of many old burdens. Moreover, Great Britain, in the midst of a depression, was more concerned with unemployed factory workers at home than with the former slaves in the West Indies. With a growing annual deficit and the need for a new income tax to balance the budget, Parliament sought to reduce the costs of administering the empire; and it started by withdrawing the salaries of the special justices, who had since 1834 overseen the decisions of local magistrates in the sugar colonies. Commenting disapprovingly from Bridgetown, Grey differed from Mac-Gregor in his opinion of the local justices of the peace: he did not believe that without supervision they were capable of impartiality. The governor apprehended the danger that resident planters and local officials might still combine to enforce unfair labor regulations, and he doubted that there was much likelihood of finding Negroes sufficiently educated or experienced to oversee the courts.[51]

Church leaders in Barbados and in Great Britain persisted in the hope that religion and education would eventually have beneficial effects on the inhabitants of both races in the West Indies, and Bishop Coleridge continued to convince local leaders that religion in particular served a useful purpose by encouraging orderly conduct. Still eager to assist Coleridge's prodigious efforts, the legislature at Bridgetown in 1840 increased rectors' salaries to £300 per annum and provided the curates with yearly stipends of £75, generous sums by current standards.[52] Meanwhile, in keeping with the attempts of the British government to economize in the colonies, many members of Parliament were beginning to think that local governments should pay a larger part of their religious costs in order to reduce Great Britain's share. Noted politicians of both parties in the home country were beginning to feel that the West Indian clergy had been too lavishly indulged, a suspicion that deepened in 1841 when Bishop Coleridge announced his intention to retire on a pension of £1,000 per annum. Many British leaders complained that while Parliament had provided for such a pension in 1824, the bishop was not entitled to retirement until it was offered by the imperial government. Russell considered the amount so excessive that authorities in London should refuse to grant it. Expressing his misgivings of the extravagant livings enjoyed by clergymen generally in the West Indies, Russell declared: "It is not ... desirable that the Bishop of Barbados should be in receipt of an income equal in amount to that of the Governor-General, and in reality placing the Bishop in a position of far greater pecuniary advantage, since he was exempt from taxation and had no private expenses.... I do not consider it favourable to the advancement of the great ends of the Episcopal Institution in the colonies that the Bishop shall be placed in a station which in respect both of rank and emolument elevates him far above any other person holding either a civil or military employment there, and even above the wealthiest of the agricultural and commercial classes."[53]

The new British government formed in September 1841 by Peel decided to allow the bishop to retire, but the Colonial Office continued to stress that the colonies should bear the principal part of their religious expenses in order to lighten the burden on British taxpayers. In 1842 Parliament passed an act lowering the salary of Coleridge's successor from £4,000 to £2,000 per annum and proportionally diminishing the amount paid from imperial funds to supplement the stipends of other Anglican churchmen in Barbados and its neighboring colonies. As intended, the money supplied by Parliament after 1842 paid only a portion of the ministers' and curates' salaries. The new Barbadian bishop, Thomas Parry, was compelled to appeal for additional funds locally; the legislature at Bridgetown agreed to supply them, provided no part of the funds was used outside of the colony. As Parliament further reduced its support of the church in Barbados, from £7,700 in 1842 to £3,500 in 1847, the local council and assembly assumed a progressively larger share of ecclesiastical costs.[54]

The bishop's power of appointment was also of concern to the imperial government. Commenting in 1833, Sir Lionel Smith had declared that the prelate, having acquired the authority to name all rectors, ministers, curates, and other church officers in Barbados and the Leeward and Windward islands, had attained a degree of control over the religious body exceeding that of the Crown in Great Britain, while the governor had no patronage over any department of the government. The Colonial Office also expressed its concern over numerous complaints from local inhabitants against the ill-trained clergymen in the West Indies; in 1845 it authorized governors to alternate with bishops in filling vacant benefices. Parry objected that such an unusual arrangement would weaken the influence of the bishop over the church, but the imperial government was determined that as long as Great Britain contributed toward clerical salaries in the colonies, it owed the British public some assurance that qualified ministers would be appointed.[55]

In the same way that authorities in London thought that religion was important as a moral influence on Barbadians, they believed education to be a beneficial stimulus. There was some doubt that instruction provided in Barbados was suited to the Negroes' needs: most teachers, for example, emphasized the fundamentals of reading and writing, which they taught from scriptural texts. After 1840 Harrison's Free School offered a more sophisticated range of subjects, including Greek and Latin, but the half-dozen Moravian establishments were the only schools in the locality that stressed agricultural and vocational training. As Parry explained, "we do not attempt to train trades and agriculture, which are better learnt among the realities of business than [in] mimic[king] shops and farms." Such attitudes contrasted sharply with educational practices in Jamaica, where the legislature paid supplementary grants to institutions offering training in agriculture, industrial arts, and household skills. According to a local official at Kingston, the Jamaican peasantry not only surpassed the Negroes of Barbados in advanced farm practices, but the women in Jamaica were also better taught in cooking, sewing, and child care.[56]

As important as leaders in London considered blacks' education to be, Parliament nevertheless began in 1840 to reduce its annual grant to West Indian schools, and in 1845 it abolished the grant altogether. The Colonial Office had hoped that the masses would be willing to support schools by paying tuition for their children, but a change had taken place in the laborers' attitude toward education. During the ten years following emancipation in 1834 blacks were eager for their children to attend classes, but by 1845 they could see that formal training did not necessarily lead to a rapid rise in economic status. Many Negroes were unwilling to pay tuition, and, as a result, scores of places of instruction were forced to close. Alfred Caldecott explained a few years later that workers' enthusiasm for education had died. The long-established day school on the Codrington estates had only a few children enrolled, and the master was irregular in attendance. Many of the local Sunday classes had died out; most teaching was under the supervision of untrained and apathetic amateurs, and the principal of Codrington College said that he knew of only one good school on the island.[57]

The Barbadian legislature, however, was eager to support public education, and in 1846 it appropriated £750 as the first in a succession of local grants for the bishop to use to sustain the church's efforts in education. Governor Grey hoped that the legislature would ultimately create schools administered by secular officials rather than the church because he favored giving more emphasis to practical rather than to religious topics, but the imperial government regarded the elimination of church influence in education as a radical change that it could not support. Even Gladstone, known for his liberal views, opposed the transfer of education from religious to secular control in the West Indies.[58]

Another concern in the West Indies was the lack of efforts to relieve the hardships of the poor. When blacks emerged from apprenticeship in 1838 and the last ties with their former owners were severed, workers were expected to be fully responsible for their own support. This attitude was reflected in the strict vagrancy laws that were enacted throughout the former slave colonies, and it was an outlook that the Colonial Office shared with the island legislatures. Glenelg urged the West Indian governments to provide money for the relief of orphans and destitute invalids, but British leaders were skeptical of all comprehensive plans to relieve the poor. Even Glenelg was convinced that "large bodies of men [in the former slave colonies] would always be found ready to avail themselves of such an opportunity of gratifying the love of inaction and repose, to which the climate [of the tropics] so disposes the inhabitants of every class." He urged that the worst examples of distress be relieved with public funds but only after every application for assistance had been carefully reviewed by a board of taxpayers, as was the practice in Great Britain. As expected, this advice from London strengthened the Barbadian planters' determination that no permanent scheme of poor relief be adopted, and humanitarians argued to no avail that Barbadian Negroes deserved help because they were the most industrious workers in the West Indies.[59]

This did not mean that there was no relief whatever for the poor in Barbados. The local council and assembly, like other West Indian legislatures, provided temporary funds to assist victims of hurricanes, droughts, and epidemics, and the parish vestries supplied small sums to aid orphans and destitute mothers. Many inhabitants supported private charities, such as St. Paul's Meal Society, the Odd Fellows Club, and St. Michael's Clothing Society, but in relation to the number of poor persons the amount provided by private charity was small. A few workers also provided for their own relief by organizing societies whose members assessed themselves every month to create a general fund. At the time of Davy's visit to the West Indies in the early 1850s, a society's dues in Barbados were 1s. ½d. a month. This same amount was paid weekly to members who were ill, and £1.13s.4d. was provided for burial costs.[60]

· The care of sick persons who could not support themselves became a serious problem. Numerous travel accounts from the West Indies testify to the fact that the medical care given the slaves by their owners, administered on the estates by hired physicians, was more than adequate. During the apprenticeship period Negroes continued to enjoy the same medical attention, with the exception of the free children, left unattended on all but a few estates. After apprenticeship ended, when it became necessary for the masses to pay their own living costs, many were unable to afford medical care, and laborers, accustomed to free medical attendance as slaves, were reluctant to pay medical fees. Recognizing that the poor needed health care, a group of Barbadian merchants, planters, and professional people created in 1840 a General Hospital Society, whose aim was to provide a center for the free treatment of indigent persons. The first hospital in Barbados thus came into being in 1844, at a cost of £4,000, supplied entirely by private subscription. Its operating costs were ultimately assumed by the legislature, and when Schomburgk visited the island in 1847 he referred to the establishment as "the brightest instance of the benevolent feeling of the Barbadians."[61]

The greatest concern of the planters, however, was their own economic well-being. From the *Barbados Blue Books* and other statistical accounts, it is apparent that sugar production declined significantly during the decade following the end of apprenticeship in 1838 (table 4.1). Exports from Barbados in 1839 were down to 395,109 cwt. (19,775 tons) from 473,587 cwt. (23,697 tons) in 1838 (table 4.2), and it was not until the 1850s that they again reached the level of 400,000 cwt. per annum. St. Kitts (because of the unusual fertility of its soil) was the only colony among those listed where the planters managed to achieve a modest increase in sugar production from 1839 to 1842 (table 4.3).

Table 4.1. Sugar Produced in Barbados, 1835–48

Year	Hogsheads[a]	Year	Hogsheads
1835	24,189 (17,234)	1842	21,545 (15,628)
1836	24,815 (18,621)	1843	23,233 (17,452)
1837	31,320 (22,286)	1844	21,913 (16,435)
1838	31,786 (23,679)	1845	23,432 (17,590)
1839	27,231 (19,755)	1846	20,016 (15,124)
1840	13,319 (10,374)	1847	32,257 (23,451)
1841	17,140 (12,855)	1848	26,887 (20,165)

SOURCES: *PP*, 1852, 51:442; Deerr, *History of Sugar*, 1:194.
a. Figures appearing in parentheses represent the number of tons estimated by Deerr.

The adverse effects of diminished output were partly offset by a rise in sugar prices, which reached a peak of 49s.1d. per hundredweight in 1840; while a decline in the world's retail cost of the product eventually followed, prices remained relatively stable until 1847. As a consequence, Barbados' exports stayed above £600,000 per annum in value except in 1841, when the figure dipped to £531,871 (table 4.2), because dry weather the previous year had resulted in an unusually small crop of 13,319 hogsheads. Throughout the period 1838–46, Great Britain continued to buy the bulk of the Barbadian sugar crop. The planters hoped to increase their sales to American buyers, but exports to the United States did not average £2,000 per annum.[62]

The new economic requirements thrust on the planters by the end of forced labor—a need for large sums of capital to finance plantation improvements and for money to pay wage labor—led to the creation of new

Table 4.2. Barbados' Sugar Exports, 1837–47

Year	Quantity of Sugar Exported in Cwt.	Average Price Per Cwt. in London[a] (£. s. d.)	Total Value of All Exports (£)
1837	445,713	1.14. 7	897,990
1838	473,587	1.13. 8	960,368
1839	395,109	1.19. 2	731,262
1840	207,484	2.19. 1	b
1841	257,105	1.19. 8	531,871
1842	312,503	1.16.11	855,712
1843	348,505	1.13. 9	688,256
1844	328,708	1.13. 8	681,000
1845	351,484	1.12.11	691,309
1846	300,000	1.14. 5	773,405
1847	b	1.18. 3	881,159

SOURCE: *Barbados Blue Books*, 1838–46, CO 33/49–56.
a. Excluding duty.
b. Figure missing at time of research.

financial institutions in the British West Indies. Local banks were created in British Guiana and Jamaica, and as early as 1837 the Colonial Bank of London had established branch offices throughout the former slave colonies. Two years later a group of Barbadian planters and merchants created the West India Bank, which likewise founded branches in several neighboring islands. The high market price of sugar and the decline in production that followed the end of apprenticeship provided incentives for the planters to search for more scientific methods of cultivation, and in 1845 a group of proprietors established the General Agricultural Society of Barbados.

Table 4.3. Great Britain's Sugar Imports from the West Indies, 1831–42

Colony	Increase or Decrease 1835–38 Compared to 1831–34 (%)	Increase or Decrease 1839–42 Compared to 1831–34 (%)
Barbados	+24	−11
British Guiana	+ 9	−62
Dominica	−33	−26
Grenada	−20	−52
Jamaica	−15	−52
Montserrat	−50	−41
Nevis	−40	−48
St. Kitts	−13	+ 5
St. Lucia	−12	−12
St. Vincent	− 5	−40
Tobago	−36	−47
Trinidad	− 7	−15

SOURCES: *PP*, 1846, 44:196; Burn, *Emancipation and Apprenticeship*, p. 367.

Among its objectives were promoting the use of new fertilizers, introducing new varieties of cane and livestock, and cultivating timber. The society tried to stimulate interest in these new ideas by holding annual fairs, and it was especially eager to acquaint the estates with improved machinery for manufacturing sugar. The planters of British Guiana were already ahead of the West Indian sugar proprietors in experimenting with modern mechanical devices; Barbadian planters were slow to abandon their traditional methods; many were reluctant to spend the money required to improve their sugar mills, and some even opposed the use of metal plowshares, which they feared would harm the soil. Nor did they give serious consideration to Governor Grey's recommendation of growing poppies for the production of opium, needed in Great Britain for medical purposes. Apart from temporarily augmenting the production of aloes and cotton, local estates continued for a time to rely on sugar as their principal and virtually only export.[63]

Conscious of their increased production costs after apprenticeship had ended, the estate owners who controlled the council and assembly felt that other economic classes in Barbados—the merchants and laborers—should start to bear a larger share of the colony's financial burdens. Planters complained that fiscal requirements of administration had always been met by levying rates on their houses and lands; as the need for revenues had expanded, other imposts had been collected on their mills, horses, carriages, exports, and imports. As early as 1779 the legislature had imposed a tax on freedmen who earned a livelihood by huckstering, although Handler indicates that such fees were not collected for many years. In 1820 the council and assembly began to tax porters and boatmen, and in 1836 they added licenses for butchers and other retail tradesmen. But the additional revenue was insufficient to meet the higher expenditures proposed in the lower house. A new jail, augmented religious and educational facilities, and enlargement of the police force had contributed to a doubling of the expenses of governing the island between 1835 and 1840, and in 1840 the colonial government experienced a deficit of £3,491.[64] That same year the Barbadian legislature decided to impose an ad valorem duty of 1 percent on all imported merchandise; Bridgetown merchants objected that the new tax raised the retail price of food, clothing, and all other items needed by the workers and thereby laid an additional burden on the class least able to pay it. Replying in the assembly for the planters, Clarke observed in anger that the flourishing appearance of the shops suggested that the merchants alone had reaped a profit from emancipation: the planters had been obliged to pay out thousands of pounds annually in wages, which the Negroes promptly spent for necessities and for such luxuries as wine and tobacco. He urged a rejection of all appeals to lower the existing duty; in response in 1841 the Barbadian legislature advanced the ad valorem duty to 3 percent.[65]

The increased customs duty produced in 1843 a surplus of £42,703, which Governor Grey believed was far beyond the current needs of the colony. He saw that such high import duties, in addition to increasing the cost of living, discouraged ships from coming to obtain Barbadian sugar: "It ought always to be borne in mind, not only that the island cannot flourish without trade, but that at present there are no means of supporting trade, unless its sugar can keep its place in the accustomed markets, or new ones can be found and opened. The island, with an overflowing population, depends in a great degree on foreign countries for its supply of corn and flour, and biscuit. It has no extensive fisheries, no timber, nor fuel, nor iron, nor any sort of metal; nor cotton, linen, nor wool for clothing. All these must be bought, and the only produce or manufacture by which they can be bought at present is Muscovado Sugar. Never was there a community, the prosperity of which so absolutely required a rejection of all notions of self-dependence, and a recognition of the necessity of mutual reliance, and a general intercourse amongst nations. Unity with England, and open trade with all the world are the cardinal points of the prosperity of Barbados." Heeding his advice, the legislature passed an act reducing the ad valorem duty back to 1 percent.[66]

Table 4.4. Effects of British Possessions Act of 1842 on Imperial Duties in British Colonies

Imported Foreign Article	Rates before 1842	Rates after 1842
Linen, paper, leather, clocks, watches	30%	7%
Silk	30%	15%
Glass	20%	15%
Cotton, textiles, tobacco, soap	20%	7%
Miscellaneous unenumerated articles	44%	15%
Fish, blubber, fins, other fish by-products	prohibited	15%
Salt fish	prohibited	2s. per cwt.
Tea	prohibited	1d. per lb.
Salt and cured meats	12 s. per cwt.	3s. per cwt.
Wheat flour	5s. per barrel	2s. per barrel
Cocoa	5s. per cwt.	1s. per cwt.

SOURCE: Stanley to the Governors of the West India Colonies, 30 July 1842, CO 854/3.

Trade statistics clearly indicated the great extent to which the island was dependent on importing food. A calculation shows that in 1842 two-thirds of the inhabitants were living on external supplies, mainly cereals, flour, and salt meat from Great Britain.[67] After 1842 there were several changes in Barbados' import trade as a result of some important modifications in imperial customs imposed in the colonies on foreign goods. Such imposts had been assessed on manufactures, foodstuffs, and other articles of non-British origin in order to give an advantage to producers of similar goods in various parts of the British Empire, but in 1842 Parliament passed the Possessions Act, which greatly reduced the protective margin in the colonies. Such necessities as wood and fertilizer were admitted to the West Indies free of all tariff; foreign whale oil, fish, and tea were taxed at very moderate rates compared with what they had been in the former schedule of customs (table 4.4). The lowered duties on foreign goods resulted in augmented imports of corn, ground meal, wheat flour, salt meat, and butter, principally from the United States. The figures in the *Barbados Blue Books* indicate that the value of American imports into Barbados nearly doubled, from £108,434 in 1842 to £201,211 in 1846. From the standpoint of the inhabitants' needs, the most beneficial effect of the Possessions Act of 1842 was a drop in retail prices (table 4.5).

Table 4.5. Average Prices of Food and Livestock in Barbados, 1842, 1843

Article	1842 (£. s. d.)	1843 (£. s. d.)
Horned cattle per head	20. 0. 0	16. 0. 0
Horses	35. 0. 0	30. 0. 0
Sheep	3. 0. 0	2. 5. 0
Goats	2.10. 0	1. 5. 0
Swine	2.10. 0	1.15. 0
Milk per gallon	1. 8	1. 0½
Butter per lb.	1. 6	1. 3
Cheese per lb.	2. 0	1. 3
Beef per lb.	1. 0	.10
Mutton per lb.	1. 3	1. 0½
Pork per lb.	.10	. 6½
Rice per lb.	18. 9	16. 8
Wheat bread per lb.	. 5	. 3¼

SOURCE: *Barbados Blue Books,* 1842–43, CO 33/52–53.

The last years of Grey's governorship in Barbados coincided with the free trade movement and a demand in the home country for the overhaul of laws governing the admission of foreign and colonial produce to Great Britain. Among the custom duties that the free traders wished to reduce or abolish was the high prohibitive tariff of 63s. per hundredweight on non-British sugar. Governor Grey, a believer in limited protection for colonial produce, foresaw shortly after his arrival at Barbados that Parliament would eventually lower the duty on foreign cane products because the British colonies were incapable of satisfying the needs of consumers in the home country. As shown, British West Indian production had fallen after apprenticeship ended; as a result, the average per capita consumption in Great Britain had declined from 23½ lbs. in 1811 to 16 lbs. in 1842. British industrialists, motivated by their own reasons for wanting to keep the price of food as low as possible, complained that British workers were forced to pay 7½d. per pound for the worst quality of raw sugar, while laborers in foreign countries obtained the best refined sugar for 4½d.[68]

Planters in the British Caribbean, who expressed themselves through the

West India Committee and other friends in London, warned that any attempt to lower the duty on foreign sugar would force them to reduce wages so that they could compete with the slave-operated plantations of Cuba and Brazil. British leaders from both parties nevertheless agreed that Parliament should act on the needs of consumers at home, and the London *Times* was convinced that there was no longer any reason for Great Britain to support the ex-slaves by giving a premium to British colonial sugar. Even more astonishing was the attitude of Sir Henry Taylor. One of the original authors of the parliamentary emancipation act of 1833, he now believed that abolition had "placed the negroes within the danger of a larger access to sudden prosperity than human nature can well bear," and the wage decline that was likely to follow the admission of foreign sugar to Great Britain would serve to make the blacks more industrious.[69]

The resulting Sugar Duties Act of 1846 called for an annual reduction of the duty on foreign sugar until 1851, when the duty on the non-British product would be equalized with the colonial product at 14s. per hundredweight. In communicating the unfavorable news to the legislature, Governor Grey expressed the hope that the result would not be as disastrous as many supposed: "I feel that there is a sure guarantee, at least, of justice being done; and of a settlement of these questions taking place, which will have in it some degree of permanence and solidity. I am almost in hopes, instead of the injuries you apprehend, that boons are about to be conferred upon you, and seeing that in all respects you hold the most advantageous position in the whole of the British West Indies, I am confident that you have nothing to fear." But these bold assurances had little effect on the planters, who gloomily awaited final ruin.[70]

In the circumstances, Governor Grey was convinced that Barbados should try to meet the competition with foreign sugar by augmenting its exports to Europe and America. He believed that one way the island could attract more foreign ships to Bridgetown was by marking the dangerous shoals off the south coast with a lighthouse. As early as 1836 the imperial government had offered to provide half the construction costs of such an undertaking, but the legislature had been unwilling to assume any part of the burden. The changes in sugar duties in 1846 convinced the Barbadians that a lighthouse was needed, and the legislature finally passed a bill to divide the expense of erecting the facility. In keeping with Great Britain's policy of reducing expenses in the colonies, London authorities were no longer enthusiastic about supporting the costs of public works in the overseas territories. But in response to pressure from British shipping interests at home, the imperial government contributed a token sum of £3,000 toward the required improvement.[71]

The governor also called to the attention of the legislature the need to rebuild the island's roads, long neglected by the parish vestries responsible for their upkeep. Unwilling to cooperate with other parishes in establishing an adequate highway system, such local bodies lacked the funds to employ trained engineers and road-builders; the result was a disconnected array of crooked lanes so unusable during the rainy season that the planters were forced to send their produce to the port at Bridgetown by slow and expensive coastal barges. The controversial tariff acts passed in Barbados in 1841 and 1842 provided enough revenue for the construction of better roads, and, responding to Grey's urgent advice, the council and assembly finally established a general fund for the construction of an integrated network of roads connecting the colony's eleven parishes. The responsibility for building and maintaining roads was also placed in the hands of a central highway board appointed by the governor and headed by a certified engineer. Barbados ultimately acquired two hundred miles of the best roads in the West Indies.[72]

The need for improved internal transportation suggested that there was a use for a railroad in the colony, and in 1845 a group of British promoters under Sir Robert Schomburgk arrived to study the possibility. The governor enthusiastically endorsed the idea, which he believed would greatly lessen the cost of shipping sugar from the interior to the port. The time had arrived, he urged local commercial interests, for Barbados to acquire necessary tools for massive production and worldwide competition. Addressing a group of estate owners and merchants, Grey confidently predicted that "European capital and the miraculous power of European machinery will work a new life throughout the mass of the new world, and great changes in the institutions and life of the inhabitants must take place."[73] A shortage of local capital and the unwillingness of the British government to make a loan to Barbados prevented the building of the proposed railway, but the governor's advice was not altogether overlooked by the planters; during the next decade they invested heavily to mechanize their plantations.

Both MacGregor and Grey believed emphatically that the interests of the sugar proprietors and the workers were identical and that the well-being of one depended on the prosperity of the other. Colonial Office leaders also thought frequently in such terms. It is important to question the compatibility of the interests of the white and black races in the West Indies, because even a simple analysis suggests that their needs were inimical. From the start of sugar cultivation, the estates required an abundance of labor, operating at maximum efficiency and producing large crops at the lowest cost. Admittedly, the plantation system did not always achieve such results. But after 1838, with the end of unpaid labor, estate owners unavoidably tended to regard wages as a detriment to profit. They discovered that in places with the highest pay, the quality of the work was at its lowest.[74] When former slaves were able to acquire land, they usually tried as hard as possible to avoid plantation employment. But conditions were different in Jamaica and British Guiana than in Barbados, where the number of workers greatly exceeded the demand and where there was little available land. As a consequence, Barbadian workers not only had to be content with low wages but were expected to provide their best effort in order to avoid losing employment altogether.

Circumstances suggested that the planters of Barbados would have an easy time under a system of hired workers. But the transition from apprenticeship to wage labor was beset with difficulties, which the legislature tried to overcome by adopting laws to regulate contracts, punish vagrancy, and discourage crime. For a time, sugar production in Barbados declined somewhat, and the legislature was prepared to adopt even stronger measures. Glenelg, who opposed the harsh treatment of Negroes, promptly disallowed the Barbados contract law, which he thought was an unfit example for other legislatures in the West Indies. It was but a short time, however, before the outlook of statesmen in London changed. After 1839 the attitude of such colonial secretaries as Russell was manifestly more sympathetic to the planters than had been the case, and when the Barbados legislature passed a new contract law in 1840 it was promptly confirmed.

Barbados arrived at a moderate but undramatic level of prosperity under Sir Charles Grey, who believed that for the moment neither planters nor workers had any serious cause for complaint. An unrestricted exodus of laborers probably would have resulted in higher wages in Barbados, but the superior wages paid in such places as British Guiana were greatly offset by the rugged living conditions and the Colonial Office was reluctant to encourage migration from one former slave colony to another. The imperial government, however, undertook to foster an exodus of workers to the West Indies from Asia under the watchful supervision of commissioners in London, and the question arises why it did not allow such a monitored emigration to take place from Barbados. Technically, there was no law which prevented the masses from leaving, although there were restrictions on the activities of emigration agents. But for twenty years after 1841, Barbadian workers themselves showed no enthusiasm for abandoning the island. However difficult their circumstances, the former slaves were attached to their country, proud of their British heritage, and scornful of other places in the West Indies.

The cooperation of Barbadian workers, despite occasional signs of discontent, was an important reason why emancipation was not as injurious to planting interests in Barbados as it was elsewhere. At least part of the credit must be given to the planters and the local legislature. For the most part, the estate owners' mood following the end of apprenticeship was conciliatory, and in turn the Barbadian council and assembly eventually repealed many of the harsh laws enacted after 1834 in fear of the working class. Meanwhile, many of the practical arrangements that arose in Barbados between employers and laborers, such as the work-rent system, evolved outside the provisions of the law. Momentarily the proprietors were satisfied with a modest return on their investments; workers' houses, although not luxurious, were adequate, and food costs were moderate. Wages were low compared to those of British Guiana, but the Barbadian laborers did not suffer from want. For a brief period, a community of interest had arisen between planters and workers.

5. Barbados and Free Trade, 1846–1856

THE EFFECTS of the Sugar Duties Act, which ultimately deprived the colonies of the protection their products had enjoyed in the mother country, provided the dominant theme in British West Indian history after 1846. The enactment of this unpopular measure caused Barbadian estate owners to complain that their plantations were "fast dying a sort of natural death."[1] The amounts of Cuban sugar imported into Great Britain from 1845 through 1851 (table 5.1) readily demonstrate why British Caribbean planters generally were deeply concerned.

At the beginning of 1846 many of Barbados' planters expected that the resulting depression in the sugar industry would fall as heavily on them as on proprietors in the neighboring colonies. The failure of the West India Bank at Bridgetown and the bankruptcy of several British firms on whom the estates of Barbados had relied for credit produced a local shortage of working capital, which in turn led to a reduction of wages. Hardships were aggravated by a simultaneous shortage of American cereals, which currently were being diverted by crop failures and high prices in Europe.[2]

Despite financial stress, Barbados in 1847 produced 32,257 hogsheads (23,451 tons) of sugar, compared to 20,016 (15,124 tons) in 1846. William Reid, Grey's successor, urged the planters to augment their production further by eliminating wasteful agricultural practices. "Few things strike a stranger more on his arrival at Barbados," he illustrated, "than the bad state of the working cattle, and seeing ten and sometimes twelve weak oxen

drawing in a Waggon." Cultivation of pastures had been so neglected since
the end of slavery that it was now necessary to feed the cattle on imported
hay. Machinery used to manufacture sugar in Barbados was old and obso-
lete. The planters were understandably reluctant to adopt new methods
because they were not in a position to assume additional risks; and if Great

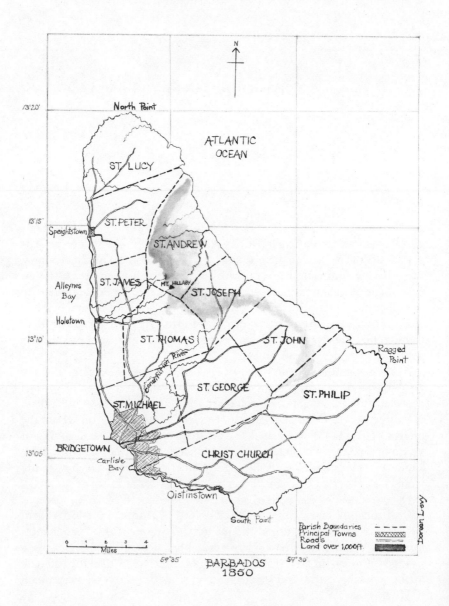

Britain expected them to invest in implements and tools in order to provide the home country with cheap sugar, Reid believed that Barbadian sugar deserved protection from the slave-grown product of Cuba. Otherwise he foresaw that the proprietors in the British colonies would be forced to lower wages still further, which would jeopardize the "consummation of the greatest act of human legislation."[3]

Because of a disagreement with the Colonial Office concerning the dismissal of a judge in the Windward Islands, Reid resigned unexpectedly in 1848. The vacant governorship was filled by Sir William Colebrooke, former governor-general of the Leeward Islands. Although an able and impartial administrator, he was not Reid's equal as an agricultural expert.[4] By the time Colebrooke arrived in late 1848, sugar prices had dropped to

Table 5.1. Great Britain's Cuban Sugar Imports and Average Prices of Sugar on London Market, 1845–51

Year	Cwt. of Cuban Sugar Imported into Great Britain	Average Price per Cwt. in London[a] (£. s. d.)
1845	197,460	1.12.11
1846	499,906	1.14. 5
1847	875,420	1. 8. 3
1848	694,203	1. 3. 8
1849	664,264	1. 5. 4
1850	489,502	1. 6. 1
1851	811,081	1. 5. 6

SOURCE: PP, 51:9442. For figures indicating Cuban production after 1850, see Deerr, History of Sugar, 1:131.
a. Excluding duty.

23s.8d., the lowest since 1831, which temporarily motivated the planters of Barbados to grow food crops, for exportation to the neighboring islands. Nearly 40,000 acres were planted in eddoes, yams, guinea corn, and vegetables in 1848; and while the value of Barbadian sugar exports fell by more than £200,000, the increased emphasis on food production not only resulted in augmented sales to such places as Jamaica and Trinidad but also led to a £93,000 reduction in imports from abroad. The following year, when the price of sugar rose slightly, the proprietors again curtailed food cultivation in order to produce cane.[5]

The period of Colebrooke's governorship was characterized by a rapid transition to scientific agriculture. Wider separation of the seedlings and heavy applications of fertilizer produced more vigorous canes and resulted in a saving of labor formerly wasted on weak plants. Cane trash, which hitherto had been burned as rubbish, was used for animal fodder.[6] Summarizing the achievements of the Barbadian estates after 1850, a local journal boasted:

> What then, and how great are our improvements? To begin with the field; ten years ago the system of farming, or jobbing out fields to the labourers to weed by the week was unknown; now it is universally practiced; ten years ago the first ploughing match had not come off; now there is scarcely an estate that will admit of their use, in which the plough, grubber, and horse hoe are not daily at work; and to these two improvements conjointly we owe the comparative steadiness of our labour market, the destruction of devil's grass, the beautiful thyme-bed appearance of our fields, and under providence the unprecedently large crops which have crowned our efforts. Let us pass to the mill; ten years ago there were not a dozen horizontal mills in the whole island, now it is hardly too much to say that there are as many in every parish, and more to follow every day. Next, look in at the boiling house; ten years ago there was scarcely a planter in Barbados who knew what a vacuum pan was, or had any idea of the possibility of evaporating cane juice at a lower temperature than that produced by a roaring fire under an open taiche; now there are four vacuum pans, besides the plant at the Refinery [established in 1846 at Bridgetown]; and Gadesden-pans innumerable, and other means and appliances which have been more partially adopted; and above all, ten years ago we were unacquainted with those valuable adjuncts to the production of good sugar, Pre-cipitators, and Centrifugal Dessicators; now they are coming so rapidly into fashion, that we shall not be surprised if the man who is unprovided with them next crop is accounted a very slow coach indeed.[7]

The effects of such innovations on Barbadian sugar harvests can be seen in the sugar export figures (table 5.2). In 1852 Barbados produced approximately a third of all the sugar in the British West Indies, causing Starkey to conclude that the changes in Great Britain's sugar tariffs, far from dooming Barbadian entrepreneurs, only spurred them to augment their efforts.[8]

One of the most beneficial effects of the intensified activity in Barbados was the elimination of a number of heavily indebted proprietors who could not keep up the pace (table 5.3). These were probably more numerous than contemporary observers realized. Between 1851 and 1861 the local court of chancery officially foreclosed on thirteen estates only, but the number of failing plantations sold privately by lawyers was more than ten times that figure. The West Indian Royal Commission of 1897 reported that properties sold in Barbados in the decade 1851–61 averaged 192 acres in size, somewhat larger than the median by Barbadian

Table 5.2. Sugar Exports from Barbados, 1848–56

Year	Hogsheads[a]	Year	Hogsheads[a]
1848	26,887 (20,165)	1853	34,692 (29,003)
1849	32,257 (24,456)	1854	41,839 (33,323)
1850	34,976 (26,232)	1855	37,071 (29,628)
1851	38,922 (39,192)	1856	43,582 (31,622)
1852	48,785 (37,150)		

SOURCES: *Barbados Blue Books*, 1848–56, CO 33/58–66; Deerr, *History of Sugar*, 1:194.
a. Figures in parentheses represent the number of tons estimated by Deerr.

standards. Writing in 1854 that several planters were being forced to sell, Davy stated that at least fifteen large plantations were broken up shortly after the passage of the Sugar Duties Act; one of the desirable effects of this was to make possible an increase in the number of landholders, from 1,874 in 1840 to 2,998 in 1847. But the Colonial Office was mainly interested in making land available to purchasers of small plots, presumably Negroes. On this subject Schomburgk commented in 1840 that there were 934 owners of plots of less than ten acres in Barbados, and Davy seemingly assumed, although he did not clearly state, that there was an increase of unspecified

Table 5.3 Estates Sold in Barbados, 1851–60

Year	No. of Estates Sold	Acreage	Average Price per Acre (£)
1851	44	8,356	51
1852	2	313	48
1853	—	—	—
1854	8	1,744	56
1855	7	1,865	46
1856	28	5,982	51
1857	23	5,452	58
1858	21	2,496	65
1859	20	4,037	65
1860	7	373	86

SOURCE: *West India Royal Commission Report* (London, 1897), C. 8657, App. C, pt. 3, p. 207. According to British law, property could not be sold before the existing debts against it were paid. In 1854 Parliament passed the West Indian Encumbered Estates Act, which created special courts in the colonies and in London where estates could be sold by judicial decree. The sum from the sale was divided among the creditors, and the purchaser acquired the estate free of debt. This arrangement was voluntarily accepted in Tobago, St. Kitts, St. Vincent, and Jamaica, but the Barbadian legislature preferred to rely on the island's own court of chancery and declined to create an encumbered estates court. See Walker to Newcastle, 14 March 1865, CO 28/200.

numbers of such small landholders after 1846. Parts of the liquidated estates undoubtedly were also absorbed by neighboring planters, since the *Barbados Blue Books* registered an increase in the average size of sugar plantations, from 178 acres in 1850 to 185 in 1871.[9]

The decline in the number of estates in the British West Indies was also a standard by which the adverse effects of the Sugar Duties Act were measured. The figure shrank dramatically in Jamaica, from 508 in 1848 to 330 in 1854, and Green mentions a plantation valued at £80,000 which was sold for £500. In British Guiana 135 out of 308 plantations were abandoned between 1846 and 1853. At Trinidad, where 206 estates were operating in 1838, nearly 30 large estates had been shut down by 1849; and nineteen of the island's most important proprietors had accumulated an aggregate indebtedness of £370,000.[10]

Relying on the quantities of sugar harvested in the West Indies as still another measure, Noel Deerr's statistics in his *History of Sugar* reveal that the parliamentary act of 1846 was not followed by anything as drastic as the decline in production attributed to the abolition of slavery in 1834 or the termination of apprenticeship in 1838. The data show that during the years 1836 to 1846 there was no significant increase in output except in Barbados (table 5.4). But in the decade that followed the Sugar Duties Act, production rose in Antigua, Barbados, British Guiana, Dominica, Nevis, St. Kitts, St. Lucia, and Trinidad and fell off markedly in Grenada, Jamaica, Montserrat, St. Vincent, Tobago, and the Virgin Islands.

The decline in the growth of sugar that took place in various colonies resulted from a combination of causes: absentee ownership, negligent administration, lack of investment capital, and labor shortages. When Sewell described the West Indies in 1861, he indicated that similar factors had caused Tobago and Grenada to sink to the level of "the ruined islands." The decline of 25 percent which took place in Jamaican production between 1846 and 1856 was attributed mainly to the shortage of labor, but even adoption of modern agricultural tools by the planters did not lead to an improvement in crop size.[11]

In contrast, Dominica and St. Lucia experienced an increase in production of over 30 percent during the decade following Great Britain's adoption of free trade in 1846. Davy ascribed results in both places to the metayer sharecropping system, which France had introduced earlier when the Windward Islands were under its control. He believed that the arrangement, though frequently disdained by workers, at least gave them an opportunity to survive.[12] But even with a 30 percent increase in crop size, planters' profits in Dominica and St. Lucia were small.

Commenting on Antigua's slightly increased productivity after 1846,

Davy explained that its estates, like those of Barbados, were favored by an oversupply of laborers. Many proprietors in Antigua were concerned because workers were acquiring their own land and cottages, but according to Davy the size of the holdings was so small and the quality so poor that the majority of Negroes were forced to rely at least partly on plantation employment. At the same time, inferior soil conditions and recurrent droughts in Antigua also limited the size of the crops: during the decade following the Sugar Duties Act, average annual sugar production in Antigua was less than 10,000 tons. Such a figure was too small for the planters to realize any significant profits in a market where the price of sugar was steadily falling.[13]

Table 5.4. Sugar Production in British West Indies, 1826–36, 1836–46, 1846–56

Colony	No. Tons Produced 1826–36	No. Tons Produced 1836–46	% Change	No. Tons Produced 1846–56	% Change
Antigua	84,531	86,351	+ 2	93,511	+ 8
Barbados	154,079	174,675	+13	282,848	+62
British Guiana	552,120	383,634	−31	395,663	+ 3
Dominica	24,535	21,781	−11	28,494	+31
Grenada	103,577	57,903	−44	47,958	−17
Jamaica	676,584	382,288	−43	284,817	−25
Montserrat	10,860	6,566	−40	1,289	−80
Nevis	24,678	13,558	−45	15,075	+ 1
St. Kitts	49,803	47,016	− 6	52,842	+12
St. Lucia	31,708	26,123	−18	34,680	+33
St. Vincent	117,206	74,203	−37	73,284	− 1
Tobago	48,035	33,914	−29	26,414	−22
Trinidad	137,616	146,892	+ 7	214,552	+46
Virgin Islands	8,818	3,567	−60	1,220	−66

SOURCE: Deerr, *History of Sugar*, 1:194–203.

The story was somewhat different in British Guiana and Trinidad. Later, during the 1860s and 1870s, the Demerara proprietors benefited from a very large increase in productivity, but in the period 1846–56 they were not able to augment the average size of their yearly crop by more than 3 per cent. Swampy soil conditions and the unchecked migration of Negroes from the estates to independent villages were the main reasons for these limited results. In contrast, Trinidad enjoyed much larger gains, partly because the fertility of the soil resulted in bigger plants. In fact, the size of the canes was such that they choked out weeds, thus eliminating the need for weeding. Yet the estates in Trinidad were often said to be ragged and untidy, and the sugar was inferior by Barbadian standards.[14]

Despite the fact that production was increasing in a few places in the West Indies, the costs of growing sugar after 1846 were of concern to planters everywhere. The contradictory information supplied by numerous writers makes it difficult to estimate the actual expense in the colonies, but costs were rising everywhere. Green showed that the money required to create a hundredweight of sugar in British Guiana increased from 6s.8d. in 1831–35 to 25s.10d. in 1845–47. The need for sophisticated drainage and milling machinery in the colony after 1847 resulted in additional costs, which only the larger estates could afford. Adamson noted that labor costs in the mainland colony decreased from $70 per hogshead in 1841 to $42.66 in 1851. This presumably meant that in British Guiana machinery costs were met by reducing laborers' wages. In Trinidad, however, wages remained high and machinery was introduced at a slower rate than in British Guiana, but the principal problem was the high interest on borrowed capital, as high as 45 percent per annum.[15]

Production costs in Barbados were among the lowest in the British West Indies, mostly because there was a great surplus of workers and almost no land for them to use to support themselves. The estates did not require great amounts of borrowed capital, and the presence of a large number of proprietors who administered their affairs in person resulted in prudent management. Another advantage lay in the northeast trade winds, which enabled the planters to rely on windmills instead of expensive steam engines to operate their crushing machines and boilerhouses. But costs were also rising in Barbados. The thin soil was incapable of producing large crops without the addition of fertilizers; the degree of the island's dependence on foreign imports could be gauged by the value of guano purchased from Peru, which rose from £39,000 in 1855 to £64,224 in 1857. Many thought that Barbados' estates were at the height of their prosperity, but others saw more clearly that planters' increased gross income was accompanied by diminished net profit. Davy's estimate, made in dollars (4s.2d.), reveals the typical expenses of a plantation after 1846 (table 5.5).[16]

The reduction of wages to 7d. and less per day was the only major cost that was lowered in Barbados after 1846, while the cost of borrowing capital was the principal increased expense. A large proportion of Barbadian planters now needed loans, for which they were required to pay interest charges in excess of 11 percent per annum. Commenting in 1848 on the effects of loans from speculators in Bridgetown as well as in London, Reid predicted that the estate owners would soon be "in bondage to the Merchants [in both places] and I see but small hope of their being able to free themselves." Meanwhile, the costs of plantation supplies were steadily rising, as were the salaries of the managers, bookkeepers, and overseers. The records of Easy Hall Plantation indicate an increase of more than 500 percent in expenses over a twelve-year period. The plantation's average cost of cultivating and manufacturing a hundredweight of raw sugar rose from 3s.9d. in 1834 to 19s.1½d. in 1846.[17] While some estates were able to produce sugar more economically than others, the planters were too easily satisfied with the increased volume of exports; many failed to give due consideration to the fact that rising production was paralleled by declining prices (table 5.6).

The course of world affairs in the 1850s temporarily exerted a favorable influence on the Barbadian economy. Because of the general demand for

Table 5.5. Plantation Expenditures in Barbados, 1847

Cultivation, including wages for field hands	$3,000
Manager's salary	480
Bookkeeper's salary	96
Apprentice	32
Book poster	64
Coopersmith	100
Blacksmith	60
Plumber	30
Millwright	50
Wheelwright	60
Carpenter	60
Mason	30
Making 100 hogsheads containers, including staves, hoops, and nails	400
Lumber	200
Stores: oats, oil, meal, provisions, etc.	200
Foreign manures	500
Freight of produce to shipping port	150
Taxes and export duties	150
Loss on stock	300
Wear and tear on machinery	650
Total	6,612

SOURCES: Davy, *The West Indies*, pp. 141–42. For other estimates of estate expenditures in Barbados in the nineteenth century, see Colebrooke to Newcastle, 7 June 1843, CO 28/178.

goods resulting from the Crimean War, the price of sugar rose gradually, from 20s. per cwt. in 1854 to 34s. in 1857.[18] Statistics reflect the effect of such increased prices on Barbadian exports, the bulk of which continued to go to Great Britain (table 5.7). The planters of Barbados were also encouraged by an enlargement in exports to the United States, from £8,825 in 1853 to £92,919 in 1857, but trade relations with Canada were unimpressive. In 1853 Barbadian exports to all of British North America amounted to less than £1,200. In the following year, the governor-general of Canada proposed a tariff-free exchange of West Indian sugar for Canadian wheat, which Colebrooke enthusiastically endorsed; Colonial Secretary Molesworth

Table 5.6. Barbados' Sugar Exports, Selected Years

Year	No. of Hogsheads	Value (£)	Average Price per Hogshead (£)
1842	21,545	671,515 (667,895)[a]	31
1847	32,257	653,980 (645,140)[a]	20
1852	48,785	738,884 (731,775)[a]	15

SOURCES: Colebrooke to Earl Grey, 22 July 1848, CO 28/168, to Newcastle, 7 June 1853, CO 28/178.
a. Statistics in parentheses represent corrected figures.

disapproved because the proposal discriminated against parts of the world not included in the arrangement.[19] Colebrooke felt that the imperial government had no right to interfere with a scheme which would lessen Barbados' dependence on supplies from the United States, a foreign power, and he pointedly asked whether Great Britain was justified in forbidding free trade between two parts of the empire when it had already approved reciprocity between Canada and the United States. The Colonial Office admitted that the famous treaty between the United States and Canada was at variance with the British principle of free trade, because it created special conditions that did not apply to all countries. But, as Taylor explained, Great Britain had made the exception because of political, not commercial, considerations.[20]

However questionable it may have been that the estates prospered greatly after 1846, there can be no doubt what effect the Sugar Duties Act had on

Table 5.7. Barbados' Exports, 1848–58 (£)

Year	Total Value of All Exports	Compared to Previous Year
1848	659,073	−224,086
1849	791,744	+132,671
1850	831,534	+ 39,790
1851	887,627	+ 56,093
1852	951,726	+ 64,099
1853	775,322	−176,404
1854	945,849	+170,527
1855	790,330	−155,519
1856	971,028	+180,698
1857	1,345,361	+374,333
1858	1,468,449	+123,088

SOURCE: *Barbados Blue Books,* 1848–58, CO 33/58–68.

workers. Barbados was entering a time of heightened economic activity that fitted David B. Davis' description of booms, in which laborers were generally overworked and underpaid. In 1847–48, wages were lower in Barbados than in any other British West Indian colony except Montserrat and Tortola (table 5.8). At the same time, the reduction in the cost of imported food, following the passage of the British Possessions Act of 1842, proved to be temporary. Even with large food crops in 1847, the price of most essential items rose markedly in the 1850s. The average daily pay in Barbados also gradually increased to 10d., but by 1858 higher food costs resulted in a real loss to the workers (table 5.9). In contrast, according to Douglas Hall, 9d.

Table 5.8. Average Daily Wages in the West Indies, 1847–48

Colony	Average Wage per Diem (d.)	Colony	Average Wage per Diem (d.)
Antigua	7½	Nevis	10
Barbados	7	St. Kitts	12½
British Guiana	20½	St. Lucia	15
Dominica	10	St. Vincent	10
Grenada	9	Tobago	11
Jamaica	15	Tortola	7½
Montserrat	6	Trinidad	25

SOURCE: Treasury to Merivale, 13 September 1848, with Earl Grey to the Governors of the West India Colonies, 15 September 1848, CO 854/4.

per day in Jamaica was sufficient in 1858 to buy enough meat and cornmeal for a family of four.[21]

Colebrooke believed that lower real income caused the inferior health and general poor state of the masses of Barbados compared to the people of the Leeward Islands. In contrast to the 1840s Barbadian workers were seen in tattered clothes, and many children were altogether unclothed. Laborers appeared haggard and forlorn, and there was an increase in the number of persons convicted of stealing food. More women were at work than in previous years, and, while the planters criticized mothers for neglecting their offspring, they preferred to hire females, whom they considered more regular than males in their work habits. Police magistrates and other civil and religious authorities frequently stated that former slaves were able to increase their earnings by cultivating sugar on their land allotments during their free time. Davy observed in 1854 that a few workers in Barbados had produced as much as 25 hogsheads a year, which meant a supplemental income of about £400 annually. But such cases were clearly exceptional; only a small number of Barbadian Negroes produced enough sugar of their own for more than three or four hogsheads a year.[22]

One of the few topics on which religious teachers, British humanitarians, and West Indian planters agreed after emancipation was that marriage and family life were needed as stabilizing influences among workers. Local records of the 1650s indicate that the idea of wedlock was exceedingly popular among the early white settlers of Barbados, and other accounts show that many brides were enlisted from English and Scottish brothels and prisons. Several twentieth-century authorities on society in the West Indies disagree on whether the laws and practices of Barbados specifically prohib-

Table 5.9. Food Costs in Barbados, 1848, 1858

Article	1848 (£ s. d.)	1858 (£ s. d.)
Wheaten flour per barrel	1. 7. 6	1. 18. 0
Milk per gal.	. 8	1. 4
Butter per lb.	1. 0	1. 8
Cheese per lb.	1. 0½	1. 6
Beef per lb.	. 7½	. 8
Mutton per lb.	.10	1. 0
Pork per lb.	. 6¼	. 7½
Rice per cwt.	16. 8	1. 2. 8

SOURCE: *Barbados Blue Books*, 1848–58, CO 33/58–68.

ited slaves from marrying. Greenfield says that prior to 1826 it was unlawful for a Barbadian slave to marry; Handler says that the rite was never prohibited to the slaves by law—on the contrary, he cites statistics showing that slave unions occasionally took place in Barbados.[23]

Following emancipation in 1834, the number of marriages among persons of all races rose, from 634 in 1835 to 1,909 in 1839. Presumably the increase was among the former slaves, since concubinage was infrequent among whites. After 1839 there was a decrease in the number of weddings performed annually in Barbados; in 1845, only 651 couples were lawfully united. Greenfield has said that marriage and family institutions were usually separate among the former slaves and their descendants throughout the West Indies, and a high illegitimacy rate was common in all of the former slave colonies. Yet he appears to imply that there was an important difference which set Barbados apart from the neighboring islands, because he believes that Barbadian family forms were totally unassociated with Africa or slavery[24] and that mating traditions were traceable instead to medieval English practices. Greenfield sees a connection between the English trothplight, which allowed a couple to cohabit without being formally married, and the Barbadian custom that permitted a female to form a mating relationship with the consent of her parents. Similarly, he believes that in

England as in Barbados a female would cohabit with a man of her choice but that she was more likely to marry him if he owned property.

There is also a possibility that married males played a more important role in Barbados than in the other West Indian colonies. The authority of the father in Barbados varied in proportion to his ability to maintain members of the household. After 1846 it became increasingly difficult for the males to support their dependents fully from their own wages, so that many women began to leave the home during the day in search of work; children as well were compelled to toil in order to earn their keep. Such conditions probably had a weakening effect on family structure, yet blood ties remained sufficiently intact that when Barbadian males chose at a later date to emigrate in search of employment abroad, they regularly sent money to their wives and offspring at home.[25]

It was an indisputable fact, however, that the quality of home life declined markedly after 1846. Colebrooke observed in 1849 that the living quarters of the workers in Barbados were bleak and unsanitary compared with those of Antigua. A few Barbadian planters displayed an interest in creating new dwellings for the laborers, but the proprietors were unwilling to secure the rights of the occupants with leases. Nor did the Negroes always choose to rent from their employers. Many preferred instead to camp in their own crude huts, made from the remains of boxes and crates, which could be quickly disassembled and moved in the event of a disagreement with the employer. The system clearly was not conducive to stable family conditions. According to a local physician, "There is absolutely less of home feelings, and of affections, and attachments, and less of domestic comfort, and even of domestic cleanliness than existed in the condition of slavery. Some of the dwellings of our peasantry are positively wretched. Composed of fragile and decayed materials, they scarcely afforded protection from the weather, while the interior is dirty and comfortless."[26]

The legislature recognized that the condition of many dwellings posed a threat to public health, and in 1851 it adopted a sanitation code requiring all new habitations to be constructed of masonry. Parishes were expected to provide central places for the disposal of rubbish, and dead persons were to be buried in licensed cemeteries rather than on their own premises. These rules did not come in time to prevent an epidemic of cholera in 1854, when more than 20,000 people perished in three weeks. The heavy toll was partly the result of the generally weakened condition of the people, many of whom, according to Colebrooke, were "attenuated from inadequate subsistence." Many improvident blacks were so much in need of new quarters that they moved into houses where occupants had recently died of cholera and, in their ignorance of the basic procedures for controlling the disease, needlessly sacrificed their lives.[27]

Eager to avoid such disasters in the future, Colebrooke engaged a civil engineer from Trinidad to recommend sanitary improvements for Bridgetown. The resulting report was not hopeful: "Few towns can offer a greater accumulation of evils from want of good sanitary measures than this city." The water supply was polluted, and fresh drinking water was so valued that hucksters were able to sell it from private wells by the pint. Once regarded as the most opulent and attractive city in the British West Indies, Bridgetown was now crisscrossed by a disorderly patchwork of crooked, muddy lanes. Shops and houses were dark and unpainted, with tattered facades that served as gutters to divert the heavy flow of rainwater into the streets. Open canals and cesspools were used to remove sewage from the most expensive homes, and, in the words of the engineer, "such are the dirty, indolent, and inconsiderate habits of the lower classes in Bridgetown, that... the filth is thrown down in the streets and thoroughfares, in any place where the absence of the police allows it to be done with impunity." Commenting on the condition of the cemeteries, he added that the scene was "too disgusting and dreadful to dwell upon."[28]

As a first step toward improving public health, particularly that of the workers, Colebrooke appealed to the legislature for funds to drain the swamps adjoining Bridgetown. But the governor lacked the influence in the assembly to obtain the money for such an undertaking. He explained, with apparent dissatisfaction, "the influence of the proprietors of Sugar Estates so entirely predominates in the Legislature & their views are so exclusively directed to objects of more immediate interest to themselves, that their support to any local undertaking of this magnitude, which would draw labor from the country, is not to be expected."[29]

Although the imperial government was unwilling after 1845 to contribute financially to the support of education in the colonies, Earl Grey continued to stress industrial training as the key that would eventually enable former slaves to achieve material prosperity. As he explained in 1847: "It would be impossible to adduce an instance of any Country of which the Agricultural and commercial prospects were so absolutely dependent on the instruction of the Lower orders as those of the West Indies are at the present time. Instruction not only makes labour intelligent and orderly but creates new wants and desires, new activities, a love of employment and an increased alacrity both of the body and the minds; and there is probably no example of a well-instructed population which is not also active and eager to work.

PRECAUTIONS

AGAINST

THE CHOLERA.

Extracted from the Notifications of the General Board of Health in England.

First Instruction.

Guard against Looseness of the Bowels and Purging.

Before a person has a decided attack of Cholera, there is usually for a few hours or longer, some looseness of the bowels or purging. If this looseness is attended to at once, the disease is generally stopped. This looseness is often unaccompanied by pain, but this must not put any one off his guard, as to the importance of this warning. If a person is purged let him go to bed, be kept quite warm, and if he is cold, apply bottles of hot water, or bags filled with hot salt, or bran, to the stomach and feet. Let him take immediately eight drops of laudanum in a wine glass of hot and weak brandy and water; the same dose should be repeated every 2 hours, as long as he is purged: and should be given night and morning for one or two days after the purging has stopped.

Second Instruction.

What is to be done if a Person is seized or taken with Cholera.

This comes on with cold, giddiness, sickness, vomiting and purging of what looks like dirty water, or rice and water. Let the patient get into a hot bed, and be well covered with blankets; apply bottles of hot water, or bags filled with hot salt, sand, or bran, to the stomach, spine, and feet; be sure he is not exposed to a draught or cold, the object being to get him into a sweat. Put a large poultice of mustard and hartshorn or vinegar, or a cloth dipped in turpentine over the stomach, and keep it on 15 or 20 minutes. Give the person 15 drops of laudanum, with a teaspoonful of brandy, rum, or other spirit in the absence of brandy, in a little hot water; a little ginger or cloves may be added. This medicine may be given every hour for 6 hours, *but not longer*; it must be then left off. When the patient begins to sweat, give him some hot tea, with a teaspoonful of brandy in it, and keep him warm in bed. The dose of the above medicine should be diminished one-half for Children under 7 years of age, and one-fourth for Infants under 3 years of age.

Third Instruction.

Medical advice should be got *as soon as possible*, in any case of seizure, as the delay of even one hour may cause death.

Fourth Instruction.

On Food.

All kinds of uncooked fruits and salads, cucumbers, celery, and pickles had better be avoided; also oysters, lobsters, crabs, mussels, or other shell fish.

The most wholesome articles of food are well baked bread, good biscuits, rice, oatmeal, and good potatoes or yams; solid food is better than fluid.

Fifth Instruction.

On the Danger of Spirits, Rum, Beer, &c.

It is a very common notion that the use of brandy, whiskey, rum, wine, and the like, is good as a protection against Cholera. This is a total and fatal mistake: in every country and town where Cholera has broken out, drunkards, and those who drink freely, have been the first and greatest sufferers from the disease.

Sixth Instruction.

Against exposure to Wet and Cold.

Wet and cold should as much as possible be guarded against, by warm dry clothing; sudden changes of temperature should also be avoided.

Seventh Instruction.

Concerning Cleanliness and Ventilation.

Nothing is of greater importance as a protection against Cholera, than cleanliness of person and of dwelling, and a good supply of fresh pure air. It is, therefore, indispensable to remove all filth from and around dwellings; to limewash living and sleeping apartments; to admit freely pure air; and especially to guard against over-crowding and a foul atmosphere.

European experience has confirmed the experience of India, that Cholera is not contagious. There is no danger from infected persons; the true danger is continuing to live in infected districts, in close, damp, and filthy dwellings. If the neighbourhood be damp or filthy. remove to a dry and clean locality as quickly as possible.

Printed at the " Globe Office."

Instruction, therefore, when provision shall be made for imparting it speedily and effectually, may be rendered the most certain of all methods for equalizing the supply of Labour with the demand; and on the other hand, the prosperity which a sufficient supply of Labour would create, may well be expected, by promoting scientific and mechanical improvements, and retaining amongst the negroes a cultivated and intelligent race of Proprietors, to assist civil order and the advancement of all classes."[30] As an indication of what changes were needed in the West Indies, Grey included a list of recommendations drawn up by J. P. Kay-Shuttleworth, the noted authority on British school practices, who emphasized the importance of health, diet, cleanliness, and recreation. Practical experience should be provided in gardening, sewing, cooking, land surveying, mechanics, drawing, livestock management, and modern agriculture, and special attention should be given to bookkeeping, vocal music, grammar, religion, and economic theory. Similarly there was a need for proper instructors, who could be secured by creating teacher-training institutions. But the first steps in furthering popular education were for the legislatures in the West Indies to increase their grants, abolish tuition fees, and make instruction compulsory for all children.[31]

Responding to these recommendations, in 1850 the Barbadian legislature passed an act providing £3,000 for public instruction for two years. Management of the schools was transferred from the bishop to a committee consisting of a few members of the council and assembly and an assortment of other residents, and provision was made for the appointment of a qualified inspector of schools. The legislature did not introduce any new curriculum, which continued to concentrate on religious and moral training, nor did it sanction compulsory attendance because there were instances when child labor was necessary for the support of the family. Nevertheless, the increased attention to education resulted in doubling the enrollment of the day schools, from about 3,000 in 1849 to 6,000 in 1854. Green has shown that the amount of money spent in Barbados per capita in 1850 was 5s.2d., compared to 1s.6d. per person in Great Britain, and there was no doubt that the educational establishment in Barbados exceeded that of all the other colonies in the British West Indies, at least in size.[32]

Another way in which Colebrooke thought that the laborers in Barbados should advance themselves was by seeking the franchise. Freedmen had made an intensive effort toward enfranchisement during the 1830s, but in the 1850s neither whites nor blacks showed much interest in the colony's political life. The *Barbados Blue Books* indicate that in the assembly elections of 1854, the total number of persons casting ballots was 76. Ten years later, out of 417 qualified electors in Bridgetown, only 13 voted.[33] The proportion of registered voters on the island to the total population was unaltered during the thirty years after the end of slavery despite a noteworthy increase in the number of persons inhabiting the colony (table 5.10).

Prescod was the only person of African descent to serve in the lower house until 1874, when William Conrad Reeves was elected. Once suspected in London as a radical, the outspoken Prescod served with distinction and made numerous practical suggestions to the assembly. A greater number of Negro leaders undertook an active part in the affairs of Jamaica, yet many of its inhabitants were also indifferent to politics: during local elections in 1863, out of a population of nearly 450,000, only 1,457 voters came to the polls.[34]

Disappointed with the lack of concern for public and civic matters, Colebrooke looked forward hopefully but somewhat unrealistically to a time when a politically active white and black population would realize that

Table 5.10. Registered Voters in Barbados, 1834–64

Year	Population	No. Registered Voters	Percentage Population Registered
1834	110,080	1,026	0.9
1844	122,198	1,103	0.9
1854	135,939	1,359	1.0
1864	152,727	1,444	0.9

SOURCES: *Barbados Blue Books*, 1834–64, CO 33/46–74; Schomburgk, *Barbados*, p. 208.

it was to their mutual advantage to collaborate in the solution of common problems. A few months before his retirement in 1856, Colebrooke wrote: "It is well known that the victims of the slave trade have with few exceptions been drawn from the most peaceable and inoffensive of the African tribes, and that the fidelity of the native African has been generally proverbial in the West Indies. And it is now abundantly evident that if the white and black races had originally been suffered to grow up together in the possession of equal rights and free from the prejudices of caste and colour these colonies possessing a moral and intelligent mixed population might have been the most prosperous and civilised dependencies of the Crown.... And if the popular institutions of the colonies should be preserved and improved their future welfare may be ultimately established on a stable and durable foundation."[35]

Colebrooke's sympathetic attitude toward the masses was not shared by officials in London. Twenty years earlier the depressed condition of the West Indian Negroes had attracted much attention in the mother country, but the declining conditions of the former slaves failed to arouse much notice after

Drawn on Stone by W.L. Walton from a Sketch by Hodges.

BRIDGETOWN IN BARBADOS.
Taken from Grand View Villa.

Hullmandel & Walton Lithographers

1850. Leaders on both sides of the Atlantic agreed that blacks were largely the cause of their own backwardness. The stereotype of the lazy Negro was gaining ground, and William Wilberforce's son, the Bishop of Oxford, was sufficiently influenced by this attitude to characterize the entire race as a people who naturally hated labor, whereas he believed that the peasantry in Great Britain loved labor for the sake of it. Such a view failed to recognize that the more hopeless the condition of the worker, the less incentive he had to exert himself for improvements that were unattainable. Seeking to refute the image of the black man as an incurable idler, Davy wrote: "It is a mistake I perceive even fallen into by some of the friends of the race.... What I have witnessed convinces me of it. The vigorous, quick walk of the negro going to his work; the untiring zest and exertions made by the negro lads on holiday at cricket, not in the shade, but fully exposed to the sun; the extra labour of the negro when cultivating his own plot of ground...often commencing before dawn by moonlight, and recurring to it after the day's work.... Other circumstances might be adduced in corroboration, such as...the willingness with which he undertakes task work...the industry and perseverance he displays in reclaiming ground...from a waste, bit by bit by changing its character to that of fertility...breaking up rocks, collecting soil....He who has witnessed...this indefatigable industry will be disposed probably to over-rate rather than under-rate the activity of the negro, and his love of, or rather...his non-aversion to labour, for I believe, comparatively few even of our English peasants truly 'love labour for the sake of labour.' In the best of them labour is an acquired habit, and habit, according to the old adage, is second nature, and so too with the negro."[36]

But local whites and many leading persons in the home country continued to regard the former slaves as mentally and morally inferior, and they continued to judge them by qualities that they believed to be inherent in the Negro race. They praised the masses for their fidelity to their masters, their good-natured mirth and spontaneous exuberance, and their benign unawareness of things supposed to have moral or esthetic meaning for whites. Likewise, they criticized the Negroes for their untrustworthiness, shiftlessness, thievish habits, and untruthfulness. As Thome and Kimball wrote, "they resemble grown children, improvident and careless to a lamentable degree."[37] As long as this attitude persisted, little or nothing would be done to ameliorate the declining status of the workers.

———————

The economic aftermath of the Sugar Duties Act of 1846 imposed new pressures on the British West Indies and greatly heightened competition among world sugar producers. The aim of British statesmen was to increase the amount of cheap sugar available to workmen in Great Britain and thereby effect a savings in factory wages, which in turn would enable British manufacturers to compete with the rising industrial output of European powers. This goal suggested that the British colonies were to sink or swim in open competition with other countries. Yet Great Britain was still eager to keep sugar production alive in the West Indies, and while more restrained than in former times in offering help, the imperial government nevertheless continued to provide occasional loans, emigrant laborers from India and China, and technical advice on trade and agriculture.

The aim of most planters in the West Indies after 1846 was to discover a way to survive under the new economic conditions. The reactions of the Caribbean proprietors varied according to different local conditions, but the aim everywhere was to keep up with the large crops being produced in the foreign West Indian colonies. To achieve this goal, British West Indian estate owners experimented with machinery and new agricultural methods. Ultimately their efforts increased the size of the crops in places, but much of the gain was eaten away by rising production costs and declining sugar prices. Their only expense that diminished after 1846 was wage labor, and in no place was this more apparent than in Barbados. As a result, such writers as Starkey and Green have tended to exaggerate somewhat the success of the Barbadian estates after 1846.[38] Some of the local owners undoubtedly continued to prosper for a time, but many encountered difficulties hitherto unknown in the history of the colony. The local court of chancery was forced to dispose of a significant number of heavily encumbered properties.

The social and economic impact of Great Britain's free trade policy was manifestly detrimental to the workers in the West Indies: Colebrooke noted the effects of lowered wages on the health of the Barbadian Negroes, and higher food costs reduced the masses to deprivation and hardship. From statistics collected it may be concluded that the conditions of Barbadian laborers in the 1850s were the worst in the West Indies;[39] and it can be shown that they became even worse during the 1860s and 1870s. In contrast, there were places in the area where Negroes were obtaining land; if they did not free themselves from the estates altogether, they nevertheless enjoyed adequate wages and lower living costs. Perhaps the most imaginative efforts on behalf of the masses occurred in Jamaica, where enterprising individuals turned their attention from sugar to cotton, silk, and copper and where many of the new ventures were financed and managed by Negro shareholders and directors. For a variety of reasons these efforts did not succeed, but they were an indication of the energy and ingenuity that would serve the people of Jamaica at a later date, when conditions were more conducive to success. At the same time, some writers considered that superior wages and independent villages gave the workers of British Guiana a great advantage, but the effects of disease and harsh treatment there gave Barbadian workers reason to pause before undertaking the voyage to the mainland colony.[40]

The traditional prejudices against the African race continued to harden, not only in the colonies but also among prominent political and religious leaders in Great Britain. Even before the Sugar Duties Act of 1846, British statesmen endeavored to discourage laborers from abandoning their duties on the estates by proposing to levy heavy taxes on individuals acquiring land.[41] Leaders such as Earl Grey continued to hope that there was yet some basis for the proprietors and workers to share mutually in the benefits of the plantation system, and he believed that education and vocational training were the keys that would lead to such an outcome. But the elaborate scheme proposed by Kay-Shuttleworth to train Negro mechanics, land surveyors, draftsmen, and engineers served no purpose to the planters of Barbados. What was still needed was an endless supply of workers to cut cane at the lowest wage.

6. Barbados at Mid-Century, 1856–1875

THE HALF DECADE following Colebrooke's departure from Barbados in 1856 was characterized by additional increases in productivity under the new governor, Francis Hincks, a former premier of Upper Canada. The Colonial Office expected that Hincks, a financial expert, would make a useful contribution toward improving agriculture and commerce and toward the betterment of the Negroes' economic plight. These expectations were unfulfilled, mainly because Hincks' interest continued to be Canada rather than the West Indies.[1] On two occasions when he was absent from Barbados, his duties were performed for several months by the island's colonial secretary, Sir James Walker. When Hincks was transferred in 1862 to the governorship of British Guiana, the imperial government chose Walker as his successor in Barbados. Ultimately Hincks returned to Canada to become the first minister of finance under the new dominion government of 1867. The governorship of Barbados was the last episode in Walker's long but drab career in the colonial service. He contributed little to the solution of economic problems. Preoccupied with the small details of local administration, he was typical of many West Indian governors after 1850. He has been described as a "careful rather than an able administrator."[2]

The statistics found in the *Barbados Blue Books* suggest that the colony prospered abundantly under Hincks and Walker. The average annual production of sugar in the colony continued to rise, from 36,000 hogsheads (29,000 tons) in 1846–56 to 46,000 hogsheads (35,000 tons) in 1856–66. This upward trend tended somewhat to offset the adverse effects of the decline in the price of sugar, from 29s.5d. per hundredweight in 1856 to 20s5d. in 1866.[3] Exports during the decade after 1856 averaged close to £1 million per year (table 6.1).

Because British mortgage-holders reserved the exclusive right to market Barbadian sugar in the home country and there were no established arrangements for selling British West Indian products in foreign countries, Great Britain continued to be Barbados' chief customer. Owing in part to the disappearance of Louisiana sugar from the market during the American Civil War, Barbados augmented its exports to the United States, from less than £10,000 in 1855 to £137,303 in 1865 and to £199,552 in 1868.[4] But such an

Table 6.1. Barbados' Imports and Exports, 1857–67

Year	Exports (£)	Imports (£)	Excess of Exports over Imports (£)
1857	1,345,361	976,306	369,055
1858	1,468,449	1,225,118	243,331
1859	1,255,571	1,049,236	206,335
1860	984,294	941,761	42,533
1861	1,075,374	923,874	151,500
1862	1,067,612	913,141	154,471
1863	981,142	878,208	102,934
1864	925,957	910,081	15,876
1865	1,161,159	953,334	207,825
1866	1,246,844	988,081	258,763
1867	1,245,501	989,503	255,998

SOURCE: *Barbados Blue Books*, 1847–67, CO 33/57–77.

increase did not significantly compensate for the island's dependence on food from the United States. In fact the American share of imports into the island continued to rise, from 16 percent of the total in 1850 to 44 percent in 1863. At the same time, a temporary decrease took place in British goods imported into the colony (table 6.2).

In the midst of these changing trends, it is not easy to gauge the profitability of the island estates after 1856. While it is clear that the volume of Barbadian exports was increasing, it cannot be assumed that profits were augmented to a comparable degree—there are no reliable statistics to determine the planters' net gains. Much of the available data cannot be trusted because the planters and managers who supplied the figures on sugar production probably exaggerated crop size in order to reassure creditors in Great Britain.[5] But the key to judging the profitability of local agriculture was connected as much with the attendant expense as it was with the size of the crops. According to Hincks, the average cost of producing a hogshead of sugar in Barbados in 1857 was £6.17s.2d. compared to £10.12s.0d. in 1834, a decrease that he attributed to a reduction in laborers' wages. The reduced costs, he believed, were sufficient for the planters to enjoy relatively high profits. Writing at length on Barbadian agriculture after emancipation, Hincks explained that the abolition of slavery had materially benefited the planters, because the expense of paying wages to each person actively at work in the fields and mills was less than providing every Negro with food, clothing, and shelter, regardless of whether such individuals were able to contribute any useful work. Seeking to prove that labor was more efficient

Table 6.2. Barbados' Imports from Great Britain and the United States, 1857–67

Year	British Imports (£)	Percentage of British Imports in Relation to Total Imports	American Imports (£)	Percentage of American Imports in Relation to Total Imports
1857	475,855	48	244,933	25
1858	631,756	51	411,675	31
1859	447,124	42	375,975	36
1860	420,266	44	316,215	33
1861	369,651	42	330,308	35
1862	343,845	37	361,514	39
1863	304,174	34	393,106	44
1864[a]				
1865	366,053	38	346,107	36
1866	379,724	38	343,270	35
1867	389,543	39	356,379	36

SOURCE: *Barbados Blue Books,* 1847–67, CO 33/57–77.
a. Figures missing at time of research.

in Barbados after emancipation than before, Hincks cited the example of a Barbadian estate that was worked before 1834 by 230 slaves, whose combined efforts produced 150 hogsheads annually; after 1834 the same plantation was able to produce a third more per year with only 90 laborers. The average amount of sugar produced per worker during slavery was barely 1,000 pounds a year, but under the new system free laborers each succeeded in producing 3,000 pounds. No other colony in the Caribbean Sea could claim such a marked increase in productivity on the part of its workers.[6]

Other observers, such as Sewell, saw symptoms of economic decline in Barbados. Contrasting the appearance of Bridgetown in 1859 with its opulent look of former times, Sewell noted: "A stranger ... upon first landing would hasten to proclaim it an exhausted city, once, possibly the centre of a flourishing business and emporium of great wealth, but now almost abandoned in ruin and decay.... I was first struck with the narrow streets and the ruined appearance of the houses. It seemed to me as though no attempt had been made to repair their dilapidated condition within half a century. The paint was worn away from roof and wood-work, and the mortar which had fallen from the walls had never been replaced save in few cases. Around each dwelling of more than ordinary Barbadian pretensions there was generally an unfinished wall, with broken pieces of glass on the top to protect the property from the trespass of the wicked. In going from my lodging house ... I was obliged to traverse several acres of vacant lots, which were overgrown with wild cactuses and studded with moss-covered ruins. They lay in the very heart of the city—the 'burnt district,' as it was called because of a fire of twenty years' standing."[7]

Reviewing Hincks' dispatches to London, Taylor was unable to agree that intensified production had benefited the proprietors in proportion to their efforts. Walker declared with greater certainty in 1859 that "the system of forcing large crops without reference to the cost, and the neglect of all those rules which give husbandry its name, has become a perfect mania." He concurred with Reid's assessment of a decade earlier that the economic future of the colony was jeopardized, and he cited the need for expensive imported fertilizers to replace the nutrients taken from the soil by excessive planting, the increased dependence on foreign food to substitute for the home-grown staples no longer produced by the estates, the disappearance of pastures required to support cattle, and the declining quality of Barbadian sugar, a result of large-scale production. Moreover, profits from the in-creased production of sugar were being siphoned off by British merchants and mortgage-holders who, in Walker's words, "have an immediate interest in the shipment of every pound of sugar which can be extracted from the land, and from the importation of all the additional supplies which must necessarily be brought to sustain a large crop, and the articles of food for both man and beast, the growth of which on the spot has been displaced by the sugar cane."[8]

The mirage of quick riches from the sugar trade continued to lure spec-ulators in Great Britain and the other British West Indian colonies into brisk competition to acquire any estates that might be put up for sale in Barbados. The effect was to augment Barbadian land values by about 20 percent between emancipation in 1834 and the adoption of free trade in 1846. Walker demonstrated that the value of plantation property in Barbados rose even more dramatically in the two decades following the adoption of free trade. At the same time, many estates previously managed by resident owners were now being directed by hired overseers representing new owners. Commenting on the new operators, Walker observed, "Whether as the representatives of absentee proprietors or as owners of estates which they

The History of Barbados,

BY

SIR ROBERT H. SCHOMBURGK K.^T.

Drawn on Stone by W.L. Walton from a Sketch by Hedges.

Hullmandel & Walton Lithographers.

TRAFALGAR SQUARE IN BRIDGETOWN.

London:

LONGMAN, BROWN, GREEN AND LONGMANS PATERNOSTER ROW.

1847

have purchased at ruinous prices ... the interest of which generally absorbs the entire profits of their crops, these industrious and skillful men plod on from year to year, and end just where they commenced, with a load of debt, which necessitates the transfer of the property to some other, of whom there are scores ready to pass through the same ordeal. By these latter transactions the general prosperity of the Colony is not affected, however calamatous they may prove to individuals. The land which they acquired on such hard terms is kept up to the highest mark of cultivation to secure such a return as will enable the holder to pay the interest on his liabilities; and more than this ... he seldom does." He conceded that there were still a few unencumbered planters in Barbados who "shine out with a lustre which reflects the most beneficial rays round them," but many of the wealthiest proprietors were also leaving the island and hence, he feared, "the best blood of the place is squeezed out of it and sent to England never to return in any shape."[9]

The serious effects on the workers of low wages, expensive food, and increasing unemployment aroused the concern of such colonial secretaries in London as Labouchere and Newcastle, who suggested that the current plight could be remedied by a modest increase in wages. In reply, Hincks impatiently insisted that the Negroes of Barbados were to blame for their own poverty, since there were places in the Caribbean Sea within a few hours' sailing time where cheap land and good wages could be had. Commenting also on the prevailing wage rate, Sewell declared that the Barbadian masses were substantially worse off after 1850 than they had been as slaves. He believed that what was needed was an effective arrangement for bargaining with their employers, but in 1858 the planters acted to suppress the first feeble effort in Barbados to form a workingmen's association, whose leaders they denounced for "attempting to arouse unjust suspicions in the minds of the ignorant touching their rights ... [and endeavoring] to jeopardize the successful system of plantation management as now adopted."[10]

The conditions of workers in Barbados continued to worsen, and in 1857, at the very moment that racial troubles in India were exciting feelings of agitation against whites, the commander of the military forces at Bridgetown, Sir Arthur Cloet, warned the Colonial Office of the danger of an impending rebellion. He feared that recent signs of unrest in British Guiana, St. Lucia, and St. Vincent also forecast a violent explosion in the West Indies, and Barbados, the most densely populated island in the Caribbean area, was especially vulnerable. "I have lived all of my life amongst the black and coloured races," he wrote, "and I look upon the innate hostility of the black man toward the white to be as distinctly pronounced as the divine declaration of the personal enmity between man and the serpent." Many persons, remembering the bloody Easter uprising of 1816, shared Cloet's fears, and in 1859 Walker informed the Colonial Office that a large number of people were arming themselves with knives and guns. The following year saw an increase in looting on estates, and 3,727 workers were arrested in 1863 for stealing. In jail the impoverished blacks became so violent that the governor reluctantly agreed to revive corporal punishment as part of prison discipline.[11] Eventually he was forced to approve several acts restoring the severe criminal penalties that the legislature had abolished in the 1840s. The jailer at Bridgetown, believing that the individuals confined in 1863 were already unduly punished by their circumstances, released 1,961 prisoners to prevent their dying in the cells. Even when freed, scores of starving workers perished in the roadways on their way home. Another local official complained, "so great has been the pinch ... that with many even the absolute necessities have been with great difficulty procured." Such hardships did not appear to trouble the planters, Walker wrote. As Hall has pointed out, the condition of the workers in Antigua was so superior to those of Barbados that the lives of the Antiguans could be described as endurable.[12]

Eager to reduce the threat of racial disorders in Barbados, a group of absentee planters in Great Britain petitioned the legislature in 1857 to provide such funds to the clergy as would enable them "to employ the further agents required to carry the glad tidings of the Gospel to ... each labourer, [and] by ... the sale of Bibles and friendly admonitions to raise the general character of the People." The legislature was willing to provide additional grants for the objectives, and Walker thought that it was important for Parliament also to support moral training in the West Indies. But the imperial government was no longer prepared to pay large sums for such purposes, and when Bishop Parry retired in 1866 after twenty-five years of service the Colonial Office announced that henceforth it intended to rely on a local minister to perform the duties of bishop in Barbados at a much reduced salary. Walker strongly opposed the attempt on the part of British officials to reduce religious expenditures, and he also believed that a theologian of British birth and training was needed to serve as bishop. A local minister would have little success in attracting the respect of the blacks, he explained.[13] Meanwhile the imperial government had decided to end the British taxpayers' responsibility to support the church in the colonies, and in 1868 Parliament passed an act relieving itself of the burden of defraying the salaries of the Anglican clergy in the West Indies as the incumbents died or retired. This was seen by the colonies to mean that they alone were responsible for maintaining the clergy in the future, a goal which the Colonial Office thought that the Caribbean dependencies could achieve if they reduced costs by merging into a single diocese. The policy therefore envisioned that the bishoprics of Barbados and Jamaica would be united, but neither Walker nor his successor, Rawson W. Rawson, believed that such an arrangement was practical because of the diversity of creeds in the West Indies. The former French colonies, for example, were predominantly Roman Catholic, and the British islands had several rival Protestant sects.[14]

In 1870 the imperial government decided that in the circumstances it was expedient to disestablish the Anglican church altogether in the West Indies. The Barbadian legislature responded by saying that in the current tense situation in the working classes, it was ready to pay the salaries of the bishop and to provide for all the other costs of maintaining the established church. The colonial secretary, Granville, opposed such an arrangement and advised Rawson that the imperial government would not permit the legislature to provide any funds for the Church of England unless it also contributed to the other church groups in Barbados. Nor did he think that the colonial government should have a voice in the selection of the bishop or any other clergymen; henceforth each religious body, being autonomous, should manage its own affairs without the intervention of local authorities.[15]

Rawson believed that such a doctrine meant that church control would fall into the hands of the laity or the masses, an outcome that he predicted the legislature would not accept. In his words, the members of the council and assembly were "unwilling to break up the foundations of their Church ... well-cemented by usage and showing no signs of decay, with the object of building upon a different foundation, which might or might not prove as sound and stable." So determined was the legislature, he urged, that any attempt to frustrate its effort to preserve the established religion would almost certainly "stir up some serious strife." In response to this blunt warning, the imperial government allowed the Barbadian legislature to provide salaries for a bishop and other Anglican ministers, on the understanding that the legislature would also provide token support to Methodist, Moravian, and Roman Catholic churchmen in the island. Thus Barbados became the only colony in the diocese to maintain the established church under the conditions required by the imperial government. Electing the opposite course, the Windward Islands disestablished the Anglican religion altogether.[16]

The colonial legislature and imperial government agreed that education should continue to be relied on as a way of teaching the Negroes to live more productive lives, although Great Britain was no longer prepared to give financial support to public instruction in the colonies. In 1858 the Barbadian legislature raised the educational grant to £2,500, and in the following year the local inspector of schools assessed the results of several successive increases. He saw that the Negroes had regained their confidence in learning and were sending the children to school in greater numbers than they had ten years earlier. Daily classes were springing up everywhere, and many old buildings were being replaced. Schoolrooms, which only a few years before had been destitute of furniture and equipment, were now liberally supplied, and an increase in the number of properly trained teachers was being encouraged by awarding certificates of merit and appropriate raises in pay. In 1860 the same official found that there was not a single locality in Barbados farther than a mile or two from a good school. In fact, he said, the problem was the opposite. In some neighborhoods, places of instruction were so near each other that it was becoming difficult to obtain the required attendance in all of them.[17]

The legislature, nevertheless, continued to augment the amount of money allocated each year for educational purposes, to £3,000 in 1867, £4,000 in 1870, and £4,600 in 1874, making it possible for some 30,000 students to attend day school in 1873, compared to 3,000 in 1849. But leaders in London questioned the quality of the public instruction in the colony, and in 1876 the British government engaged the inspector of schools in Jamaica to evaluate Barbados' educational practices. The resulting report characterized the facilities as lavish, lacking in planning, and based on antiquated instructional techniques. The teachers, who continued to neglect vocational training, relied on a curriculum that, as in the 1840s, emphasized the scriptures and classical writings but did not relate meaningfully to the daily lives of the people.[18]

The Barbadian legislature characteristically rejected a recommendation from London calling for restrictions on child labor in order to encourage more young persons to attend school. It argued that daily labor was not as harmful as idleness and that the childrens' wages were needed more than ever for the support of the family.[19]

Whatever good fortune favored the estate owners of Barbados from 1850 to 1869 was followed by a succession of ruinous droughts and crop failures during Rawson's term as governor. The output of sugar in 1869, just over

Table 6.3. Barbados' Sugar Exports, 1867–76

Year	Hogsheads[a]	Value (£)
1867	51,304 (46,725)	800,970
1868	58,250 (50,960)	857,250
1869	32,150 (26,465)	479,550
1870	39,360 (34,363)	591,990
1871	53,788 (47,166)	804,465
1872	39,167 (34,372)	586,140
1873	37,337 (32,669)	560,055
1874	47,289 (41,337)	709,300
1875	65,012 (56,875)	975,100
1876	37,848 (32,676)	567,700

SOURCES: *Barbados Blue Books*, 1866–78, CO 33/76–88; Deerr, *History of Sugar*, 1:194.
a. Figures appearing in parentheses represent the number of tons estimated by Deerr.

26,000 tons, was the smallest since 1837. "The parched condition of the soil, the emaciated state of the cattle, and the crippled means of the planters," Rawson wrote, combined to form a picture of distress seldom known in the island.[20] There was a brief respite from the drought in 1871, but the recurrence of dry weather the following year heightened the distress of the inhabitants. Exports during Rawson's term were irregular (table 6.3). Because of drop in production, the colony was no longer able to rely on sugar sales abroad to pay for its imports, resulting in unfavorable balances of trade (table 6.4). The reduced size of the harvests likewise had an effect on the style of living in Barbados, and even the whites were forced to limit their consumption of such luxuries as tobacco, coffee, and butter. The worst hardships continued to fall on the masses; 30 percent more persons were convicted in 1870 for stealing food than had been in 1869. The legislature was always ready to acknowledge the intense and apparently hopeless distress of

Table 6.4. Barbados' Annual Balance of Trade, 1869–78

Year	Balance of Trade (£)	Year	Balance of Trade (£)
1869	− 90,796	1874	+ 91,519
1870	− 96,847	1875	+287,417
1871	+106,658	1876	− 63,611
1872	−103,587	1877	− 46,221
1873	−169,731	1878	− 24,321

SOURCE: *Barbados Blue Books*, 1866–78, CO 33/76–88.

the working class, yet it continued to oppose the adoption of a general plan of relief for the poor because it thought that any form of public assistance would encourage idleness. Glenelg had expressed the same fear a quarter of a century before. As Walker explained, the old belief that the Negroes were governed by an uncontrollable urge to avoid work continued to dampen the sympathy that the island's leaders might have had for the poor.[21] Commenting on the reluctance of the legislature to provide assistance, a visiting clergyman castigated the attitude of the council and assembly as "shameful and inhumane parsimony," while he characterized the amount of relief given as a "miserable pittance." Whatever public funds were granted for the support of indigents in Barbados arose primarily from the efforts of the eleven parish vestries, and in 1872 the local bodies contributed no less than £10,000. The parochial officials seemed to be more keenly aware of the people's suffering than were the members of the legislature.[22]

Even with the added support of numerous private charities the economic status of the laborers continued to decline, a trend vividly demonstrated in 1872 by a riot following the accidental sinking in the harbor of the *Cuban*, a ship belonging to the West India Steam Packet Company. When the vessel's submerged cargo, valued at £180,000, was salvaged by the consignees and brought to the pier, police had to be summoned to halt the looting. As Rawson explained, the people thought that Jesus Christ had sent the ship as a gift for their relief, and the crowds were so determined to carry away the goods that they did not disperse until one person was killed and seventy-seven were arrested.[23]

Concerned over Barbados' inability to provide full employment for the workers, Rawson conducted a census in 1871; it revealed that the number of inhabitants had increased from 135,939 to 161,559 in twenty years, notwithstanding the death of 20,000 cholera victims in 1854 and a high infant mortality rate.[24] The population density of Barbados in 1871 was 906 persons per square mile, compared to 284 in Antigua, 93 in Trinidad, and 25 in British Guiana. The census figures also disclosed that the proportion of blacks in Barbados had risen in the ten years since 1861 from 88 percent of the total to 89.8 percent. During the same period, the proportion of whites declined from 11.7 percent to 10.2 percent. The survey also showed some interesting facts relating to occupational distribution in Barbados. More than a quarter of the total population was employed in agriculture and another quarter was listed as unemployed. A small proportion of the inhabitants was engaged in activities not related to agriculture (table 6.5).

As early as 1863, Walker had recommended that jobless blacks be encouraged to settle in the neighboring colonies; the council and assembly responded hesitantly by authorizing bona fide estate owners from other colonies to recruit needed laborers. During the next decade, about 13,000 Barbadians departed for British Guiana; in 1873 the legislature agreed to supply £200 a year to assist needy emigrants, provided that they were not currently employed by a local planter.[25] But when foreign agents from the Dutch and Danish West Indies arrived to advertise the higher wages in their areas, the imperial government itself expressed its opposition to any general exodus of laborers to non-British territories. Commenting, however, on the growing burden of unemployment in the island, the Colonial Office noted with concern that not many persons appeared to be leaving.[26] The Barbados superintendent of emigration saw the danger more clearly: "If the limit of food production has been reached, but population goes on increasing, it is a

Table 6.5. Occupations in Barbados, 1871

Occupations	No. Persons[a]	Occupations	No. Persons[a]
Agricultural workers	42,270	Sailors, etc.	1,720
Unemployed	40,829	Porters	1,558
At school	29,080	Artisans	1,499
Domestics	14,486	Accountants	953
Seamstresses	8,868	Various	1,633
Engineers and mechanics	6,848	Military	777
Traders and hucksters	4,620	Professional and teachers	569
Washerwomen	3,795	Civil officers	446
Proprietors and administrative employees	1,863	Other laborers	231

SOURCE: Rawson to Kimberley, 22 August 1872, CO 28/216.
a. There may be minor inaccuracies in the figures given by Rawson.

necessary consequence that poverty should be increasing also. The rate of increase of poverty, measured justly by the amount of poor relief [provided by the parish vestries] is most serious, and suggests the remark that if pestilence does not decimate the people before the arrival of the year 1881, a large emigration must be encouraged; otherwise the burden of poor relief will become intolerable, for the hearts of liberal vestrymen never will devise liberal things to save the most needy [in] distress."[27]

With leaders in London and Bridgetown mutually opposed to emigration on a large scale, it appeared that punitive measures remained the sole means of controlling the restless masses. Several years earlier, the imperial government had condemned the harsh treatment of convicts in Barbados, but in 1869 Colonial Secretary Granville urged Rawson to impress the inhabitants with a "wholesome dread of the prison," which he hoped would discourage further crime. Officials in London authorized the Barbados jail commissioners to reintroduce the treadmill at the main prison. Writing from London, Sir

Julian Pauncefot, the Colonial Office's legal assistant under secretary, expressed the current unfavorable opinion of the black race generally: "The truth is that the negroes are incorrigible idlers and prefer living in filth and squalor and disease to working more than is absolutely necessary to keep the wolf out. This they can do [in many places] with two days' work a week with the help of stolen sugar cane, and the charity of ministers of religion and other benevolent people, who cannot convert them to habits of industry and yet cannot bear to see their wretched condition. This is such an admitted fact as to be a 'platitude,' but I think it should not be lost sight of in future justice to the planters, on the question of the 'oppressed negro.'"[28]

Such an attitude on the part of British officials encouraged planters to adopt more forceful methods; as a result hundreds of cases were brought against the Negroes. Accused of insubordination, breach of contract, unauthorized absence, tardiness, negligence, and improper performance of duty, workers had no choice but to satisfy the demands of their employers or to submit to long sentences of hard labor.[29]

Such efforts failed to alter the habits of the laborers, and in the opinion of many humanitarian observers the Negroes of Barbados were already rendering full value for the amount of wages they received. Commenting on current efforts to coerce the masses, Sewell wrote: "The planting interest ... may be characterized as one of unqualified selfishness. But it has not the merit of being prudent, sagacious, or far-seeing selfishness. Extravagant in all that pertained to their own ease and luxury; penurious when the improvement, moral, social, or political, of the people was in question; tenacious of their aristocratic privileges, opposed to reform ... the planters themselves have done all they could to retard the progress of the ... [colony], and to aggravate the evils which an ill-planned and untimely scheme of emancipation entailed.... Theirs was not the broad, grasping selfishness of a powerful oligarchy wise enough to combine their own aggrandizement with that of the nation at large; but it has been from first to last a narrow-minded selfishness that pursued crooked paths to accumulate gain at the expense of the public weal, and to the infinite detriment of the colonial credit."[30]

Notwithstanding vigorous efforts by planters generally after 1856, sugar production continued to be disappointingly low throughout most of the British Caribbean colonies, particularly in Jamaica, where there was a large number of plantations and a sparse labor supply. In the Windward and Leeward islands, crops were too small to bring any profits. In contrast the proprietors of British Guiana and Trinidad achieved noteworthy improvements in output by introducing foreign workers and sophisticated machinery; but both expedients were costly, and the introduction of migrants from China and India had the additional disadvantage of complicating race relations. The planters of Barbados also eventually resorted to new tools and methods but to a lesser extent than British Guiana and Trinidad, and Barbadian estate owners never had to pay high wages, both reasons for Barbados' ability to produce large crops at low cost. But as the unit price of sugar continued to fall after 1856, the island's entrepreneurs saw that, if profits were to be maintained, still larger harvests were necessary. Such a goal could not be achieved without heavy applications of imported fertilizer and use of expensive machinery, both of which required the planters to rely more heavily on funds from British creditors. While these endeavors resulted in larger crops, profits dwindled, a growing number of planters failed to repay their loans, and Barbadian agriculture became speculative and risky. The recurrence of droughts after 1869 and the rise of the beet industry made it difficult for Barbadian planters to operate at a profit. As early as the 1840s, beet sugar began to make inroads into the trade marts of London and Amsterdam. By 1857 beet sugar producers were supplying a quarter of the world's sugar; in 1884 they contributed over half (53.4 percent) of the total sugar production.[31] Neither Starkey's *Economic Geography of Barbados* nor Green's impressive work on *British Slave Emancipation* sufficiently emphasizes the total effect that beet competition had on the West Indies.

From a humanitarian point of view, it is important to consider the economic status of the masses in the West Indies after 1856. Wages appear to have diminished somewhat after that, even in British Guiana, Trinidad, and Jamaica, but the workers in these three places continued to benefit from good pay and from the sale of such crops as pimiento, cocoa, cotton, and arrowroot.[32] Another advantage in these colonies was cheap, locally grown food. The cost of food in Barbados after 1856 was increasing, probably because planters had reduced the amount of land used for growing laborers' provisions. Taking into account the low wages in the island, it is not difficult to understand why riots and looting occurred during the 1860s and 1870s, and it was no mystery why the governors, military commanders, and planters feared rebellion. The Barbadian legislature undertook to avert such an event by devoting large sums of money to religious and educational programs, neither of which was of much practical benefit to the workers. But it was at the church and schoolhouse that the masses were dissuaded from violence. Where such moral training failed, the Colonial Office recommended the substitution of penal sentences.

7. The Political Background,
Federation Crisis, and Aftermath

BritISH officials speculated for more than two centuries on the need for increased administrative efficiency and reduced government costs in the West Indies, and as early as 1626 Lord Carlisle appointed a common governor-general to administer Barbados and the Leeward Islands. But because of the distance separating the Leewards from Barbados, the proprietor allowed them to be ruled by their own lieutenant-governors and local legislatures. Officially the governor-general possessed superintending power over the whole group, but the colonists who lived outside Barbados so deeply resented any interference from Bridgetown that in 1671 the Crown detached them altogether and gave them their own governor-general, who ruled from St. Johns in Antigua.[1]

Seeking to unify the management of the several territories under his administration, the first governor-general of the Leeward Islands, Sir William Stapleton, decided in 1683 to invite local governments to send delegates to a general legislature, the first attempt to bind the colonies into a closer union. But insular prejudices were strong, and in 1684 the local assemblies rebuffed a proposal to standardize laws throughout the archipelago. From time to time Stapleton's successors also called meetings of the general legislature, but virtually all suggestions put forth by the governor-general failed to pass. The last session was held in 1798.[2] A century and a half later, A. B. Keith explained that the islands were too jealous and their leaders too fond of their local dignities and privileges to allow a central government to form.[3]

138

Among the British officials of the next century who were impressed with the advantages of the British West Indian federation was Lord Goderich. He decided in 1833 to join Barbados and the Windward Islands under a governor-general at Bridgetown, but he allowed the Windwards to retain their separate legislatures and lieutenant governors. Unwilling to irritate the local legislatures on the eve of emancipation, he decided that for the moment no effort should be made to create a general legislature.[4]

A few years later, in 1837, Sir William Colebrooke wrote from Antigua to recommend the restoration of the Leeward Islands' general legislature, but local hostility was so pronounced that the Colonial Office hastily denied any intention of forcing federation on the colonies. Sir Evan MacGregor in Barbados saw that the West Indian legislatures were weary from many long and unavailing struggles with the imperial government and thought that no further external pressure should be applied on them.[5] When Lord John Russell showed an interest in federation shortly afterward, MacGregor gave his reasons why the idea of union was unpopular in the West Indies. The planters were reluctant to participate in meetings held at a distance in other islands; variations in historical traditions, social institutions, and economics made a uniform system of government impractical; and such debt-free colonies as Barbados were unwilling to share their revenues with their poorer neighbors.[6] The Barbadian Council was reluctant to send envoys to a general legislature because it feared that much time would be wasted in petty discussions and that disagreement in the general legislature would paralyze legislation for all of the colonies.[7]

However faint the prospects for unification, British officials continued to promote ways of coordinating the administration of the West Indies. Stephen complained that the Colonial Office practice of seeking the concurrence of so many different legislatures to any policy was so complicated that it threatened to undermine completely the most important aims of the imperial government. Referring to the reams of correspondence on such subjects as wages, contracts, voting rights, the militia, and prison discipline, Stephen confessed that he was bewildered by the perplexity of simultaneous discussions with nineteen different islands. It was understandable, he added, that the colonies were eager to enact their own laws, but he was convinced that the great majority of the colonists would be better served by abolishing the local legislatures: "I believe that few men, perhaps no man, can have so deep a sense as I have of the absurdities and evils ... of these assemblies. The great vice of them all ... is ... that they place boundless irresponsible power in the hands of a small, privileged class ... being moreover composed of half-taught, ill-mannered, and ill-judging people. I never, for example, doubted that such bodies as the Legislature of Nevis and Montserrat were in the nature of a broad farce exhibited on the stage of human society. The Assembly of Jamaica has crowded into the last 27 years a greater amount of blunder than perhaps any other Legislature on earth."[8]

Financial waste, inconsistent and illogical laws, and endless disputes between various branches of the legislature were further proof of the inability of the colonies of the West Indies to govern themselves. A century after emancipation Wrong said that it was a mockery to regard such societies as self-governing. Yet this unfavorable characterization did not always apply to the Barbados Council and Assembly, whose acts the Colonial Office frequently cited as models for other colonies. Stephen believed, though, that most of the laws passed in Bridgetown were the work of one or two members of the legislature into whose hands the others routinely delivered their votes. Commenting on the island's numerous statutes, he wrote, "I have always supposed that ... I was reading the work of some one man ... who is the real legislature on all subjects ... and it seems to me that almost all of the good legislation in the world is the result exactly of this system, namely, a dictatorship in the form of popular government."[9]

There were occasions when opposition by Barbadian political leaders to British policy exasperated London authorities. In 1835 Lord Aberdeen observed that over a period of two hundred years the legislature had devised a method to interfere with the governor's control by transferring many of his powers to boards consisting of its own members. The council and assembly had created a dozen bodies to regulate such matters as finance, public works, education, health, the militia, prisons, and defense. Altogether independent of the executive's control, such boards quarreled over questions of jurisdiction, issued contradictory rulings, exceeded authorized expenses, purchased defective supplies, and abandoned expensive public works before their completion. Reviewing the confusion, Governor Grey urged the legislature in 1844 to bring these numerous groups under his supervision by allowing him to appoint salaried administrators to oversee their activities. But the council and assembly opposed the suggestion because the members feared it would diminish their claim to self-government.[10]

A few years later Colebrooke frankly admitted that the government of Barbados ran more efficiently and intelligently than that of any other British colony in the West Indies. Its boards generally had carried on their work with commendable energy and industry, he wrote, and they usually reported in a businesslike and thorough manner. Such results could be attributed to the fact that the legislature was composed mainly of resident planters, whereas in many of the other islands government was left in the hands of less knowledgeable leaders. But the principal defect in Barbados was that the numerous boards and committees were sometimes unable to agree on matters requiring an immediate decision, and Colebrooke believed also that Grey's objections to financial confusion were justified. In order to overcome these difficulties he asked the legislature in 1854 for the authority to appoint a single official to serve as a coordinating chairman of the boards. Similarly, the activities of the council and assembly could be synchronized by creating an executive committee consisting of members appointed by the governor from both houses. Such a group would be in a position to speak officially for the governor in the legislature and to advise him at the executive level, as done in Jamaica. But the Barbadian legislature rejected the plan by a narrow vote of 11 to 9. Prescod, the only black member of the assembly, voted in favor of Colebrooke's suggestion.[11]

Dismissing the possibility that the legislature would voluntarily agree to political reform, Colebrooke urged the Colonial Office to pursue a more forceful policy and to introduce the executive committee system in Barbados by order-in-council rather than to wait for the council and assembly to act. At the same time, he thought that the imperial government should give additional consideration to federation in the West Indies. He was convinced that a merger of Barbados and the Windward Islands would greatly improve the public business of the colonies, eliminate corruption, and reduce administrative costs. Sound financial practices would be assured by allowing the governor to appoint an executive committee of members of both houses of the general legislature who would have the exclusive right to prepare financial estimates and control money votes. It would also be advantageous to consolidate the judicial establishments in the colonies, while the existing legislatures could be continued for local purposes only. The governor felt that these reforms were so badly needed that an act of Parliament should be used to overcome the opposition.[12]

While Colonial Office leaders were aware of the advantages of political unity in the West Indies, they were also becoming increasingly reluctant to resort to parliamentary intervention in the colonies, except in emergencies such as the Canadian revolution of 1837. Taylor was convinced that any interference from London would arouse enough resentment in Barbados to delay reform indefinitely. Recalling the imperial government's unsuccessful attempt to suspend Jamaica's constitution in 1838, he wrote: "There is in ... [Colebrooke's] despatches much well-reasoned and intelligent, but I am afraid useless discussion of the reforms required in the constitutions of the W. Indian Legislatures.... The evils have long been undoubted and undisputed, & Sir W. Colebrooke has vainly cherished for many years the notion of abating them by the convention of a General Legislature.... The essential question is ... where the power resides ... & whether it resides in any body which can be induced to exercise it? The local Legislatures have the power to purify themselves, but the Assemblies are closed corporations, the members of which are returned by a small per centage ... of the population—they are unamenable to any public opinion.... The Gov. and Lt. Govs. ... look to the authority of Parliament, & in truth it is by that authority & in no other way, that any essential reforms can be accomplished. But, is any Govt. in these days strong enough to go to Parliament.... I confess that I shd. be more reluctant than I once was to advise such a course. The circes. were much more critical in 1838 when there was also a very strong anti-slavery feeling *with* the Govt. & *against* the Assemblies. The bill for the suspension of the

Table 7.1. Barbados' Revenues and Expenditures, 1860–76 (£)

Year	Revenue	Expenditures	Deficit	Surplus
1860	94,752	110,873	16,121	
1861	98,049	115,895	17,846	
1862	93,682	93,461		221
1863	102,572	104,795	2,223	
1864	107,391	104,384		3,007
1865	98,870	99,383	513	
1866	103,935	95,838		8,097
1867	98,348	99,783	1,435	
1868	105,545	99,370		6,175
1869	102,606	105,481	2,875	
1870	104,932	105,709	777	
1871	119,492	122,347	2,855	
1872	117,652	125,040	7,388	
1873	123,676	121,797		1,879
1874	123,869	123,961	92	
1875	132,122	126,844		5,278
1876	117,057	123,727	6,670	

SOURCE: *Barbados Blue Books*, 1860–70, CO 33/80.

Jamaica Assembly then brought in (which originated with myself, though it was only half the measure I had proposed, for my proposal went the length of suspending all the W. Indian Assemblies) overthrew ... [Lord Melbourne's] Govt."[13]

In reply the governor argued that there was more support for federation in the West Indies than the Colonial Office was aware of, and he considered that the people were "entitled to claim the interposition of Parliament to enable them to unite." A year later, his successor, Hincks, wrote to say that Colebrooke had been greatly deceived in counting on much support for federation in Barbados, but he did believe that local leaders were beginning to realize that some practical political reforms were needed. Hincks felt that Colebrooke's suggestion calling for a separate executive committee, a reform recently adopted in St. Vincent and Grenada, was also greatly needed in Barbados. But the Colonial Office continued to avoid constitutional modifications not supported by local leaders, and Taylor doubted that such approval could be obtained.[14]

Yet the lavish spending habits of the Barbadian legislature were beginning to attract unfavorable attention from public officials in London as well as from important local residents. A succession of deficits was incurred by the Barbados government from 1860 through 1876 (table 7.1). The Colonial Office was aware that the council and assembly of Barbados had sanctioned many extraordinary expenditures to finance a number of beneficial public works, including a freshwater supply for Bridgetown, a new town hall and marketplace, a modern prison at Glendiary, and improved harbor facilities. But the members of the legislature had a long history of carelessness with public money, as shown by examples cited by Bruce Hamilton from the legislative session of 1844. Early in January a member of the assembly had moved for a vote to grant the island's treasurer an annual salary of £200, which the house promptly did. The same day, another member gave notice of a forthcoming bill to raise the salaries of the clerk of the public market and the toll-gatherer. In March a motion was presented to grant an unspecified sum of money to the general hospital. The following month several assemblymen introduced petitions for a loan to a parish chuch, a grant of money to the president of the council, and various funds for the maintenance of lepers, the payment of jurors who had served at a recent trial, and the relief of a destitute widow.[15] As was the custom in the Bridgetown legislature, practically all such matters were approved without appropriate investigation or debate.

As loathe as the imperial government was to interfere in the colonies' internal affairs, the Jamaican uprising of 1865 greatly increased its determination to enlarge executive power in the West Indies, and Gladstone's colonial secretary, Granville, announced in 1868 that the Leeward Islands would soon be joined into "one Colony, with one Governor, one Council, one Superior Court, and one Corps of Police." The governor-general of the Leeward Islands, Sir Benjamin Pine, encountered heavy opposition to the proposal in Antigua but finally gained the concurrence of legislatures in the island group, a feat made possible because the imperial government had recently packed the legislatures with nominated majorities. In 1871 Parliament, believing that it had won the support of the people of the Leeward Islands, passed an act reestablishing the general legislature. But because Parliament allowed the colonies to retain their separate legislatures, the plan fell short of establishing a full federation.[16]

In 1869 Granville instructed Rawson to feel out leaders in Barbados and the Windward Islands on the possibility of unification. But Rawson replied that unless the imperial government converted the legislature in Bridgetown into a nominated chamber with a majority obedient to the Crown, he saw no possibility that it would agree to such a step. The governor thought that leaders in Grenada, St. Vincent, St. Lucia, and Tobago would not resort to extreme measures in opposing the plan, but, commenting on the obduracy of the Barbadian legislature, he said, "The Assembly here is composed with a few exceptions of incompetent narrow-minded men, who love the power which that body has wielded fo. generations—who know that they would have no chance of being admitted into a nominated council or single chamber; and will therefore resist this change to the last. They would not appreciate the distinction of Barbados being the seat of the government for the whole archipelago; they would be afraid of competition with the selected representatives of the other islands; jealous of their having a voice in legislating for Barbados and other communities. Barbados is their all and enough for them."[17]

Nevertheless, Rawson thought that there was a chance of achieving other political reforms in Barbados. The legislature's excessive corruption, he wrote, its encroachment on the executive power, and the inability of both chambers to agree on important matters were serious enough to justify Colonial Office intervention. Perhaps if the imperial government allowed the legislature to continue discrediting itself, the inhabitants themselves would eventually insist on substituting a more efficient single chamber composed of a nominated majority and only a few elected members. Hoping to expose the weaknesses of the existing system of government, Rawson addressed the legislature in 1869 on its prevailing methods of conducting business. It was a waste of time, he declared, to call together so many committees and boards whose members did not even pretend to understand the details under consideration, and, however inefficient such bodies had proved to be, the governor, responsible to the Queen for the good government of the island, could not interfere either to move them to beneficial acts or to prevent them from error. These comments deeply offended many leading citizens, and the *Agricultural Reporter* responded by castigating the governor's remarks as "high handed and arbitrary." The *Barbados Times* complained that "narrow minds are capable of doing anything save that which is liberal." Meanwhile, efforts from London to promote the adoption of unicameral legislatures in the Windward Islands heightened the suspicion that the Colonial Office would soon make a similar attempt in Barbados. By 1870 the feeling in Barbados against Great Britain was so pronounced that Rawson cautioned the colonial secretary that the assembly was "up in arms."[18]

By this time, Rawson was more convinced than ever that federation was neither feasible nor desirable. The experiences encountered by Pine at Antigua strengthened his conviction. The economic benefits of federation in the Leeward Islands were illusory, Rawson wrote; the financial standing of the colonies was unchanged; and there was no improvement in administration. Hence, the governor recommended that the scheme to join Barbados with the Windward Islands should be dropped and that the imperial government should concentrate instead on creating a unicameral legislature with a nominated majority in Bridgetown. If necessary, an act of Parliament should be passed to overcome local opposition. Anticipating approval of this suggestion in London, Rawson confidently informed the legislature that an important constitutional change could be awaited involving the creation of a strong executive body. But officials in London continued to disavow any suggestion that Parliament would override the wishes of the local inhabitants in the colonies, and Granville hastily advised Rawson not to rely on any means of effecting reforms in Barbados other than persuasion.[19]

A major difference of opinion was developing between the governor and the Colonial Office. Rawson doubted that any major political changes in Barbados were possible without an act of Parliament, which the imperial government opposed as too forceful a measure. The appointment of Lord Kimberley as colonial secretary in 1870, however, led to more vigorous efforts to overhaul the West Indian governments, and the new permanent under secretary, R. G. W. Herbert, believed that Rawson should be ordered to give federation much stronger support than he had in the past. Herbert also thought that, as an important first step, the courts of Barbados and the Windward Islands should be unified. But Rawson had already advised against such an undertaking, which would be opposed by the numerous petty officials who derived a living from the local tribunals. Furthermore, he feared that the influential inhabitants of Barbados were so suspicious that federation was the ultimate aim of the imperial government that they would view any political changes as preliminary to ending the existing separate administrations.[20]

Within a few months Rawson's attitude changed somewhat, and his thoughts returned to the feasibility of a single chamber. The council and assembly were deadlocked on a public works bill, and he believed that if the most influential member of the assembly, Brandford Griffith, could be persuaded to propose a unicameral system there was a chance that the legislature would accept the plan. Reluctant to rekindle local opposition, Rawson waited a year before allowing Griffith to publish an article on the benefits of a single chamber. When the publication finally appeared in 1872, it suggested that a unicameral body consisting of a combination of elected and appointed members would reduce waste and inefficiency, minimize the loss

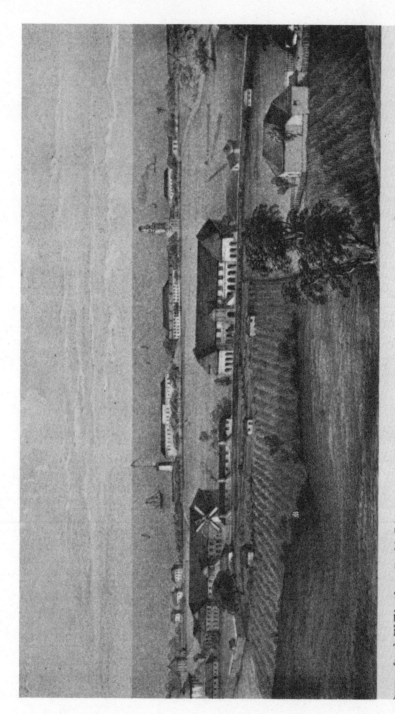

Drawn on Stone by W.L. Walton from a Sketch by Hedges.

Bulman del & Walton Lithographed.

ST ANN'S GARRISON IN BARBADOS

of the members' time, and prevent the passage of "crude measures" requiring future amendments. Griffith realized that many Barbadians took pride in their self-governing status under the existing constitutional arrangements, and, as a concession to their feelings, he believed that the elected membership in the new legislature should have a majority of one, a compromise that the governor endorsed as a reasonable alternative between crown colony rule and self-government.[21]

The legislature reacted with such fiery indignation that Rawson, shaken by the outcry, warned Kimberley against attempting any political changes whatever. Kimberley was sufficiently annoyed by the governor's wavering to rebuke him severely for failing to support the imperial government's policies.[22] But Rawson was unwilling to accept responsibility for Great Britain's failure to carry out its aims in the West Indies. The blame rested with the mother country itself, he insisted, because it had failed to give the governor the firm support necessary to overcome local opposition. "The governor needs three things," Rawson wrote, "straw wherewith to make his bricks, a plan of the edifice he is desired to erect—and orders to erect it." He continued to question the advantages of federation; but if the imperial government was determined to effect a merger of Barbados with the Windward Islands, the Colonial Office should seek to overcome the objections in Barbados by guaranteeing that it would be the seat of the federal government and appointing the two most influential members of the Barbadian council, Sir John Sealy and Sir Charles Packer, to important administrative positions. Mollified by Rawson's explanation, Kimberley expressed his reluctance to buy off the opposition in Barbados. But he did not reject the recommendation, if it was needed as a last alternative.[23]

When Disraeli succeeded Gladstone as prime minister in 1874, Lord Carnarvon replaced Kimberley at the Colonial Office. These changes did not produce any important modification in the attitude of the imperial government toward federation, but Carnarvon prepared to offer a compromise to appease Barbados. The island would be allowed to retain the existing bicameral system provided that it agreed to strengthen the influence of the governor by creating a separate executive council to assist him in important administrative matters. But by this time, Rawson was again in the throes of old fears: he was convinced that the existing council, which acted as a second chamber and as an executive board for the governor, would not consent to transfer any part of its powers to a new executive council. The upper chamber, he warned, had lately found a new leader, Nathaniel Fodringham, "an impetuous, obstinate man, commanding much influence and strongly opposed to federation." Taking brief notice of these comments, Carnarvon concluded that it was hopeless to press for any changes in

Barbados as long as Rawson was in charge. John Pope Hennessy, his successor, would arrive in 1875.[24]

In May 1875 Rawson was temporarily replaced by Lieutenant Governor Sanford Freeling of Dominica, pending the arrival of Hennessy, former governor of the Bahamas. During the six months between Hennessy's appointment and his arrival in Bridgetown, many Barbadians wondered uneasily what political measures were being prepared for them in London. The recent introduction of nominated unicameral legislatures in several neighboring colonies heightened the suspicions of local leaders, and in June a large public meeting took place at Bridgetown to protest any similar constitutional change in Barbados. The principal spokesman was Fodringham, who anxiously foresaw that the inauguration of a single chamber would be followed by an attempt to federate Barbados with the Windward Islands, a radical experiment that would cause confusion, discord, and poverty to spread to Barbados. Only one planter, Sir Graham Briggs, spoke in favor of the imperial government's intentions in the West Indies.[25]

Freeling nervously reported the feelings of the local inhabitants to his superiors in London, but the Colonial Office was not surprised. "Nor were I a Barbadian," a functionary noted, "do I think I should be an advocate of becoming a Crown Colony, as ... [Barbados] was said to have a Revenue equal to its expenditures and no debt."[26] Moreover, the union of Barbados with the other colonies would probably lead to the emigration of Barbadian workers and a consequent reduction in the supply of cheap labor.

Throughout the summer of 1875 the planters of Barbados openly strove to persuade the Negroes that the plan being devised in London was of great disadvantage to them because, they alleged, federation would produce a renewal of slavery, reduced living standards, and heavy taxes to pay for the increased cost of governing the other islands. Therefore, the supporters of federation were the real enemies of the people and the opponents were their friends. Replying to such distorted charges, the attorney general, Hugh Semper, an advocate of West Indian unification, complained that he was made a target by antifederation leaders and was pointed out to the working class as an object of distrust, to the extent that his servants left him and he was warned from several sources that his life was in danger. Likewise, Briggs was cautioned by a note which stated that "murder is intended for you.... Shot you will be, by a cosmopolite."[27]

Conscious of the rising tension, Freeling urged the legislature to provide penalties for the punishment of malicious gossip; this caused Fodringham to react, in Freeling's words, "in an excited manner" in the council. A few days later, the acting governor opened the annual session of the legislature with the unpopular reminder that the town hall jail was again in an unfit state. The place was in such a condition, he declared, that he was entitled under the provisions of the West Indian Prisons Act to close the establishment altogether. Summarizing the effect of his remarks for the colonial secretary, Freeling noted they had probably caused some offense, but he hoped that the imperial government would approve of his "exposing scandals" instead of waiting for Hennessy to begin the irksome work. After expressing mild astonishment at the acting governor's inapt remarks, the legislature unexpectedly became involved with a problem arising from a contested election in St. Thomas Parish. Freeling suggested that the question could be solved by a ruling from the attorney general; but when the assembly rejected the suggestion and decided to call for a fresh election in St. Thomas, Freeling suddenly dissolved the legislature.[28] The members were understandably taken aback, and it was in this strained atmosphere that Hennessy arrived four days later, on November 1.

In his first dispatch from Barbados, the governor complained of the impulsive act on the part of his predecessor, which had aroused mistrust and made it more difficult to raise the delicate question of federation. Seeking to allay the irritation, Hennessy staged a series of receptions and social events at the governor's mansion; he was rewarded when the local newspapers expressed friendship toward him. A few days later the new executive spoke reassuringly to a second session of the legislature. It would soon be his duty to suggest a few ways for improving the administration of Barbados and the Windward Islands, he declared, but in such an old and contented community as Barbados he recognized that the governor should always respect "the conservative spirit of local traditions." Above all he intended to honor the privileges and powers of the existing council and assembly.[29]

At the same time, Hennessy privately invited several members of the legislature to discuss a variety of general problems affecting Barbados and the Windward Islands, whose mutual benefit, he said, would be served by introducing a limited number of common administrative arrangements. He had already jotted these down in a draft proposal entitled "The Six Points." Specifically he recommended making the auditor general, prisoner exchange system, lunatic asylum, lazaretto, police force, and judicial system into joint ventures. Reporting to Carnarvon, Hennessy believed if it was made clear that the new arrangements preserved the existing constitution of Barbados and the independence of the treasury from those of the other islands, he could expect the Barbadian legislature to pass a resolution approving the Six Points. Carnarvon was elated. Bearing in mind the problems he had recently experienced in his efforts to improve the government of South Africa, the colonial secretary believed that Hennessy had acted wisely in soothing the opposition in Barbados. But Herbert, the permanent under secretary, thought that the governor had blundered by agreeing to uphold the Barbadian constitution.[30]

In January 1876 Hennessy summoned the council to implement his proposals, and, after opening the discussion in the upper chamber, he left Barbados for a three-week tour of the Windward Islands. The governor's absence gave Bridgetown newspapers a chance to express themselves freely, and the *Agricultural Reporter* reviewed the Six Points in detail. Now that the people had time to reflect on what Hennessy was about to do, the editor commented that "public opinion, which at first was perfectly taciturn, has been gradually aroused to a sense of the situation." He added that the present mood was something akin to the calm "which not infrequently precedes atmospheric discharge." In particular, the editor suspected that federation would ultimately entail the creation of a general legislature in which the representatives of the Windward Islands would outnumber those from Barbados. Another local journal, which had expressed its initial confidence in Hennessy, now declared that only a "swashbuckler military blockhead... could fail to discriminate the constitutional adjustment" currently being contemplated in London.[31]

Returning from the neighboring colonies, Hennessy informed Carnarvon that the views recently expressed in Barbados did not necessarily reflect the opinion of the people generally. A full-scale discussion of federation would take place in the legislature in February, and he was hopeful that his proposals would be carried in both houses. The colonial secretary thus continued to expect a favorable outcome in Barbados, but Pauncefot was anticipating that the legislature would "trample" on the Six Points. When the assembly debated the proposals in February, its members defeated them unanimously.[32]

At the same time, Carnarvon added to the discontent in Barbados by instructing Hennessy to appoint a new executive council, its four members to constitute a body separate from the existing council. Deprived of its power to advise the governor on important administrative matters, the latter continued to function only as a legislative chamber. This change had been considered for many years, and Carnarvon thought that leaders in Barbados would concur in the reform, which he declared was adopted in all of "the great colonies."[33] But the change had a further inflammatory effect in Barbados.

Despite the great dissatisfaction of the upper chamber, Hennessy still hoped to win support for federation by appealing to both legislative houses on humanitarian grounds. Addressing a joint session on 3 March 1876, he noted sympathetically that many planters had suffered the adverse effects of free trade. But they should realize that many tradesmen and laborers had endured worse hardships, and he hoped that "no intelligent person who loves Barbados" would fail to see that the aim of the imperial government was to assist the needy inhabitants. He believed also that local leaders should have an interest in uplifting the poor, in order to lessen the distressing crimes that accompanied poverty. Consequently it was important to obtain employment and fair wages for the working class, and the main advantage of federation was that it would provide the masses with a natural outlet from the island. The members of the legislature, who had always feared such an outcome, were stunned; but when the governor left the chamber and entered his carriage, a crowd of excited Negroes swarmed around and carried it through the streets on their shoulders.[34]

Hennessy promptly advised Carnarvon that his appeal had produced a good effect and that the Six Points still had a chance of passing. A few local politicians and white shopkeepers, he wrote, were persisting in an effort to confuse the Negroes, but he did not believe that they would succeed. What Hennessy appears to have greatly misunderstood was that it was no longer possible to allay the planters' bitter feelings against him. Even before the speech of March 3, a group of white inhabitants joined to form the Barbados Defense Association, an organization dedicated to oppose "the measures which ... [the Colonial Office and] its emissaries are resorting to in their endeavors to carry out ... [their] policy here."[35] A few days later Hennessy wrote to warn Carnarvon that a heightened spirit of defiance was also developing in the legislative council. He suspected that the leading member, Sealy, was offended by the recent creation of a separate executive council, and he thought that another important member, Packer, was likewise a "jealous opponent of the Government." As Hamilton noted in his lively book on the federation issue, excitement was rising, with the supporters and opponents of federation doing their utmost to win whites and blacks to their side. "If the Six Points pass today," one white shopkeeper told a group of Negros, "I shall be able to buy you as slaves tomorrow at 12 o'clock."[36] Similarly planters complained that the governor had promised that federation would give every Negro free land and two shillings a day. The Barbados Defense Association meanwhile added to the turmoil by calling public meetings to ridicule federation. It advertised in a public handbill:

No Confederation! No Confederation!
Spacious Hall
Magic Lantern Exhibition

On Monday, Wednesday, and Friday evenings, March 27, 29th, and 31st, will be exhibited very fine views of various parts of the world, comic scenes, etc. Fun! Fun! Fun! Also cartoons, conundrums, side scenes, comic views on the political and local issues of the day. Several

Drawn on Stone by W.L.Walton from a Sketch by Hedges.

Holhmandel & Walton Lithographers

ST JOHN'S CHURCH AND HACKLETON'S CLIFF

scenes on the following and kindred subjects: Barbados, before, during, and 10 years after the millenium.... The Six Points. The angels of this millenium. Weak points of some of the angels. What they want and why. What the people say about it, etc.[37]

Because of the time lag in transmitting dispatches by ship across the Atlantic, the Colonial Office took several weeks to react to Hennessy's communications. Commenting on the speech of March 3, Herbert observed with satisfaction that at last the legislature had found an executive who was its master in message writing. On March 21, however, an important absentee planter in Great Britain, Sir Charles Trollope, wrote to the colonial secretary to demand Hennessy's recall. He complained that the governor was spreading revolutionary ideas to the Negroes, bit by bit and by means of "side winds, innuendo, and manipulation." In another letter the chairman of the West India Committee objected to Hennessy's efforts to promote emigration. He feared that the governor had greatly underestimated the importance of a large working class. "But for the relative cheapness of labour caused thereby in the production of the staple," he admitted, "the Island would not be as successful as it is."[38]

Both Carnarvon and Herbert promptly came to Hennessy's rescue, but the colonial secretary was shaken a few days later by a cable from the Barbados Defense Association indicating that a riot had occurred at Mount Prospect Plantation. The message was that a number of blacks had tried to break up a meeting of antifederation partisans, and it had resulted in stone-throwing and pistol shots. Subsequent cables added details: several estate owners were injured, many whites were threatened, females were molested, and a repetition of the Jamaica rebellion of 1865 was expected. Carnarvon was sufficiently troubled by the news to cable Hennessy, who was to make it clear that no scheme of federation would be forced on the colony against the inhabitants' wishes and to take steps to prevent any additional excitement among the Negroes.[39]

A few weeks later, in April, a deputation from the Barbados Defense Association arrived in London to complain that Hennessy had deliberately inflamed the workers, and in so doing he had relied on the lowest class of emissaries, including a quack doctor, bankrupt planter, and convicted forger. Together with Briggs, the only respectable supporter of federation, they had deceived the ignorant masses, who were "delighted to hear of anything that would bring them higher wages, or what they prefer ... plenty to eat and sleep without work."[40]

Leaders in Great Britain were beginning to wonder whether the supporters of federation had made any exaggerated promises to the workers. On

April 18, two days after Herbert had expressed such a concern in a Colonial Office minute, the federation issue in Barbados suddenly came to a head when a crowd of blacks assembled at Byde Mill Estate, a large plantation in the eastern part of the island. They demanded an increase in wages; when the managers refused, the laborers on several neighboring estates joined the angry crowd to raid the cane fields and provision grounds. The frightened managers and overseers summoned the police, and a clash followed in which an undetermined number of laborers were slain. Equipped with this information, the absentee planter and representatives of the Barbados Defense Association in London advised Carnarvon that the governor had fomented a rebellion. The rioting continued for three days, at the end of which Hennessy cabled that all signs of disturbance had ceased. Four hundred rioters were in jail, thirty persons were injured, and eight inhabitants had been killed.[41]

An important letter, which appears to be the only relevant source omitted in Hamilton's comprehensive account of the federation crisis, was meanwhile sent by the president of the Barbados Legislative Council to the West India Committee in London. In it the official, Dr. Grant Thomas, advised that nothing short of recalling Hennessy would restore tranquillity to the colony. He explained that the masses, who somehow had been informed of the wrongs perpetrated against them by the planters, were influenced by a hazy notion that federation would open the way to increased wages and the possession of land. How far the governor had acted to spread such ideas was not known; but after an auspiciously friendly beginning with the members of the legislature, he was now openly declaring the constitution of the colony to be "vicious in the extreme" and without parallel in any part of the British empire. Hennessy had also accused members of the council and assembly of disloyalty because they opposed his views. After all this, who could wonder at the outbreak that spread such alarm throughout the island by exciting "that peculiar element in the character of the Negro which varies according to circumstances from the docility of a child to the ferocity of a savage"? Believing as they did that the plan of the governor entitled them to a community of goods, they began pillaging the fields and shouting, "Hurrah for Confederation," "God bless Confederation," "God bless Pope Hennessy." Next they proceeded to destroy livestock and to break into houses. "What but murder could possibly have been the next step?" Thomas asked.[42]

Thomas' letter led the Colonial Office to decide that it was important to settle the agitation in Barbados as soon as possible but that, as long as Hennessy remained in the island, no solution was likely. Carnarvon was reluctant to remove Hennessy, but in October, Herbert persuaded the colonial secretary to transfer him to another colony. The next month, Hennessy was appointed governor of Hong Kong.[43]

The next governor of Barbados was Captain George Strahan; during his administration Parliament considered converting Barbados into a crown colony. Commenting on the political problem in the island, a former governor, Hincks, advised that the whites would probably accept such an arrangement, which would make the imperial government responsible for controlling the blacks.[44] But Carnarvon, sensing that any attempt to deprive Barbados of its elected lower house would stir up renewed resistance, offered a compromise. If local leaders authorized the governor to appoint two officers of the crown to sit with the assembly, he would allow the existing political arrangements in Barbados to continue. The Barbadian legislature, still unwilling to admit appointed members, rejected the offer.[45]

The solution to the political problem in Barbados was found in 1881, when the legislature passed an act creating a new executive committee consisting of several members appointed by the governor from the council and assembly. The new body possessed several important exclusive powers, including the initiation of all money votes and the preparation of an annual budget. There were no further constitutional changes of any significance until the end of World War II. Meanwhile, authorities in London decided to suspend the effort to federate Barbados with the neighboring colonies,[46] and in 1885 they likewise agreed to abolish the loose union that had united Barbados and the Windward Islands under a common governor-general since 1833. It was not until the Montego Bay Conference of 1947 that the imperial government again urged the West Indies to consider the possibility of forming a federation. Despite the imperial government's renewed attempt to promote the principle of unification, the idea was still unacceptable to the colonial governments. In 1965 the Barbadian legislature resolved in favor of total separation from the other islands, and in the following year Barbados became an independent state.

One of the main problems on which the Colonial Office focused interest was the need for political reform in the West Indies. Whether its aims could have been accomplished by relying on different methods than those that were employed or by entrusting the implementation of policies to different personalities are matter for conjecture. But there are a number of facts that explain why the policies failed in Barbados.

British statesmen did not clearly distinguish what they hoped to achieve. Such officials as Stephen, Taylor, and Herbert complained repeatedly of the inefficiency, waste, and corruption that in varying degrees characterized the Caribbean colonies. But the experience of two centuries of colonial administration had shown the imperial government that political change could succeed only if supported by the inhabitants. As a consequence, the Colonial Office was reluctant to apply any forceful pressure or coercion.

During the 1840s the imperial government envisioned a few simple modifications in the British West Indies, such as the subordination of the numerous legislative committees and boards to the governor's control. In the following decade it sought a more comprehensive change entailing the creation of separate executive committees consisting of members appointed from both houses of the legislature by the governor. Jamaica, along with the Leeward and Windward islands, eventually accepted the modification, but Barbados, fearing the loss of its right to self-government, rejected it. By 1860 the economic status of the British West Indies had worsened to the extent that the cabinet in London was beginning to visualize the need for financial grants and loans, which it was unwilling to provide unless it had control over the use of such funds. The Colonial Office therefore pressed for the introduction of unicameral legislatures comprised of members appointed by the crown. The Morant Bay uprising of 1865 ultimately persuaded Jamaica to accept the arrangement. Within a short time the Leeward Islands also surrendered their elected legislatures, and by 1875 the Windward Islands followed suit. In the end, the Bahamas and Barbados were the only surviving examples of what was known as the old representative system. But the financial condition of Barbados was markedly superior to that of the neighboring islands, and the legislature saw that there was no need for it to submit to imperial control.

The movement to federate the British West Indies had a much longer history than the effort to create appointed legislatures, but it was a disappointment from the beginning. The Leeward Islands federation of the seventeenth century was an admitted failure. For all practical purposes, the origin of the policy which eventually resulted in the disturbances of 1876 may be traced to a Colonial Office memorandum of 1868 entitled "Proposed Re-arrangement of Governments of Trinidad & Windward & Leeward Islands."[47] The proposal was characterized by a vague uncertainty; it shifted from a highly centralized union of islands on the one hand to a mere sharing of administrative facilities on the other. This explains why officials in London sometimes referred to the suggested arrangement as a federation and at other times as a confederation. Interpreting the indecision as a sign of weakness, the opposition forces in Barbados used it to full advantage.

The blame that Kimberley and Carnarvon placed on Rawson for his failure to push more vigorously for unification was undeserved. As long as the imperial government was unwilling to override local opposition, there was no possibility that the Barbadian legislature would accept federation. Kimberley's hope that federation in the Leeward Islands would eventually demonstrate the advantages of unification by lowering government costs likewise ended in disappointment—it resulted instead in increased expense. Ultimately Rawson was forced to agree with local leaders in Barbados that little or nothing was to be gained by federation, but he did not make this opinion public.

When Freeling became acting governor of Barbados in 1875, the irritation of Barbadian leaders was further aggravated by his unwarranted dissolution of the legislature. When Hennessy arrived several months later, the local gentry were already prejudiced against him. Hennessy saw that there was a need to reassure local leaders that no important constitutional change was contemplated. Hamilton's criticism that the improvident executive deserved for making such a pledge is unduly severe.[48] Yet it was undeniable that the unauthorized promise misled the inhabitants and greatly weakened the hand of the colonial secretary. The Six Points were scarcely more than a half step in the direction of coordinating the affairs of the colonies. But many leaders in Bridgetown reacted warily, and it should not have been a surprise on 3 March 1876, when the governor recommended federation as a remedy to the working classes' low wages, that such a suggestion would immediately solidify the opposition against him.

Despite the confused accounts of the riots at Mount Prospect and Byde Mill, it is clear that the gullible laborers were the victims of distorted claims originated by the antifederation faction, which expected that the disorder would lead the Colonial Office to recall Hennessy. A few overenthusiastic supporters of colonial unification may also have made unrealistic promises to the Negroes, but there was no evidence indicating that Hennessy had deliberately incited them. The riots demonstrated the lengths to which opponents of the measure were willing to go to defeat it.

Apart from the imprudent speech made by the governor on March 3, there were other reasons why the acceptance of federation at Bridgetown was improbable. The colony had more than two centuries of uninterrupted self-rule; and while the admiration expressed by Green and other writers for the island's political institutions may have been somewhat exaggerated,[49] there was nevertheless a conspicuous difference in the quality of government in Barbados and in the Windward Islands. By 1875 the neighboring colonies had lost their elected legislatures, and, more important, their treasuries were empty. Moreover, the historical background, social habits, language, and religion of Barbados were distinctly British, to the extent that the island was often referred to as "Little England." In contrast the Windwards had been for a long period of time under French control. As Rawson remarked, the circumstances were such at Bridgetown that leaders would not even have wished it to become the capital city of the proposed federation.[50] It is impossible to say whether they would have reacted differently if the imperial government had insisted. When Parliament left no doubt in 1833 that slavery would be ended, the planters had been sufficiently realistic not to resist the imperial will.

It is also interesting to speculate on the reasons why Great Britain did not abolish self-government in Barbados after 1876. The island had undergone a dangerous crisis; the landed proprietors themselves saw a parallel between the federation riots and the Jamaica uprising of 1865, which had induced the legislature at Kingston to vote for its own destruction. But local leaders in Barbados continued to trust in their ability to govern the colony, and they believed that the imperial government would not force any radical measures on them because contemporary opinion in Great Britain was inclined to respect traditional rights and to deplore arbitrary intervention. The Executive Committee Act of 1881 was as much political change as the Barbadian legislature was willing to accept.

Concerning the economic status of Barbados, in 1875, the year preceding the federation crisis, the colony produced 56,875 tons of sugar, which was the largest crop in its history thus far. There was a temporary decline in the next three years, after which the island returned to its former high volume of productivity. But owing to the rapid rise of the sugar beet industry in many parts of the world, sugar prices dropped from 24s.6d. per hundredweight in 1877 to 10s.6d. in 1899 (see table 7.2).

Such was the effect of the falling price of sugar that, in the ten years from 1886 to 1896, as many as 155 proprietors unremorsefully shed their moribund estates, and there was also a sharp drop in land values, from £63 to £27 per acre. Under such pressure, many absentee planters, who were estimated to own a third of the arable land in Barbados, decided to sell at a loss; their properties passed into the hands of new owners, who were in a better financial position to introduce advanced methods of cultivating and manufacturing sugar. A few central factories had been established in the past, but now several others were added.

The continuing decline of sugar prices and the devastation of the cane fields by moth bores led the imperial government in 1896 to appoint a royal

Table 7.2. Barbados' Sugar Exports, 1875–99

Year	Tons Exported	Price per cwt.[a] (£ s. d.)	Year	Tons Exported	Price per cwt.[a] (£ s. d.)
1875	56,875	1. 0. 0	1888	63,882	13. 0
1876	32,676	1. 1. 6	1889	57,106	16. 0
1877	43,545	1. 4. 6	1890	74,606	13. 0
1878	38,073	1. 4. 0	1891	44,226	13. 6
1879	50,001	19. 0	1892	51,849	13. 6
1880	47,439	1. 0. 6	1893	58,765	14. 3
1881	45,073	1. 1. 3	1894	57,967	11. 3
1882	48,269	1. 0. 0	1895	33,331	10. 0
1883	46,242	19. 0	1896	45,170	10. 9
1884	54,263	13. 3	1897	51,257	9. 3
1885	52,649	13. 6	1898	46,878	9. 6
1886	40,047	11. 9	1899	40,442	10. 6
1887	60,263	11. 9			

SOURCE: Deerr, *History of Sugar*, 2:531.
a. Excluding duty.

commission to investigate economic conditions throughout the British Caribbean colonies. It concluded that the state of Barbados' agriculture was the worst in the West Indies, and it urged several measures to assist the former slave colonies as a whole. Among the recommendations was the suggestion that Great Britain should once again provide financial support for colonial sugar producers. Two years later, Parliament responded by establishing the Imperial Department of Agriculture in Barbados; in 1902 it voted £250,000 in loans to assist planters in financing crops and purchasing new machinery.[51] Although the amount of aid was small, there were some beneficial results. In subsequent years the sugar industry experienced a series of rises and declines characterizing commodity enterprises. But the period of Barbados' unique economic success was over. The island faded into the empire's backwater, where many of the neighboring colonies had languished since the end of slavery.

Notes

1. Prelude to Emancipation in Barbados, 1627–1833

1. Jerome S. Handler, *The Unappropriated People: Freedmen in the Slave Society of Barbados*, p. 29.
2. Richard S. Dunn, *Sugar and Slaves: The Rise of the Planter Class in the English West Indies, 1624–1713*, p. 104. See also Thomas Clarkson, *The History of the Rise, Progress, and Accomplishment of the Abolition of the African Slave-Trade*, 1:111; Robert H. Schomburgk, *The History of Barbados*, pp. 94–95; J. S. Parry and P. M. Sherlock, *A Short History of the West Indies*, p. 175.
3. Handler, *Unappropriated People*, p. 12; Handler, "The Amerindian Slave Population of Barbados in the Seventeenth and Early Eighteenth Centuries."
4. Dunn, *Sugar and Slaves*, pp. 6, 55–56.
5. Ibid., pp. 59–72. See also Otis P. Starkey, *The Economic Geography of Barbados*, pp. 57–58.
6. Dunn, *Sugar and Slaves*, p. 73.
7. K. G. Davies, *The Royal Africa Company*, pp. 65–70, 74–76, 192, 300–312.
8. Starkey, *Economic Geography*, pp. 54 ff., 117; Schomburgk, *Barbados*, pp. 75, 491.
9. Alan H. Adamson, *Sugar without Slaves: The Political Economy of British Guiana, 1838–1904*, p. 5; Handler, *Unappropriated People*, pp. 7–8; Starkey, *Economic Geography*, p. 70.
10. Quoted in Hume Wrong, *Government of the West Indies*, p. 23.
11. Starkey, *Economic Geography*, pp. 83–84; John Oldmixon, *The British Empire in America*, 2:98, 105, 127–28. For several relevant quotations from Oldmixon, see Starkey, *Economic Geography*, pp. 96–97.
12. W. L. Mathieson, *British Slavery and Its Abolition, 1828–1838*, pp. 62, 100; Oldmixon, *The British Empire in America*, 2:131. For detailed information relating to the living conditions of the slaves in Jamaica, see Thomas Roughly, *The Jamaica Planter's Guide*, pp. 80–115.
13. Starkey, *Economic Geography*, pp. 59–60; Daniel McKinnen, *A Tour of the British West Indies in the Years 1802 and 1803*, pp. 30–31.
14. J. A. Thome and J. H. Kimball, *Emancipation in the West Indies: A Six Months' Tour in Antigua, Barbados, and Jamaica in the Year 1837*, p. 57.

15. Quotes from Mathieson, *British Slavery and Its Abolition*, p. 82; see also Schomburgk, *Barbados*, p. 422.

16. Richard Hall, ed., *Acts Passed in the Island of Barbados from 1643 to 1762 Inclusive*, pp. 112–21; also quoted in U. B. Phillips, *American Negro Slavery*, p. 490.

17. Mathieson, *British Slavery and Its Abolition*, pp. 32–39; Elsa V. Goveia, "The West Indian Slave Laws of the Eighteenth Century."

18. Dunn, *Sugar and Slaves*, pp. 243, 256–61; Elsa V. Goveia, *Slave Societies in the British Leeward Islands at the End of the Eighteenth Century*, pp. 152–202.

19. W. L. Burn, *Emancipation and Apprenticeship in the British West Indies*, p. 65; Mathieson, *British Slavery and Its Abolition*, pp. 96–98. For additional information concerning the failure of West Indian courts to punish white offenders, see Hansard, 1830, 25:1186–89, 1213.

20. C. R. Boxer, *The Golden Age of Brazil, 1695–1750*, p. 9; Stanley M. Elkins, *Slavery: A Problem in American Institutional Life*, pp. 52–80; Gwendolyn M. Hall, *Social Control in Slave Plantation Societies*, passim; Marvin Harris, *Patterns of Race in America*, pp. 65–78; Franklin W. Knight, *Slave Society in Cuba during the Nineteenth Century*, pp. 59–120; Donald Pierson, *Negroes in Brazil*, pp. 111–56; Kenneth M. Stampp, *The Peculiar Institution: Slavery in the Ante-Bellum South*, pp. 141–91; Frank Tannenbaum, *Slave and Citizen*, passim.

21. David B. Davis, *The Problem of Slavery in Western Culture*, pp. 223–43.

22. U. B. Phillips, *Life and Labor in the Old South*, pp. 160–72, 191, 201–2, 213, 217; Mathieson, *British Slavery and Its Abolition*, p. 86.

23. Starkey, *Economic Geography*, pp. 70–71, 79; Alan Burns, *History of the British West Indies*, pp. 589–93.

24. J. S. Handler and Frederick W. Lange, *Plantation Slavery in Barbados: An Archaeological and Historical Investigation*, pp. 1–42, 58–102; Starkey, *Economic Geography*, pp. 98, 110; Mathieson, *British Slavery and Its Abolition*, pp. 71–72; Mayers to the Colonial Office, 18 June, 19 July 1833, CO 28/112. The mid-eighteenth century sugar boom was a possible exception to Davis' theory that the treatment of slaves was generally more brutal in areas where economic prosperity was being enjoyed by the planters: see *Problem of Slavery*, pp. 223–43.

25. Mathieson, *British Slavery and Its Abolition*, pp. 61–69; Sidney M. Greenfield, *English Rustics in Black Skin*, pp. 41–43, 146–47; George Pinckard, *Notes on the West Indies*, 1:192–448.

26. Starkey, *Economic Geography*, p. 98.

27. *PP*, 1825, 15:517; Joseph Sturge and Thomas Harvey, *The West Indies in 1837*, p. 140, also quoted in Burn, *Emancipation and Apprenticeship in the British West Indies*, pp. 65–66.

28. Handler, *Unappropriated People*, passim; Greenfield, *English Rustics*, pp. 41–47, 146–47; Mathieson, *British Slavery and Its Abolition*, p. 39; Schomburgk, *Barbados*, p. 381.

29. Quoted in F. G. Spurdle, *Early West Indian Government*, p. 9.

30. Ibid., pp. 12–13; quoted in Wrong, Government of the West Indies, p. 29.

31. Quoted in Wrong, p. 29; Searle to the Council of State, 19 September 1653, also quoted in Spurdle, *Early West Indian Government*, p. 14; Schomburgk, *Barbados*, p. 202.

32. Schomburgk, pp. 206–10; Spurdle, pp. 12, 40; Leonard W. Labaree, *Royal Government in America*, pp. 134–71; Goderich to Smith, 7 March 1833; "An Address of the Council of Barbados to the Earl of Aberdeen," 24 April 1835, with Smith to Aberdeen, 9 May 1835, CO 28/115.

33. Quoted in Greenfield, *English Rustics*, p. 47; Schomburgk, *Barbados*, pp. 381, 431–32; Burn, *British West Indies*, p. 625.

34. Quoted in Labaree, *Royal Government in America*, p. 383.

35. Quoted in Rawson to Granville, 17 September 1870, CO 28/111.

36. J. H. Bennett, Jr., *Bondsmen and Bishops: Slavery and Apprenticeship on the Codrington Plantations of Barbados, 1710–1838*, p. 1; Hansard, 1824, 10:1091–1112.

37. Schomburgk, *Barbados*, pp. 93–96; Handler, *Unappropriated People*, pp. 154–61; Bathurst to Warde, 22 January 1824, CO 29/33.

38. Bennett, *Bondsmen and Bishops*, pp. 1–5; Parry and Sherlock, *Short History*, pp. 246–48; Schomburgk, *Barbados*, p. 93; Handler, *Unappropriated People*, p. 167.

39. William H. Coleridge, "Statement of Churches, Schools, and Chapels in Barbados,"

with MacGregor to Russell, 5 December 1839. See also Coleridge's "Summary of the Number and Cost of Churches, Schools, and Chapels in Barbados to 1837," CO 28/159. Information concerning the number of churches, chapels, and schools may also be found in the *Barbados Blue Books*, 1830–65, CO 33/42–75.

40. Parry and Sherlock say (*Short History*, p. 247) that it was illegal to teach reading and writing to the slaves in Barbados, but Mathieson declares (*British Slavery and Its Abolition*, p. 107) that there was nothing in the British colonies to prevent teaching slaves to read. See also Handler, *Unappropriated People*, pp. 172, 178–79.

41. Schomburgk, *Barbados*, pp. 93, 104–23; "An Act to Consolidate and Amend Certain Acts of This Island Relative to the Central Schools," 16 March 1858, *Barbados Acts*, CO 30/26.

42. Parry and Sherlock, *Short History*, p. 247; Schomburgk, *Barbados*, p. 427.

43. Handler, *Unapropriated People*, pp. 172–75.

44. Ibid., pp. 172–89; Schomburgk, *Barbados*, pp. 93, 104–23; Parry and Sherlock, *Short History*, p. 248.

45. Algernon Aspinall, *Pocket Guide to the West Indies*, pp. 91–92; Bennett, *Bondsmen and Bishops*, p. 5.

46. For an example of the illicit trade in Negroes between the United States and Barbados, see MacGregor to Normanby, 26 October 1839, CO 28/128. On the slave registry bill, see G. W. Jordan, *An Examination of the Principles of the Slave Registry Bill*, passim.

47. Schomburgk, *Barbados*, pp. 395–98.

48. Hansard, 1823, 9:255–360; *PP*, 1824, 24:427 ff.; Lowell J. Ragatz, *The Fall of the Planter Class in the British Caribbean, 1763–1833*, pp. 412–16.

49. [R. Hamden], *A Report of a Select Committee of the Council of Barbados Appointed to Inquire into the Actual Condition of the Slaves of this Island*, passim; Burns, *British West Indies*, p. 635; *PP*, 1825, 26:205, also quoted in J. Holland Rose, A. P. Newton, and E. A. Benians, eds., *The Cambridge History of the British Empire* (Cambridge, 1940), 2:321.

50. Warde to Bathurst, 23 October, and accompanying anonymous statement of 21 October 1823, CO 28/92.

51. Anonymous statement, 23 October 1823, with Warde to Bathurst, 25 October 1823, CO 28/92.

52. Bathurst to Warde, 22 January 1824, CO 29/30, 14 February 1825, CO 29/31; Warde to Bathurst, 3 December 1824, CO 28/93; quote in Burns, *British West Indies*, p. 618.

53. Quoted in Mathieson, *British Slavery and Its Abolition*, pp. 137, 138.

54. Quoted ibid., p. 162.

55. Ibid., pp. 162–63, 175.

56. Hansard, 1826, 14:968–82, 15:1284–1366.

57. Huskisson to the Officer Administering Barbados, 18 October 1827, CO 29/31.

58. *PP*, 1826–27, 25:1, 53, 347.

59. *PP*, 1831–32, 46:279, 649, 733; resolution of the Barbados Assembly, 7 February 1832, with Lyon to Goderich, 21 February 1832, CO 28/109; Ragatz, *Fall of the Planter Class*, p. 440.

60. *Minutes of the West India Merchants*, 18 April 1831. These two lobby groups merged into a single organization in 1843 and were known thereafter as the London West India Association, or more popularly as the West India Committee. See *Minutes of the Standing Committee of the West India Planters and Merchants*, 22 March 1843.

61. Ragatz, *Fall of the Planter Class*, pp. 375–76.

62. Quoted in *Minutes of the West India Merchants*, 22 August 1832.

2. BARBADOS AND THE ABOLITION OF SLAVERY, 1833–1834

1. Extract of a letter from Lafayette to Hume, 22 January 1832, in *Minutes of the West India Planters and Merchants*, 15 February 1832.

2. Goderich to Smith, 7 March 1833, CO 29/33; Schomburgk, *Barbados*, p. 454.

3. Skeete to Goderich, 4 January, 3 April 1833, CO 28/111; Smith to Stanley, 23 May 1833, ibid.

4. "An Address of the Governor to the Council and Assembly of Barbados," with Smith to Goderich, 7 May 1833, ibid.; "Reply of the Assembly to the Governor's Address," *Journal of the Barbados General Assembly (JBGA)*, 4 June 1833, CO 31/51; Smith to Stanley, 13 June 1833, CO 28/111.

5. Quoted in Mathieson, *British Slavery and Its Abolition*, p. 252; Smith to Stanley, 23 May 1833, CO 28/111.

6. Thome and Kimball, *Emancipation*, pp. 75–76.

7. Handler, *Unappropriated People*, pp. 132–38. In 1829 there were 14,959 whites and 5,146 free colored and black persons in Barbados: see William A. Green, *British Slave Emancipation: The Sugar Colonies and the Great Experiment, 1830–1865*, pp. 11–13. For examples of prejudice of persons of mixed blood in Barbados against blacks, see Thome and Kimball, *Emancipation*, p. 76.

8. Green, *British Slave Emancipation*, pp. 14–15; Handler, *Unappropriated People*, p. 150.

9. Quoted in Handler, p. 115; see also Schomburgk, *Barbados*, pp. 381, 431–32; Prescod and other free colored petitioners to the Governor, 6 May 1833, with Smith to Stanley; Smith to Prescod and other free colored Petitioners, 13 May 1833; both with Smith to Stanley, 23 May 1833, CO 28/111.

10. "A Message of the Council to the Governor," 29 May 1833, with Smith to Stanley, 2 July 1833; Smith to Stanley, 23 May 1833; both in CO 28/111.

11. Minute of Stephen, 11 December 1833, with Smith to Stanley, 27 September 1833, CO 28/111; Stanley to Smith, 13 July, 2 September 1833, CO 29/33.

12. Hansard, 1833, 17:1191–1262. For a concise description of Stanley's original bill, see Ragatz, *Fall of the Planter Class*, p. 453.

13. "A Petition from the Council and Assembly of Barbados to the Commons in the United Kingdom," *JBGA*, 6 July 1833, CO 31/51.

14. Burns, *British West Indies*, pp. 626–27; Ragatz, *Fall of the Planter Class*, pp. 453–55.

15. *JBGA*, 30 July 1833, CO 31/51; Mayers to the Colonial Office, 18 June, 19 July 1833, CO 28/112.

16. "A Report of the Committee of the Assembly Appointed to Confer with the Committee of the Council on the Subject of Slave Emancipation," *JBGA*, 29 October 1833, CO 31/51; Stanley to the governors of the West India Colonies, 13 June, 5 September, 19 October 1833, CO 854/1. See also *JBGA*, 30 July, 15 October, 19 November 1833, CO 31/51.

17. Mathieson, *British Slavery and Its Abolition*, p. 250; "A Message of the Governor to the Council and Assembly," *JBGA*, 15 October 1833, CO 31/51.

18. Stanley to the governors of the West India Colonies, 19 October 1833, CO 854/1, also found in *JBGA*, 19 November 1833, CO 31/51.

19. Green, *British Slave Emancipation*, pp. 122–23.

20. "An Act for the Abolition of Slavery and the Government of the Apprenticed Labourers in This Island," 8 April 1834, *Barbados Acts*, CO 30/21; Lefevre to Smith, 13 June 1834, CO 29/33; Stanley to the governors of the West India Colonies, 13 June 1833, CO 854/1, also found in *JBGA*, 30 July 1833, CO 31/51.

21. Smith to Stanley, 23 May, 13 July 1833, CO 28/111; "A Message of the Governor to the Council and Assembly," *JBGA*, 21 January 1834, CO 31/51; Smith to Aberdeen, 6 March 1835, CO 28/115.

22. *JBGA*, 4 June 1833, 21 January 1834, CO 31/51; "An Act for Establishing a Rural Police in this Island," 21 July 1834; "An Act for Establishing a Police in Bridgetown," 29 July 1834, *Barbados Acts*, CO 30/21; Smith to Taylor, 4 January 1835, CO 28/115.

23. Smith to Spring-Rice, 28 July 1834, CO 28/113.

24. "A Proclamation of the Governor to the Slave Population," with Smith to Stanley, 22 January 1834, ibid. For military precautions undertaken by Smith, see Smith to Spring-Rice, 31 July 1834, ibid. On the holiday, see Smith to Spring-Rice, 3 July 1834, ibid.

25. Smith to Spring-Rice, 5 August 1834, ibid.; Green, *British Slave Emancipation*, p. 131n4.

3. NEGRO APPRENTICESHIP IN BARBADOS, 1834–1838

1. Paul Knaplund, *James Stephen and the British Colonial System, 1813–1847*, pp. 108–14.
2. Spring-Rice to Smith, 12 August 1834, CO 29/33.
3. Quoted in Mathieson, *British Slavery and Its Abolition*, p. 251.
4. "A Memorial of the Council and Assembly to the Secretary of State for Colonies," 4 November 1834, with Smith to Spring-Rice, 5 November 1834, CO 28/114.
5. "An Act to Alter an Act for the Abolition of Slavery in This Island," 3 November 1834, *Barbados Acts*, CO 30/21.
6. "A Memorial of the Council and Assembly," with Smith to Spring-Rice, 5 November 1834, CO 28/114.
7. Glenelg to Smith, 10 June 1835, CO 29/33.
8. "A Memorial of the Council and Assembly," with Smith to Spring-Rice, 5 November 1834, CO 28/114; Mathieson, *British Slavery and Its Abolition*, p. 260; Green, *British Slave Emancipation*, p. 132.
9. Glenelg to Smith, 10 June 1835, CO 29/33.
10. Mathieson, *British Slavery and Its Abolition*, pp. 243–65; *JBGA*, 24 April 1838, CO 31/52.
11. *PP*, 1837–38, 44:154; Burns, *British West Indies*, p. 634; Smith to Stanley, 8 July 1833, CO 28/111; "An Act for the Abolition of Slavery and the Government of the Apprenticed Labourers in this Island," 8 April 1834, *Barbados Acts*, CO 30/21.
12. "Reports of the Stipendiary Magistrates," with Beckles to Glenelg, 21 September, 12 October 1836, CO 28/117; with MacGregor to Glenelg, 10 November, 31 December 1836, CO 28/118; with MacGregor to Glenelg, 21 March, 10 July 1837, CO 28/119; with MacGregor to Glenelg, 1 September 1837, CO 28/120.
13. Sligo to Glenelg, 4 November 1835, CO 137/202; see also Burn, *Emancipation and Apprenticeship*, pp. 170–71, 177–78.
14. Mathieson, *British Slavery and its Abolition*, p. 246; Sturge and Harvey, *The West Indies in 1837*, p. 26.
15. "Reports of the Stipendiary Magistrates," with Beckles to Glenelg, 21 September, 12 October 1836, CO 28/117; with MacGregor to Glenelg, 10 November, 31 December 1836, CO 28/118; with MacGregor to Glenelg, 21 March, 10 July 1837, CO 28/119; with MacGregor to Glenelg, 1 September, 1837, CO 28/120; Mathieson, *British Slavery and Its Abolition*, p. 246.
16. Adamson, *Sugar without Slaves*, pp. 57–103; Burn, *Emancipation and Apprenticeship*, p. 271; Green, *British Slave Emancipation*, p. 135; Mathieson, *British Slavery and Its Abolition*, pp. 86–88; Sturge and Harvey, *The West Indies in 1837*, pp. 93, 96; Donald Wood, *Trinidad in Transition: The Years after Slavery* (London and New York, 1968), pp. 5, 7, 48–51.
17. *JBGA*, 18 August 1835, CO 31/52
18. Thome and Kimball, *Emancipation*, p. 67.
19. Ibid., p. 76; Douglas Hall, *Free Jamaica, 1838–1865: An Economic History*, pp. 3, 20, 24.
20. Kennedy to MacGregor, included as part of the "Reports of the Stipendiary Magistrates," with MacGregor to Glenelg, 21 March 1837, CO 28/119. Additional information concerning the treatment of the free black children may be found in Smith to Spring-Rice, 25 August 1834, CO 28/113; Smith to Spring-Rice, 8, 30 September 1834, CO 28/114; Smith to Aberdeen, 21 March 1837, CO 28/119.
21. Starkey, *Economic Geography*, p. 117; M. G. Smith, *The Plural Society in the British West Indies*, pp. 123–24.
22. Smith to Spring-Rice, 1 August, 30 September 1834, CO 28/114; "Reply of the Council to the Governor's Message," 16 September 1834, with Smith to Spring-Rice, 30 September 1834, ibid.; see also Green, *British Slave Emancipation*, p. 134.
23. Thome and Kimball, *Emancipation*, pp. 58, 63; Glenelg to Smith, 29 June 1835, CO 29/33.
24. *Dictionary of National Biography* (London, 1921), 4:773–74; John Davy, *The West Indies Before and Since Slave Emancipation*, pp. 93–94; Handler and Lange, *Plantation Slavery in*

Barbados, pp. 186–87; W. L. Mathieson, *British Slave Emancipation,* p. 71. Handler and Lange, however, cite several sources indicating that women attending slave funerals in Barbados usually dressed in white, while the men wore black.

25. Thome and Kimball, *Emancipation,* pp. 131, 141.

26. Quote in Mathieson, *British Slavery and Its Abolition,* p. 112; Philip D. Curtin, *Two Jamaicas: The Role of Ideas in a Tropical Colony,* pp. 162–65; Thome and Kimball, *Emancipation,* p. 137; Smith, *Plural Society,* p. 165; Wood, *Trinidad,* pp. 8–9.

27. *PP,* 1837–38, 48:113.

28. *Barbados Blue Books,* 1830–65, CO 33/42–75; W. G. Sewell, *The Ordeal of Free Labor in the British West Indies,* p. 43.

29. "Reports of the Stipendiary Magistrates," with Beckles to Glenelg, 21 September, 12 October 1836, CO 28/117; "Charge of the Chief Justice of Barbados to the Grand Jury," with Smith to Glenelg, 27 June 1836, ibid.; "An Address of Horatio N. Springer to the Assembly," *JBGA,* 29 September 1835, CO 31/51.

30. "An Act to Establish Byelaws, Ordinances, and Regulations for the Good Government of Bridgetown," 16 November 1835, *Barbados Acts,* CO 30/21; "An Act for the Abolition of Slavery and the Government of the Apprentices of this Island," 4 April 1834, ibid.

31. *JBGA,* 21 July 1835, CO 31/52; Burn, *Emancipation and Apprenticeship,* p. 167.

32. Glenelg to MacGregor, 28 November 1836, CO 29/35; minute of Stephen, 29 October 1836, with Smith to Glenelg, 27 June 1836, CO 28/117.

33. Smith to Spring-Rice, 25 September 1834, CO 28/114; Smith to Aberdeen, 6 March 1835, CO 28/115.

34. Aberdeen to Smith, 1, 10 January 1835, CO 29/33; "An Address of the Council to the Earl of Aberdeen," 24 April 1835, with Smith to Aberdeen, 9 May 1835, CO 28/115; "An Address of the Assembly to the Earl of Aberdeen," 31 March 1835, with Smith to Aberdeen, 23 April 1835, ibid.; "An Act to Provide for the Temporary Establishment of a Police in this Island," 24 April 1835, *Barbados Acts,* CO 30/21.

35. Smith to Aberdeen, 28 March, 9, 28 May 1835, Smith to Glenelg, 6 July 1835, CO 28/115. See also Green, *British Slave Emancipation,* pp. 146–47.

36. Smith to Glenelg, 8 August 1835, CO 28/116. See also Smith to Aberdeen, 9 May 1835, CO 28/115.

37. Burn, *Emancipation and Apprenticeship,* pp. 295–96, 302, 304–5, 361.

38. Minute of Stephen to Taylor, 31 August 1835, with Smith to Glenelg, 6 July 1835, CO 28/115. See also minute of Stephen to Glenelg, with Smith to Glenelg, 8 August 1835, CO 28/116; Glenelg to Smith, 31 August 1835, CO 29/33.

39. "An Act for Continuing in Force and Amending an Act for the Temporary Establishment of a Rural Police in this Island," and "An Act to Repeal Certain Clauses of the Act for Abolition of Slavery and Providing for the Government of the Apprenticed Labourers," 19 August 1835; "An Act to Amend an Act to Establish a Police in Bridgetown," 21 August 1835; all in *Barbados Acts,* CO 30/22. See also "An Address of the Governor to the Council and Assembly," 21 August 1835, with Smith to Glenelg, 22 August 1835, CO 28/116.

40. Glenelg to Smith, 13 October 1835, CO 29/33.

41. Smith to the Special Justices, 14 October 1835; "A Scale of Work to be Performed by the Apprenticed Labourers in the Island of Barbados"; both with Smith to Glenelg, 8 December 1835, CO 28/116; Mathieson, *British Slavery and Its Abolition,* pp. 267–68.

42. Smith to Glenelg, 8 December 1835, CO 28/116.

43. Mathieson, *British Slavery and Its Abolition,* pp. 246–60; quote in Schomburgk, *Barbados,* p. 473.

44. Smith to Glenelg, 24 November 1837, CO 137/221; also quoted in Mathieson, *British Slavery and Its Abolition,* p. 271.

45. Curtin, *Two Jamaicas,* pp. 97–98; Schomburgk, *Barbados,* pp. 472–73.

46. Schomburgk, p. 490. The hogshead was a measure which varied from 14 cwt. to 18 cwt.

47. Middlemore to Smith, 7 April 1835, with Smith to Aberdeen, 8 May 1835, CO 101/79;

Darling to Smith, 21 August 1835, with Smith to Spring-Rice, 9 September 1835, CO 285/41; Sligo to Glenelg, 24 September 1835, CO 137/202.

48. Hill to Stanley, 7 August 1834, CO 295/103; Colebrooke to Aberdeen, 9 April 1835, CO 23/93; MacGregor to Stanley, 19 August 1834, cited in Burn, *Emancipation and Apprenticeship*, p. 174; Smyth to Spring-Rice, 20 August 1834, CO 111/132; Sligo to Spring-Rice, 13 August 1834, CO 137/192.

49. Sligo to Glenelg, 6 September 1835, CO 137/202.

50. *JBGA*, 27 August 1833, CO 31/51, 26 January 1836, CO 31/52; *Barbados Blue Books*, 1832–38, CO 33/44–49.

51. Thome and Kimball, *Emancipation*, pp. 53–84; Green, *British Slave Emancipation*, pp. 151–61; Glenelg to Smith, 10 June 1835, CO 29/33.

52. "Report of the Number of Complaints against Apprenticed Labourers and of Assaults Committed by Employers from 1 January to 31 October 1836," with MacGregor to Glenelg, 6 December 1836, CO 28/118; "General Abstract of Cases Brought before the Special Justices of the Peace from 15 October to 30 November 1837," with MacGregor to Glenelg, 13 December 1837, CO 28/120; Sligo to Spring-Rice, 12 October 1834, CO 137/193; second quote in Mathieson, *British Slavery and Its Abolition*, p. 264. For an indication of the harsh treatment given to the apprentices in other colonies see Burn, *Emancipation and Apprenticeship*, p. 168.

53. Hansard, 1835, 37:960 ff.; Mathieson, *British Slavery and Its Abolition*, pp. 274–76; Mathieson, *British Slave Emancipation*, pp. 14–15.

54. Minutes of the Acting Committee of the West India Planters and Merchants, 17 June 1835; Glenelg to the Governors of the West India Colonies, 18 May 1835, CO 854/1.

55. Quoted in Mathieson, *British Slavery and Its Abolition*, pp. 283–84.

56. Sturge and Harvey, *West Indies in 1837*, pp. 4–6. See also various statements by Scoble with MacGregor to Glenelg, 13 December 1838, CO 28/124.

57. "A Memorial of the Bridgetown Gaol Comissioners to the Governor," 7 March 1836, with Smith to Glenelg, 9 March 1836, CO 28/117; Mathieson, *British Slavery and Its Abolition*, pp. 280–81; Burn, *Emancipation and Apprenticeship*, pp. 194, 288; Thome and Kimball, *Emanciapation*, pp. 91–92; Sturge and Harvey, *West Indies in 1837*, pp. 91–92.

58. Sturge and Harvey, p. 235.

59. MacGregor to Glenelg, 14 March 1838, CO 28/122.

60. *PP*, 1837–38, 40:367.

61. Leicester Smith to MacGregor, 22 February 1838, with MacGregor to Glenelg, 14 March 1838, CO 28/122; MacGregor to Glenelg, 2 March 1838, ibid.; "An Act to Amend an Act for the Abolition of Slavery and the Government of Apprenticed Labourers in This Island," 24 February 1838, *Barbados Acts*, CO 30/22.

62. Thome and Kimball, *Emancipation*, p. 73. For additional information concerning the difficulties experienced by the special justices because of inadequate pay, poor housing, and ill health, see Green, *British Slave Emancipation*, pp. 140–44. Further information concerning the usefulness of the special justices is also found in Mathieson, *British Slavery and Its Abolition*, pp. 225, 279, and concerning their character in Burn, *Emancipation and Apprenticeship*, p. 201.

63. Mathieson, *British Slavery and Its Abolition*, pp. 289–93; "An Address of Robert B. Clarke to the Assembly," 31 January 1837, with MacGregor to Glenelg, 12 June 1837, CO 28/119.

64. Statement of Joseph Sturge, in the *Birmingham Philanthropist*, 16 March 1837; see also the *Antigua Herald*, 20 May 1837, extracts of which are with MacGregor to Glenelg, 12 June 1837, CO 28/119.

65. "An Act to Repeal the 38th Clause of the Abolition Act of this Island," 30 March 1837, with MacGregor to Glenelg, 12 June 1837, CO 28/119; *JBGA*, 17 October 1837, CO 31/52.

66. Quote in Colthurst to the governor's private secretary, 6 June 1837, with MacGregor to Glenelg, 12 June 1837, CO 28/119; MacGregor to Glenelg, 28 June 1838, CO 28/123.

67. Buxton to Clarke, 26 June 1837, *JBGA*, 17 October 1837, CO 31/52; R. Harward, "A Memorial Addressed to H. M. Government Relative to the System of Apprenticeship," 17 November 1837, CO 854/2.

68. Mathieson, *British Slavery and Its Abolition*, p. 299; Hansard, 1838, 40:352 ff., 1284 ff.

69. Mathieson, *British Slave Emancipation,* p. 17; Glenelg to the Governors of the West India Colonies, 2 April 1838, CO 854/2.

70. "A Message of the Assembly of Barbados to the Governor," 13 March 1838, with MacGregor to Glenelg, 14 March 1838, CO 28/122; "An Address of Robert B. Clarke to the Assembly of Barbados," *JBGA,* 24 April 1838, CO 31/51.

71. MacGregor to Glenelg, 26 April 1838, CO 28/122; "An Act Terminating the Apprenticeship of Praedial Labourers," 16 May 1838, *Barbados Acts,* CO 30/22; "An Address of the Assembly to the Secretary of State for Colonies," *JBGA,* 23 April 1839, CO 31/54.

72. Green, *British Slave Emancipation,* pp. 157–59; Wood, *Trinidad,* p. 47; Smith to Glenelg, 17 May 1838, CO 137/228.

73. Mathieson, *British Slavery and Its Abolition;* pp. 301–2; Mathieson, *British Slave Emancipation,* p. 21; Green, *British Slave Emancipation,* pp. 165–67.

74. MacGregor to Glenelg, 28 June 1838, CO 28/123.

75. Mathieson, *British Slave Emancipation,* pp. 40–42; Burn, *Emancipation and Apprenticeship,* p. 371.

4. THE ADVENT OF FREE LABOR, 1838–1846

1. "An Address of Robert B. Clarke to the Assembly," *JBGA,* 3 July 1838, CO 31/52; "A Resolution of the Council of Barbados," 3 July 1838, with MacGregor to Glenelg, 4 July 1838, CO 28/123; *The Cambridge History of the British Empire,* 2:714, 718.

2. MacGregor to Glenelg, 28 June 1838, CO 28/123, 30 May 1838, CO 28/122.

3. "An Act to Regulate the Hiring of Servants and the More Expeditious Recovery of Wages," "An Act to Punish and Suppress Vagrancy," "An Act for Preventing Tumults and Riotous Assemblies and for the More Speedy and Effectual Punishment of Rioters," all in 6 June 1838, *Barbados Acts,* CO 30/22; "An Act Authorizing the Appointment of Rural Constables in this Island," with MacGregor to Glenelg, 8 July 1838, CO 28/123.

4. Glenelg to the governors of the West India Colonies, 6 November 1837, CO 854/2.

5. Glenelg to MacGregor, 31 August 1838, CO 29/35; Glenelg to the governors of the West India colonies, 15 September 1838, CO 854/2.

6. MacGregor to Glenelg, 7, 23 July 1838, CO 28/123.

7. "An Act to Authorize the Appointment of an Assistant Court of Appeals in this Island," 19 July 1838, *Barbados Acts,* CO 30/22; Green, *British Slave Emancipation,* pp. 179–80.

8. Whittingham to the War Office, 8 December 1837, CO 28/126.

9. "An Address of the Governor to the Apprenticed Labourers," 27 July 1838, Minutes of the Council, 24 July 1838, both with MacGregor to Glenelg, 11 August 1838, CO 28/123.

10. *The Barbadian,* 1 August 1838; quote in Mathieson, *British Slave Emancipation,* p. 52. See also Jones to the governor's private secretary, 10 August 1838, with MacGregor to Glenelg, 11 August 1838, CO 28/123.

11. Sharpe to MacGregor, 10 August, 1838, with MacGregor to Glenelg, 11 August 1838, CO 28/123. For additional comments on the uncooperative attitude of the workers in 1838, see Edward Clarke to Mayers, 26 September 1838, CO 28/126.

12. "A Proclamation of the Governor to the Apprenticed Labourers," with MacGregor to Glenelg, 11 August 1838, CO 28/123.

13. Quote in Edward Clarke to Mayers, 26 September 1838, CO 28/126; MacGregor to Glenelg, 22 August 1838, CO 28/123.

14. MacGregor to Glenelg, 20 September 1838, CO 28/123; "An Address of Joseph Garraway to the Labourers of St. Andrew's Parish," 12 September 1838, with MacGregor to Glenelg, 4 October 1838, CO 28/124.

15. Aberdeen to Smith, 10 January 1835, CO 29/33; Glenelg to MacGregor, 31 August 1838, CO 29/35.

16. Cuppage, Tinling, and Garraway to the governor's private secretary, 29 October 1838,

with MacGregor to Glenelg, 31 October 1838, CO 28/124; Mathieson, *British Slave Emancipation*, p. 66.

17. MacGregor to Glenelg, 16 April 1839, CO 28/127.

18. Mathieson, *British Slave Emancipation*, p. 54.

19. "An Act to Regulate the Hiring of Servants and for the Recovery and Security of Wages" and "An Act for the Suppression and Punishment of Vagrancy," both 6 January 1840, *Barbados Acts*, CO 30/23; "Reports of the Police Magistrates," with president of the council to Russell, 17 June 1841, CO 28/140.

20. Russell to the officer administering Barbados, 9 August 1841, CO 29/37; Mathieson, *British Slave Emancipation*, pp. 55, 138–39; "Reports of the Police Magistrates," with president of the council to Russell, 17 June 1841, CO 28/140.

21. Minute of Merivale, 29 April 1848, with Reid to Earl Grey, 6 March 1848, CO 28/126; Hall, *Free Jamaica*, p. 20; Normanby to MacGregor, 1 August 1838, CO 29/35. For additional comments concerning the lack of land in Barbados, see Cuppage, Tinling, and Garraway to MacGregor, 30 September 1839, with MacGregor to Russell, 26 October 1839, CO 28/128; Russell to the office administering Barbados, 9 August 1841, CO 29/37.

22. Schomburgk, *Barbados*, p. 152; Davy, *The West Indies*, p. 109; Mathieson, *British Slave Emancipation*, p. 69.

23. Smith to Glenelg, 26 July 1836, CO 28/117; "An Act to Regulate the Emigration of Labourers from this Island," 22 July 1836, *Barbados Acts*, CO 30/21.

24. Glenelg to the governors of the West India Colonies, 19 December 1838, *JBGA*, 26 March 1839, CO 31/54; "Minutes of the Council," 26 March 1839, with MacGregor to Normanby, 4 April 1859, CO 28/127; "An Act to Prevent the Clandestine Deportation of Young Persons from this Island," 26 April 1839, *Barbados Acts*, CO 30/22.

25. Numerous statements by Day, with MacGregor to Normanby, 19 September, 9 October 1839, CO 28/128, and with MacGregor to Russell, 26 October, 5 December 1839, CO 28/129.

26. The governor's private secretary to Clarke, 30 August 1839, to the police magistrates, 2 September 1839, to Thorne, 11 September 1839; all with MacGregor to Normanby, 19 September 1839, CO 28/128. See also MacGregor to Glenelg, 9 October 1839, ibid.

27. Day to the editor of the *Barbados Mercury*, with MacGregor to Glenelg, 9 October 1839, ibid.

28. Minutes of the Council, 26 March 1839, with MacGregor to Normanby, 4 April 1839, CO 28/127; see also various depositions of Barbadian emigrants to British Guiana, with MacGregor to Russell, 21 March 1840, CO 28/133. The views of the Barbados agent in London are found in Mayers to Vernon Smith, 11 December 1839, CO 28/132.

29. Prescod, "The Gagging Act," with MacGregor to Russell, 9 April 1840, CO 28/134. See also "An Act to Protect the Labourers of this Island from Impositions Practiced upon Them by Emigration Agents," 21 March 1840, *Barbados Acts*, CO 30/23.

30. Adamson, *Sugar without Slaves*, p. 43; minute of Stephen to Vernon Smith, 29 May, 8 June 1840, both with MacGregor to Russell, 9 April 1840, CO 28/134.

31. Russell to MacGregor, 26 June, 14 November 1840, CO 29/35. See also *JBGA*, 1 September 1840, 12 January 1841, CO 31/54.

32. Minute of Stephen to Vernon Smith, 8 June 1840, with MacGregor to Russell, 9 April 1840, CO 28/134.

33. Mathieson, *British Slave Emancipation*, pp. 54, 96; minute of Spedding to Stephen, 7 August 1841, with president of the council to Russell, 17 June 1841, CO 28/140.

34. MacGregor to Glenelg, 11 December 1838, with enclosures, CO 28/124; "A Proposal for a Colonial Union of the Coloured Classes," with MacGregor to Russell, 1 May 1840, CO 28/134.

35. MacGregor to Russell, 1 May 1840, CO 28/134; "A Memorial of the Assembly to the Secretary of State for Colonies," *JBGA*, 23 April 1839, CO 31/54; minute of Stephen to Vernon Smith, 19 May 1841, with MacGregor to Russell, 14 March 1841, CO 28/139; minute of Stephen to Vernon Smith, 29 May 1840, with MacGregor to Russell, 9 April 1839, CO 28/134.

36. Minute of Stephen to Sir George Grey, 18 August 1835, with Smith to Aberdeen, 22 May 1835, CO 28/115.

37. Hall, *Free Jamaica,* pp. 7–8, 136–38; Curtin, *Two Jamaicas,* pp. 58, 182–83, 196.

38. Glenelg to the governors of the West India Colonies, 15 January 1839, CO 854/2; MacGregor to Russell, 11 November, 4 December 1839, CO 28/129; Russell to MacGregor, 15 February, 24 June, 1 September 1840, CO 29/35; Russell to the officer administering Barbados, 5 August 1841, CO 29/37; Phillips to Stephen, 1 January 1840, CO 28/137.

39. "An Act to Amend an Act for the Representation of the People of this Island and to Declare Who Shall be Liable to Serve as Jurors," 6 June 1840, *Barbados Acts,* CO 30/23; MacGregor to Russell, 18 April 1840, CO 28/134.

40. MacGregor to Glenelg, 8 September 1838, CO 28/123. Of more than two hundred persons holding commissions in the militia under MacGregor, only five were colored or black. See also Darling to Russell, 17 September 1841, CO 28/140.

41. MacGregor to Russell, 20 December 1839, CO 28/129; "An Act to Establish Courts of Arbitration in this Island," 28 January 1840, *Barbados Acts,* CO 30/23; Russell to MacGregor, 14 February 1840, CO 29/35.

42. Glenelg to the governors of the West India Colonies, 30 November 1838, Normanby to the governors of the West India Colonies, 1 April 1839, both in CO 854/2; minute of Stephen to Labouchere, 6 December 1838, with MacGregor to Glenelg, 15 January 1838, CO 28/122; MacGregor to Glenelg, 15 January 1839, CO 28/127; "Report of a Committee of the Council," 3 December 1839, with MacGregor to Russell, 5 December 1839, CO 28/129.

43. Schomburgk, *Barbados,* p. 490; Darling to Russell, 17 September 1841, CO 28/140.

44. MacGregor to Glenelg, 12 May 1838, CO 28/122, 1 May 1837, CO 28/119. See also Green, *British Slave Emancipation,* pp. 147–48.

45. *Barbados Blue Books,* 1841–51, CO 33/51–61.

46. Sir Charles Grey to Stanley, 3 October 1842, CO 28/144; Stephen quoted in W. P. Morrell, *British Colonel Policy in the Age of Peel and Russell,* p. 155.

47. "An Act Taking Away the Punishment of Death in Certain Cases and Substituting Other Punishments in Lieu," 12 July 1842, *Barbados Acts,* CO 30/23.

48. Pilgrim to Sir Charles Grey, with Sir Charles Grey to Stanley, 31 August 1844, CO 28/160.

49. Mathieson, *British Slave Emancipation,* pp. 132–34, 143.

50. Sir Charles Grey to Stanley, 8 February 1845, CO 28/161.

51. Morrell, *British Colonial Policy,* pp. 150–53; Sir Charles Grey to Stanley, 16 January 1843, CO 28/156. For the imperial government's reasons for withdrawing the salaries of the special justices, see Stanley to Grey, 14 April 1842, CO 29/37.

52. "An Act for the Better Maintenance of the Protestant Clergy and the Rural Chapelries in this Island," 3 March 1840, *Barbados Acts,* CO 30/23.

53. Russell to the Archbishop of Canterbury, 14 August 1841, CO 29/36.

54. Stephen to the treasury, 8 February 1842, CO 29/36; Stanley to Parry, 20 August 1842, with Parry to Hope, 10 August 1842, CO 28/155; "An Act for the Better Maintenance of the Protestant Clergy and the Rural Chapelries in this Island," 26 January 1844, *Barbados Acts,* CO 30/24; *Barbados Blue Books,* 1842–75, CO 33/52–85; "Report of the Diocese of Barbados for 1865," CO 28/203.

55. Smith to Stanley, 26 November 1833, CO 28/111; Stanley to Sir Charles Grey, 1 November 1845, draft with Sir Charles Grey to Stanley, 15 September 1845, CO 28/162; Stanley to the governors of the West India Colonies, 4 December 1845, CO 854/2; Parry to Gladstone, 5 June 1846, CO 28/165; Earl Grey to the governors of the West India Colonies, 19 September 1846, CO 854/2.

56. Parry to Darling, 2 August 1841, Darling to Russell, 19 August 1841, both in CO 28/140; Hall, *Free Jamaica,* p. 31.

57. Russell to MacGregor, 8 April 1841, CO 29/37; Russell to the governors of the West India Colonies, 18 March 1841, with Stanley to the governors of the West India Colonies, 1 October 1845, CO 854/2; Alfred Caldecott, *The Church in the West Indies,* p. 113.

58. "An Act Authorizing Quarterly Payments for a Limited Period from the Public

Treasury towards the Moral and Religious Education of the People of this Island," 21 July 1846, *Barbados Acts*, CO 30/24; Sir Charles Grey to Gladstone, 3 August 1846, CO 28/164; Gladstone to Sir Charles Grey, 24 April 1846, draft with Sir Charles Grey to Gladstone, 23 March 1846, ibid.

59. Glenelg to the governors of the West India Colonies, 1 February 1839, CO 854/2. See also *JBGA*, 16 April 1839, CO 31/54; Sewell, *The Ordeal of Free Labor*, p. 43.

60. "Report of the Committee of the Assembly Appointed to Consider the Question of the Poor Laws," *JBGA*, 21 November 1840, CO 31/54; Schomburgk, *Barbados*, pp. 130–31; Davy, *The West Indies*, p. 100.

61. Schomburgk, *Barbados*, p. 128.

62. *Barbados Blue Books*, 1838–46, CO 33/49–56.

63. Green, *British Slave Emancipation*, p. 180; Adamson, *Sugar without Slaves*, pp. 167–73; "A Message of the Governor to the Council and Assembly," *JBGA*, 13 June 1843, CO 31/54; Sir Charles Grey to Stanley, 15 June 1843, CO 28/157; *Barbados Blue Books*, 1842–46, CO 33/52–56.

64. Handler, *Unappropriated People*, p. 127; "An Act to Regulate the Trade and Business of Butcher and to Check and Prevent as Much as Possible the Stealing of Stock," 22 November 1836, "An Act to Regulate the Sale of Bread by Itenerant Vendors," 17 August 1836, both in *Barbados Acts*, CO 30/22; *Barbados Blue Books*, 1839–42, CO 33/50–52.

65. "An Act Laying a Duty on Goods Exported and Imported in This Island," 10 December 1840, "An Act Laying a Duty on Goods Exported from and Imported into this Island," 29 December 1841, both in *Barbados Acts*, CO 30/23; Clarke to MacGregor, 22 December 1840, with MacGregor to Russell, n.d. 1840, CO 28/135. For the views of other assemblymen concerning the need for increasing the colony's revenues, see *JBGA*, 10 November 1840, CO 31/54.

66. *Barbados Blue Book*, 1843, CO 38/53; "A Message of the Governor to the Council and Assembly," *JBGA*, 29 December 1842, CO 31/53; "An Act to Amend and Continue in Force an Act for Laying a Duty on Goods Exported from and Imported into this Island," 29 December 1843, *Barbados Acts*, CO 30/24.

67. Mathieson, *British Slave Emancipation*, p. 54.

68. "A Message of the Governor to the Council and Assembly of Barbados," *JBGA*, 29 December 1842, CO 31/53; Mathieson, *British Slave Emancipation*, pp. 142–43.

69. *The Times* (London), 23 July, 9 November 1846; minute of Taylor to Earl Grey, 15 February 1846, quoted in Morrell, *British Colonial Policy*, p. 151.

70. "A Message of the Governor to the Council and Assembly," *JBGA*, 13 August 1844, "An Address of the Council and Assembly to the Governor," *JBGA*, 27 August 1844, both in CO 31/53.

71. Colebrooke to Earl Grey, 27 April 1849, CO 28/170; Hamilton to Pakington, 13 April 1852, CO 28/176; "An Act to Provide for the Erection of a Lighthouse in this Island," 14 September 1847, *Barbados Acts*, CO 30/24.

72. "An Address of the Governor to the Council and Assembly," *JBGA*, 13 June 1843, CO 31/53; "An Act to Consolidate and Amend the Laws Relating to Highways," 12 August 1845, *Barbados Acts*, CO 30/24.

73. Sir Charles Grey to Stanley, 9 December 1845, CO 28/162; "A Message of the Governor to the Council and Assembly," *JBGA*, 21 October 1845, CO 31/56.

74. Green, *British Slave Emancipation*, pp. 195–96; Adamson, *Sugar without Slaves*, pp. 38–39; Wood, *Trinidad*, pp. 53, 66.

5. BARBADOS AND FREE TRADE, 1846–1856

1. Quoted in Mathieson, *British Slave Emancipation*, p. 178.

2. Reid to Earl Grey, 24 May 1848, CO 28/168.

3. *Barbados Blue Books*, 1846–47, CO 33/56–57; Reid to Earl Grey, 24, 26 February 1848, CO 28/168.

4. *Dictionary of National Biography*, 16:883–87, pt. 2 of supplement 1, pp. 42–43.

5. Colebrooke to Newcastle, 7 June 1853, CO 28/178; *Barbados Blue Books*, 1840–47, CO 33/56–57, 1847–49, CO 33/57–59.

6. "Fifth Annual Report of the St. Philip Agricultural Society for the Year 1844," with Sir Charles Grey to Stanley, 4 September 1845, CO 28/162; Colebrooke to Newcastle, 10 May 1854, CO 28/180.

7. Quoted in Starkey, *Economic Geography*, p. 120.

8. Colebrooke to Newcastle, 7 June 1853, CO 28/178; Starkey, *Economic Geography*, pp. 114–15, 120–21.

9. Presumably an "estate" was thought to comprise ten acres or more. Starkey writes that the number of estates in Barbados remained fixed at 508 from 1865 to 1890. Figures given by Davy and Schomburgk appear to be vague and inconsistent: Davy says that there were 508 estates of ten acres or more in 1840, Schomburgk that there were 940, but they agree that the number of all landowners in 1840 was 1,874 (Starkey, *Economic Geography*, p. 178; Davy, *West Indies*, pp. 109–10; Schomburgk, *Barbados*, p. 153). For information of a later date, see Colebrooke to Newcastle, 7 June 1853, CO 28/178; Rawson to Kimberley, 22 August 1872, CO 28/216; *Barbados Blue Books*, 1850–71, CO 33/60–81.

10. Hall, *Free Jamaica*, pp. 82, 199; Green, *British Slave Emancipation*, p. 235; Adamson, *Sugar without Slaves*, pp. 161, 164; Wood, *Trinidad*, pp. 36, 124.

11. Davy, *The West Indies*, pp. 182–87, 218–27, 246–47; Sewell, *Ordeal of Free Labor*, p. 75; N. Deerr, *History of Sugar*, 1:168–69; Hall, *Free Jamaica*, pp. 96–97.

12. Davy, *The West Indies*, p. 185.

13. Ibid., pp. 397–98; Douglas Hall, *Five of the Leewards*, pp. 32–58, 96–127; Deerr, *History of Sugar*, 1:195–96.

14. Adamson, *Sugar without Slaves*, pp. 57–70, 163–69; Green, *British Slave Emancipation*, pp. 202–3.

15. Green, p. 220; Adamson, pp. 167, 175–76, 183; Wood, *Trinidad*, p. 27.

16. Reid to Earl Grey, 8 March 1848, CO 28/168; *Barbados Blue Books*, 1855–58, CO 33/65–68; Starkey, *Economic Geography*, p. 123.

17. "Accounts of Easy Hall Plantation," quoted by Pilgrim, with Reid to Earl Grey, 8 March 1848, CO 28/168; *Barbados Blue Books*, 1846–47, CO 33/56–57; Reid to Earl Grey, 7 December 1848, CO 28/167.

18. *The Cambridge History of the British Empire*, 2:728.

19. "Report of the Barbados Finance Committee," *JBGA*, 3 April 1855, CO 31/57; Colebrooke to Molesworth, 11, 24 September 1855, CO 28/183; Committee of the Privy Council for Trade to Molesworth, 26 June 1855, with Russell to the governors of the West India Colonies, 11 August 1855, CO 854/5.

20. Colebrooke to Russell, 7 August 1855, CO 28/123; minute of Taylor to Elliott, 13 September 1855, with Colebrooke to Russell, 26 July 1855, CO 28/183.

21. Hall, *Free Jamaica*, p. 181.

22. Davy, *West Indies*, pp. 92–93, 148–50; Hincks to Lytton, 22 September 1858, CO 28/188; Green, *British Slave Emancipation*, p. 323n104.

23. Dunn, *West Indies*, p. 76; Greenfield, *English Rustics*, p. 43; Handler, *Unappropriated People*, pp. 129n48, 165, 168.

24. Schomburgk, *Barbados*, p. 89; Greenfield, *English Rustics*, p. 162.

25. Greenfield, pp. 59–60, 102–3, 163–64.

26. Colebrooke to Earl Grey, 27 April, 6 October 1849, CO 28/171; "An Address of Dr. Grant Thomas to the Cliff District Agricultural Society," with Colebrooke to Russell, 9 June 1855, CO 28/182.

27. "An Act for the Protection of the Public Health of This Island," 19 February 1851, *Barbados Acts*, CO 30/25; Colebrooke to Newcastle, 27 June 1854, to Sir George Grey, 12 July 1854, both in CO 28/180.

28. Lewis N. Samuel, "General Report on the Condition of Bridgetown," *JBGA*, 28 November 1854, CO 31/57.

29. Colebrooke to Earl Grey, 9 June 1851, CO 28/171.

30. Earl Grey to the Governors of the West India Colonies, 26 January 1847, CO 854/3.

31. Kay-Shuttleworth to Hawes, 6 January 1847, with Earl Grey to the Governors of the West India Colonies, 26 January 1847, ibid. The printed enclosure in Earl Grey's circular dispatch is incorrectly signed "B. Kay-Shuttleworth," which is probably a printer's error.

32. "An Act to Provide for a More Extensive and General Education of the People of This Island," 24 October 1850, *Barbados Acts,* CO 30/25; "Report of the Barbados Education Committee to 5 October 1854," *JBGA,* 16 January 1855, CO 31/57; Hamilton to Pakington, 13 April 1852, CO 28/176; Green, *British Slave Emancipation,* p. 349n61.

33. *Barbados Blue Books,* 1854–64, CO 33/64–74; Colebrooke to Newcastle, 20 March 1854, CO 28/180.

34. Curtin, *Two Jamaicas,* p. 189.

35. Colebrooke to Russell, 9 June 1855, CO 28/182.

36. Davy, *The West Indies,* pp. 89–91.

37. Thome and Kimball, *Emancipation,* p. 282.

38. Starkey, *Economic Geography,* pp. 117–24; Green, *British Slave Emancipation,* pp. 201–2, 222, 245–46, 258, 325, 404.

39. *Barbados Blue Books,* 1866–78, CO 33/76–88. On the superior condition of workers in Antigua, see Hall, *Five of the Leewards,* pp. 32–57, 96–146.

40. Hall, *Free Jamaica,* pp. 121–56; Adamson, *Sugar without Slaves,* p. 43.

41. Green, *British Slave Emancipation,* pp. 184–88.

6. BARBADOS AT MID-CENTURY, 1856–1875

1. *Dictionary of National Biography,* 26:439–41.

2. Ibid., 59:69.

3. Hall, *Free Jamaica,* p. 270.

4. *Barbados Blue Books,* 1847–67, CO 33/57–77.

5. Walker to Newcastle, 27 September 1859, CO 28/189.

6. Hincks to Labouchere, 22 August 1857, CO 28/187.

7. Sewell, *Ordeal of Free Labor,* pp. 18–19.

8. Minute of Taylor, 28 September 1857, with Hincks to Labouchere, 22 August 1857, CO 28/187; Walker to Newcastle, 27 September 1859, CO 28/189.

9. Walker to Buckingham and Chandos, 27 November 1867, CO 28/205.

10. Hincks to Labouchere, 6 June 1857, CO 28/187; Hincks to Newcastle, 19 September 1860, CO 28/191; quote in Sewell, *Ordeal of Free Labor,* pp. 32–33.

11. Cloet to Parmure, 26 September 1857, CO 28/187; Walker to Bulwer-Lytton, 26 April 1859, CO 28/189; Walker to Newcastle, 9 August 1863, CO 28/196; Walker to Cardwell, 8 October 1864, CO 28/199.

12. "An Act to Consolidate and Amend a Law Relating to the Malicious Injury to Property," 17 February 1868, "An Act to Consolidate and Amend the Law of this Island Relating to Offences Against Property," 17 February 1868, "An Act to Consolidate and Amend the Law of this Island Relating to Larceny," 2 March 1868, all in *Barbados Acts,* CO 30/27; Walker to Cardwell, 31 October 1864, CO 28/199; "Report of the Inspector of Schools," quoted in Mundy to Cardwell, 18 October 1865, CO 28/191; Walker to Buckingham and Chandos, 27 November 1867, CO 28/205; Hall, *Five of the Leewards,* p. 58.

13. "A Memorial of the Non-Resident Proprietors of Barbados to the Council and Assembly," 16 September 1857, *JBGA,* 3 November 1857, CO 31/58; Walker to Carnarvon, 9 April 1866, CO 28/202; Cardwell to Walker, 1 March 1866, CO 29/41.

14. Treasury to the Colonial Office, 4 July 1867, CO 28/205; Buckingham and Chandos to Mundy, 27 October 1868, CO 29/41; Parry to Adderley, 5 June 1868, CO 28/207; Granville to Rawson, 28 August 1869, CO 29/41; Rawson to Granville, 17 April 1870, CO 28/211.

15. Granville to Rawson, 11 June 1870, CO 29/41.

16. Rawson to Kimberley, 10 October 1871, CO 28/215, 1 September, 3 December 1870, CO 28/212, 1 June 1871, CO 28/213; "A Resolution of the Council," with Rawson to

Kimberley, 10 October 1871, CO 28/215; "An Act to Grant an Annual Sum toward the Support of the Ministers of the Roman Catholic Church," 7 November 1871, *Barbados Acts,* CO 30/27, Caldecott, *Church in the West Indies,* pp. 142–48.

17. "An Act to Amend an Act to Provide a More Extensive and General Education of the People of this Island," 21 December 1858, *Barbados Acts,* CO 30/26; "Reports of the Inspector of Schools for 1859 and 1860," both quoted in Hincks to Newcastle, 15 October 1861, CO 28/193. For Hincks' views on the need for increased public education, see Hincks to Labouchere, 6 June 1857, CO 28/187.

18. "An Act for a Further Grant of Money for Educational Purposes," 26 June 1867, "An Act for a Further Grant of Money for Educational Purposes," 13 August 1872, both in *Barbados Acts,* CO 30/27; "An Act for a Grant of Money for Educational Purposes," 5 May 1874, *Barbados Acts,* CO 30/28; Rawson to Kimberley, 22 August 1872, CO 28/216; John Savage, "Report of the State of Education in Barbados in 1876," CO 811/6. For additional statements by Rawson on public education, see Rawson to Granville, 4 September 1869, CO 28/209.

19. Ready to the non-resident Proprietors of Barbados, 26 October 1857, *JBGA,* 3 November 1857, CO 31/58.

20. Rawson to Kimberley, 15 September 1870, CO 28/212.

21. Rawson to Carnarvon, 8 November 1874, CO 321/1; "An Address of the Assembly to the Governor," with Hennessy to Carnarvon, 30 March 1876, in *Papers Relating to the Late Disturbance in Barbados,* C. 1539; Walker to Cardwell, 3 June 1864, CO 28/198.

22. Quoted in Bruce Hamilton, *Barbados and the Confederation Question,* pp. 6–7; Rawson to Kimberley, 29 September 1873, CO 28/218. For further information concerning parochial poor relief, see Rawson to Granville, 8 June 1869, CO 28/208.

23. Rawson to Kimberley, 29 October 1872, CO 28/217.

24. Rawson to Kimberley, 22 August 1872, CO 28/216.

25. "An Act to Amend the Laws Relating to Emigration from this Island," 23 March 1864, *Barbados Acts,* CO 30/26; Walker to Cardwell, 3 June 1864, CO 28/198; Cardwell to Walker, 11 June 1864, CO 29/39; Adamson, *Sugar without Slaves,* p. 77; "An Act to Amend an Act Relating to Emigration from this Island," 18 February 1873, with Rawson to Kimberley, 8 July 1873, CO 28/218.

26. Minute of Fairfield to Herbert, 5 August 1873, with Rawson to Kimberley, 8 July 1873, CO 28/218; Hennessy to Carnarvon, 25 April 1876, in *Further Papers Relating to the Late Disturbances in Barbados,* C. 1559.

27. Quoted in Hamilton, *Confederation Question,* p. 8.

28. Granville to Rawson, 20 November 1869, CO 29/41; Walker to Buckingham and Chandos, 23 March 1868, CO 28/206; Buckingham and Chandos to the Officer Administering Barbados, n.d. 1868, CO 29/41; Minute of Pauncefot, with Hennessy to Carnarvon, 25 April 1876, CO 321/9.

29. Hamilton, *Confederation Question,* pp. 5–6.

30. Sewell, *Ordeal of Free Labor,* p. 38.

31. Adamson, *Sugar without Slaves,* pp. 190–95; Deerr, *History of Sugar,* 2:490–91.

32. Hall, *Free Jamaica,* pp. 182–200.

7. THE POLITICAL BACKGROUND, FEDERATION CRISIS, AND AFTERMATH

1. Spurdle, *Early West Indian Government,* pp. 7–11, 21–24, 41.

2. Colin Hughes, "Experiments towards Closer Union in the British West Indies."

3. Keith, *Constitutional History of the First British Empire,* p. 174.

4. Goderich to Smith, 7 March 1833, CO 29/33. See also Stanley to MacGregor, 1 March 1834, with numerous dispatches pertaining to West Indian federation, CO 28/138.

5. Coleridge to Glenelg, 14 June 1837, Glenelg to Colebrooke, 18 August 1838, in *PP,* 1840, 34:595; MacGregor to Glenelg, 9 April 1838, CO 28/138.

6. Draft of Russell to Colebrooke, n.d. December 1840, CO 28/138. See also Russell to Colebrooke 1 June 1840, in *PP*, 1840, 34:595.

7. MacGregor to Russell, 21 July 1840, CO 28/138; "Minutes of the Council," 31 March, 29 April, 6 June 1840, enclosed in the same dispatch.

8. Minute of Stephen to Taylor, 7 June 1839, with MacGregor to Glenelg, 14 March 1839, CO 28/127; minute of Stephen to Taylor, 2 December 1840, with Taylor's "Memorandum for the Plan of a West India Congress," 25 November 1840, CO 28/138.

9. Wrong, *Government of the West Indies*, p. 70; minute of Stephen to Taylor, 2 December 1840, with Taylor's "Memorandum for the Plan of a West India Congress," 25 November 1840, CO 28/138.

10. Aberdeen to Smith, 1, 10 January 1835, CO 29/33; *JBGA*, 13 August 1844, CO 31/53.

11. Colebrooke to Newcastle, 22 December 1853, CO 28/179, 20 March 1854, CO 28/180.

12. Colebrooke to Newcastle, 9 July 1855, CO 28/182; Newcastle to Colebrooke, 12 June 1854, CO 29/39.

13. Minute of Taylor to Merivale, 15 August 1855, with Colebrooke to Russell, 9 July 1855, CO 28/182.

14. Colebrooke to Molesworth, 8 October 1855, CO 28/183; Hincks to Labouchere, 28 April 1856, CO 28/185; minute of Taylor to Merivale, 28 May 1858, with the same dispatch.

15. Hamilton, *Confederation Question*, p. 14.

16. Granville to Pine, 10 April 1869, *Correspondence Respecting the Federation of the Leeward Islands*, C. 343; Hamilton, pp. 23–24.

17. Hamilton, pp. xvii, 16, 29; Rawson to Granville, 9 August 1869, CO 28/208.

18. Rawson to Granville, 9, 24 August 1869, CO 28/208, 7 September 1869, CO 28/209; "An Address of the Governor to the Council and Assembly," *JBGA*, 27 July 1869, CO 31/61; *Agricultural Reporter*, 19 October 1869; *Barbados Times*, 20 October 1869.

19. Rawson to Granville, 9 August 1869, CO 28/208; "An Address of the Governor to the Council and Assembly," *JBGA*, 9 November 1869, CO 31/61; Granville to Rawson, 2 September 1869, CO 29/41.

20. Minute of Herbert, 18 April 1870, with Rawson to Granville, 17 March 1870, CO 28/211; Rawson to Granville, 25 January 1870, ibid., 1 July 1870, CO 28/212.

21. *Agricultural Reporter*, 10, 13 September 1872.

22. *Barbados Times*, 11 September 1872; Rawson to Kimberley, 26 September 1872, CO 28/217; Kimberley to Rawson, 15 November 1872, C. 1539.

23. Rawson to Kimberley, 28 February, 9 May 1873, CO 28/218; Kimberley to Rawson, 1 May 1873, C. 1539; minute of Kimberley, 8 June 1873, with Rawson to Kimberley, 9 May 1873, CO 28/218.

24. Carnarvon to Rawson, 26 November 1874, with Rawson to Carnarvon, 7 October 1874, CO 321/1; Rawson to Carnarvon, 28 December 1874, ibid.; minute of Carnarvon, with Rawson to Carnarvon, 10 December 1874, ibid.

25. Freeling to Carnarvon, 1 July 1875, CO 321/5 (see also the same dispatch in C. 1539).

26. Minute of Cox, 2 August 1875, with Freeling to Carnarvon, 1 July 1875, CO 321/5.

27. Hamilton, *Confederation Question*, p. 40; anonymous letter to Briggs, n.d., C. 1539.

28. Freeling to Carnarvon, 24 July 1875, CO 321/5 (see also the same dispatch in C. 1539), 28 October, 10 November 1875, C. 1539.

29. Hennessy to Carnarvon, 8 November 1875, "An Address of the Governor to the Council and Assembly" 29 November 1875, both in C. 1539; Hamilton, *Confederation Question*, p. 46.

30. Hennessy to Carnarvon, 26, 29 November, 8, 9 December 1875, C. 1539; minute of Carnarvon, 4 January 1876, with Hennessy to Carnarvon, 9 December 1875, CO 321/5; Carnarvon to Hennessy 28 January 1876, C. 1539; minute of Herbert, 2 April 1876, with Hennessy to Carnarvon, 11 March 1876, CO 321/9.

31. *Agricultural Reporter*, 21 January 1876; *Barbados Times*, 22 January 1876.

32. Minute of Pauncefot, with Hennessy to Carnarvon, 28 January 1876, CO 321/9; Hennessy to Carnarvon, 9, 11 February 1876, C. 1539.

33. Carnarvon to Hennessy, 28 January 1876, C. 1539.

34. "An Address of the Governor to the Council and Assembly," 3 March 1876, with Hennessy to Carnarvon, 11 March 1876, ibid.; Hamilton, *Confederation Question,* p. 56.

35. Hennessy to Carnarvon, 11 March 1876, CO 321/9; quoted in Hamilton, *Confederation Question,* p. 57.

36. Hennessy to Carnarvon, 12 March 1876, CO 321/9; Hamilton, pp. 52–65; quoted in Hennessy to Carnarvon, 11 March 1876, C. 1539.

37. "Information for the People of the Evils of West Indian Federation," with Hennessy to Carnarvon, 30 March 1876, C. 1539.

38. Minute of Herbert, 2 April 1876, with Hennessy to Carnarvon, 11 March 1876, CO 321/9; Trollope to the Colonial Office, 16 March 1876, Hill to Carnarvon, 24 March 1876, both in C. 1539.

39. Herbert to Trollope, 22 March 1876, Carnarvon to Hennessy (telegraphic), 29 March 1876, both in C. 1539; Hamilton, *Confederation Question,* p. 65.

40. Quoted in Hamilton, p. 81. For a description of the kind of persons who allegedly supported Hennessy in Barbados, see ibid., p. 76.

41. Minute of Herbert, 16 April 1876, with Hennessy to Carnarvon, 24 March 1876, CO 321/9; West India Committee to the Colonial Office, 30 May 1876, C. 1539; Hamilton, pp. 71–85.

42. Thomas to Hill, 28 April 1876, with Hill to the Colonial Office, 19 May 1876, CO 321/14.

43. Minute of Pauncefot, with Hill to the Colonial Office, 19 May 1876, ibid.; minute of Herbert, with Hennessy to Carnarvon, 16 October 1876, CO 321/11; Hansard, 1877, 222:1977.

44. Minute of Herbert, with Strahan to Carnarvon, 10 January 1878, CO 321/9; *Toronto Daily Globe,* 13 May 1876.

45. Carnarvon to Strahan, 16 November 1877, "Reply of the Assembly to the Governor's Address," both with Strahan to Carnarvon, 26 December 1877; *Correspondence Respecting the Constitution and Administration of Barbados*; all in C. 2645.

46. Hamilton, *Confederation Question,* pp. 108–10; *Papers Relating to the Proposed Union of the Islands of Grenada, St. Lucia, St. Vincent, and Tobago* (London, 1885), C. 4482.

47. A. W. Birch, "Proposed Re-arrangement of Governments of Trinidad & Windward & Leeward Islands," December 1868, CO 28/207.

48. Hamilton, *Confederation Question,* pp. 44–52.

49. Green, *British Slave Emancipation,* p. 75.

50. Rawson to Kimberley, 26 September 1872, CO 28/217, 28 February 1873, CO 28/218.

51. C. 8657; *Barbados Report for the Years 1956 and 1957* (London, 1959), pp. 95–96.

Appendixes

Appendix 1. Barbados' Revenues and Expenditures, 1832–78 (£)

Year	Revenue	Expenditure	Deficit	Surplus
1832	25,110	18,356		6,754
1833	20,915	16,536		4,379
1834	36,220	17,841		18,379
1835[a]				
1836	42,336	29,373		12,963
1837	38,416	32,066		6,350
1838	33,081	32,342		739
1839	41,966	34,152		7,814
1840	50,335	53,826	3,491	
1841	66,434	64,674		1,760
1842	70,704	56,204		14,500
1843	95,760	53,057		42,703
1844	92,251	85,599		6,652
1845	57,751	52,347		5,404
1846	86,246	88,158	1,912	
1847	53,058	55,686	2,628	
1848	41,627	43,713	2,086	
1849	47,438	44,531		2,907
1850	54,064	47,438		6,626
1851	53,725	50,469		3,256
1852	54,096	54,978	882	
1853	61,552	68,199	6,647	
1854	59,142	71,227	12,085	
1855	58,462	69,523	11,061	
1856	85,061	70,575		14,486

Continued

Appendix 1—*Continued*

Year	Revenue	Expenditure	Deficit	Surplus
1857	82,592	80,970		1,622
1858	96,914	87,891		9,023
1859	87,595	80,352		7,243
1860	94,752	110,873	16,121	
1861	98,049	115,895	17,846	
1862	93,682	93,461		221
1863	102,572	104,795	2,223	
1864	107,391	104,384		3,007
1865	98,870	99,383	513	
1866	103,935	95,838		8,097
1867	98,348	99,783	1,435	
1868	105,545	99,370		6,175
1869	102,606	105,481	2,875	
1870	104,932	105,709	777	
1871	119,492	122,347	2,855	
1872	117,652	125,040	7,388	
1873	123,676	121,797		1,879
1874	123,869	123,961	92	
1875	132,122	126,844		5,278
1876	117,057	123,727	6,670	
1877	121,432	119,611		1,821
1878	139,192	134,308		4,884

SOURCES: *Barbados Blue Books,* 1830–78, CO 33/42–88; Walker to Newcastle, 27 September 1859, CO 28/189, 17 September 1862, CO 28/195, 21 October 1863, CO 28/197; Rawson to Kimberley, 15 September 1870, CO 28/212, 29 September 1873, CO 28/218; Rawson to Carnarvon, 8 November 1874, CO 321/1; Dundas to Carnarvon, 12 November 1877, CO 321/15. See also C. 8657.

a. Figure missing at time of research.

Appendix 2. Barbados' Exports and Imports, 1832–83 (£)

Year	Exports	Imports	Balance of Trade
1832	408,363	481,610	− 73,247
1833	553,628	461,135	+ 92,493
1834	736,006	449,790	+286,216
1835[a]			
1836	749,193	630,157	+119,036
1837	897,990	606,586	+291,404
1838	960,368	730,763	+229,605
1839	731,262	233,772[b]	[a]
1840[a]			
1841	531,872	317,336[b]	[a]
1842	855,712	276,418[b]	[a]
1843	668,256	617,131	+ 51,125
1844	681,000	604,410	+ 76,590
1845	691,309	682,368	+ 8,941
1846	773,405	631,267	+142,138
1847	881,159	561,261	+319,898
1848	659,073	432,016	+227,057
1849	791,744	591,478	+200,266
1850	831,534	734,385	+ 97,149
1851	887,627	787,977	+ 99,650
1852	951,726	767,974	+183,752
1853	775,322	571,315	+204,007
1854	945,849	377,358	+568,491
1855	790,330	644,784	+145,546
1856	971,028	841,254	+129,774
1857	1,345,361	976,306	+369,055
1858	1,468,449	1,225,118	+243,331
1859	1,255,571	1,049,236	+206,335
1860	984,294	941,761	+ 42,533
1861	1,075,374	923,874	+151,500
1862	1,067,612	913,141	+154,471
1863	981,142	878,208	+102,934
1864	925,957	910,081	+ 15,876
1865	1,161,159	953,334	+207,825
1866	1,246,844	988,081	+258,763
1867	1,245,501	989,503	+255,998
1868	1,269,674	1,134,257	+135,417
1869	935,424	1,026,220	− 90,796
1870	973,020	1,069,867	− 96,847
1871	1,298,546	1,191,888	+106,658
1872	1,021,443	1,125,030	−103,587
1873	1,024,083	1,193,814	−169,731
1874	1,140,767	1,049,248	+ 91,519
1875	1,474,910	1,187,493	+287,417
1876	964,262	1,027,873	− 63,611
1877	1,097,912	1,144,133	− 46,221
1878	1,078,411	1,102,732	− 24,321
1879[a]			
1880	1,166,389	1,170,736	− 4,347
1881	1,140,361	1,119,213	+ 21,148
1882	1,192,295	1,162,866	+ 29,429
1883	1,141,138	1,155,341	− 14,203

SOURCES: Same as Appendix 1 and *PP*, 1852, 51:442.
a. Figure(s) missing at time of research.
b. Figure does not include goods of British origin.

Appendix 3. Barbadian Exports to Various Countries, 1832–75 (£)

Year	Great Britain Including Ireland	British West Indies	British North America	U.S.A.	Total[a]
1832	283,642	108,158	7,101	6,024	408,363
1833	417,991	121,688	5,442	7,328	553,628
1834	609,990	111,321	5,587	6,464	736,006
1835[b]					
1836	621,362	112,271	2,763	11,928	749,193
1837	773,077	110,619	10,710	1,024	897,990
1838	838,215	112,215	5,362	1,458	960,368
1839	595,269	133,837	515	50	731,262
1840[b]					
1841	408,984	115,834	751	2,532	531,872
1842	717,818	134,514	122	289	855,712
1843	539,756	119,269	24	1,548	668,256
1844	539,674	134,799	152	1,258	681,000
1845	548,527	129,193	2,821	1,750	691,309
1846	609,788	157,709	190	2,848	773,405
1847	714,514	149,102	3,600	3,442	881,159
1848	554,251	95,762	1,342	5,192	659,073
1849	652,941	133,347	697	1,552	791,744
1850	672,881	151,872	1,444	2,014	831,534
1851	714,693	163,028	4,472	3,066	887,627
1852	783,801	146,986	6,115	13,002	951,726
1853	607,550	151,592	1,170	8,825	775,322
1854	782,156	135,313	6,359	9,400	945,849
1855	572,243	150,725	12,885	46,602	790,330
1856	660,959	152,426	29,014	74,510	971,028
1857	937,822	183,167	29,412	92,919	1,345,361
1858	1,096,762	195,444	31,757	58,058	1,468,449
1859	820,998	193,766	46,096	62,799	1,225,571
1860	666,756	158,823	29,944	55,445	984,294
1861	791,575	131,577	25,744	31,941	1,075,374
1862	699,656	169,369	56,892	83,716	1,067,612
1863	629,257	180,890	23,477	69,204	981,142
1864	548,952	170,602	35,036	91,097	925,957
1865	702,317	190,715	37,985	137,303	1,161,159
1866	817,980	178,070	44,299	118,298	1,246,844
1867	796,990	200,058	36,352	109,521	1,245,501
1868	666,496	198,230	138,643	199,552	1,269,674
1869	447,705	201,131	78,971	145,369	935,424
1870	544,455	193,947	65,256	110,177	973,020
1871	609,868	245,260	140,822	229,173	1,298,546
1872	470,525	221,167	124,170	107,624	1,021,443
1873	471,175	273,488	67,740	125,640	1,024,083
1874	559,566	190,324	91,224	207,604	1,140,767
1875	782,434	210,159	119,866	266,417	1,474,910

SOURCES: Same as Appendix 1.
a. Totals include exports to some countries not listed above.
b. Figures missing at time of research.

Appendix 4. Barbados' Imports from Various Countries, 1832–75 (£)

Year	Great Britain Including Ireland	British West Indies	British North America	U.S.A.	Peru[a]	Total[b]
1832	238,660	32,692	55,070	134,468		481,610
1833	272,672	31,508	73,728	62,208		461,135
1834	261,525	21,312	57,447	93,354		449,790
1835[c]						
1836	416,264	35,206	67,516	82,931		630,157
1837	390,590	19,666	71,752	92,414		606,586
1838	483,134	22,005	82,410	83,632		730,763
1839	64,611[d]	39,283	88,572	10,153		[c]
1840[c]						
1841	51,680[d]	28,738	75,488	121,955		[c]
1842	33,805[d]	28,743	69,352	108,434		[c]
1843	359,413	21,869	53,406	162,364		617,131
1844	338,381	23,538	39,742	161,252		604,410
1845	358,795	3,518	39,348	188,686		682,368
1846	320,590	39,494	33,730	201,211		631,267
1847	289,276	49,405	37,193	155,762		561,261
1848	212,585	32,441	39,475	111,130		432,016
1849	374,480	29,038	45,418	122,387		591,478
1850	464,651	36,235	48,690	128,173		734,385
1851	546,582	38,240	48,205	130,188		787,977
1852	489,282	43,191	27,771	141,035		767,974
1853	312,119	40,470	49,501	140,893		571,315
1854[c]						377,358
1855	296,098	61,733	53,226	199,944		644,784
1856	351,439	49,504	72,069	274,030	39,000	841,254
1857	475,855	45,790	101,393	244,933	11,750	976,306
1858	631,756	57,992	78,803	411,675	64,224	1,225,118
1859	447,124	57,427	77,020	375,975	28,870	1,049,236
1860	420,266	51,180	75,895	316,215	7,750	941,761
1861	369,651	48,231	85,286	330,308	[c]	923,874
1862	343,845	49,314	80,989	361,514	[c]	913,141
1863	304,174	45,440	41,292	393,106	24,750	878,208
1864	363,109	51,835	81,525	[c]	[c]	[c]
1865	366,053	49,407	86,099	346,107	49,900	953,334
1866	379,724	48,631	86,733	343,270	51,000	988,081
1867	389,543	52,573	78,754	356,379	52,600	989,503
1868	396,297	58,820	88,661	448,781	53,967	1,134,257
1869	344,875	57,846	77,440	392,976	70,000	1,026,220
1870	413,908	53,197	72,468	343,160	106,165	1,069,867
1871	546,396	37,164	79,882	417,308	45,650	1,191,888
1872	470,508	47,263	90,068	421,936	20,450	1,125,030
1873	365,189	52,106	78,210	485,275	129,725	1,193,814
1874	384,782	36,452	80,745	457,482	25,093	1,049,248
1875	443,090	35,704	92,562	483,235	63,500	1,187,493

SOURCES: Same as Appendix 1.
a. *Barbados Blue Books* do not provide import figures from Peru for 1832–55.
b. Totals include figures from countries not listed above.
c. Figures missing at time of research.
d. Figure does not include goods of British origin.

Appendix 5. Sugar Exported from Barbados, 1823–78

Year	Hogsheads[a]	Year	Hogsheads[a]
1823	24,257 (15,370)	1851	38,922 (29,192)
1824	20,256 (11,986)	1852	48,785 (37,150)
1825	22,590 (13,240)	1853	34,692 (29,003)
1826	20,220 (12,008)	1854	41,839 (33,323)
1827	17,010 (9,950)	1855	37,071 (29,628)
1828	26,789 (16,242)	1856	43,582 (31,622)
1829	22,545 (13,220)	1857	38,885 (29,181)
1830	25,111 (16,844)	1858	50,027 (37,712)
1831	26,096 (16,139)	1859	40,343 (29,568)
1832	18,757 (13,325)	1860	43,365 (32,352)
1833	27,022 (19,349)	1861	49,845 (39,705)
1834	27,318 (19,728)	1862	46,078 (35,062)
1835	24,189 (17,234)	1863	42,036 (32,500)
1836	24,815 (18,621)	1864	36,199 (26,980)
1837	31,320 (22,286)	1865	46,068 (41,307)
1838	31,786 (23,679)	1866	57,188 (50,105)
1839	27,231 (19,755)	1867	51,304 (46,725)
1840	13,319 (10,374)	1868	58,250 (50,960)
1841	17,140 (12,855)	1869	32,150 (26,465)
1842	21,545 (15,628)	1870	39,360 (34,363)
1843	23,233 (17,452)	1871	53,788 (47,166)
1844	21,913 (16,435)	1872	39,167 (34,372)
1845	23,432 (17,590)	1873	37,337 (32,669)
1846	20,016 (15,124)	1874	47,289 (41,337)
1847	32,257 (23,451)	1875	65,012 (56,875)
1848	26,887 (20,165)	1876	37,848 (32,676)
1849	32,574 (24,456)	1877	47,260 (43,545)
1850	34,976 (26,232)	1878	43,508 (38,073)

SOURCES: Same as Appendix 1; *PP*, 1852, 51:442; Schomburgk, *Barbados,* p. 150; Deerr, *History of Sugar,* 1:194.
a. Figures in parentheses represent the number of tons estimated by Deerr.

Appendix 6. Sugar Estates Sold in Barbados, 1851–96

Year	No. Estates Sold	Acreage	Average Price per Acre (£)
1851	44	8,356	51
1852	2	313	48
1853	—	—	—
1854	8	1,744	56
1855	7	1,865	46
1856	28	5,982	51
1857	23	5,452	58
1858	21	2,496	65
1859	20	4,037	65
1860	7	373	86
1861	11	2,601	46
1862	12	2,260	57
1863	15	2,607	41
1864	10	2,092	56
1865	9	2,115	50
1866	6	864	62
1867	16	2,841	57
1868	15	2,192	60
1869	12	2,337	47
1870	5	1,126	49
1871	8	1,611	61
1872	21	3,356	56
1873	8	1,425	53
1874	3	297	45
1875	7	1,892	49
1876	5	1,283	70
1877	7	811	64
1878	2	808	47
1879	—	—	—
1880	19	3,076	68
1881	12	1,613	46
1882	3	308	54
1883	3	519	53
1884	7	1,261	65
1885	—	—	—
1886	9	1,164	63
1887	3	413	26
1888	12	1,329	39
1889	36	5,629	42
1890	32	4,270	44
1891	7	1,442	26
1892	11	1,563	26
1893	23	4,899	35
1894	17	2,425	35
1895	5	522	28
1896	16	2,291	27

SOURCE: C. 8657, App. C, pt. 3, p. 207.

Appendix 7. Population Statistics, Barbados, 1851–71

A. Population of Barbados, 1851–71

Year	Population	Rate of Population Growth (%)
1851	135,939	
1861	152,275 (152,727)[a]	12.0
1871	161,559 (162,042)[a]	6.1

a. Statistics appearing in parentheses have been corrected to match figures in the *Barbados Blue Books,* 1851–71, CO 33/61–81.

B. Rate of Population Growth in Barbados by Race, 1851–71

Racial Group	Rate of Change 1851–61 (%)	Rate of Change 1861–71 (%)
White	+ 5.0	−0.2
Colored	+20.0	+9.5
Black	+11.0	+5.0

C. Racial Composition of Barbados, 1851–71

Year	No. White	% White	No. Colored	% Colored	No. Black	% Black
1851	15,824	11.7	30,059	22.1	90,056	66.2
1861	16,594	10.9	36,128	23.6	100,005	65.5
1871	16,560	10.2	39,528	24.4	105,904	66.4

D. Population of Barbados by Occupation, 1871 [a]

Agricultural workers	42,270
Unemployed	40,829
At school	29,080
Domestics	14,486
Seamstresses	8,868
Engineers and mechanics	6,848
Traders and hucksters	4,620
Washerwomen	3,795
Proprietors and administrative employees	1,863
Sailors	1,720
Porters	1,558
Artisans	1,449
Accountants	953
Various	1,633
Military	777
Professional and teachers	569
Civil officers	446
Other laborers	231

a. There may be minor inaccuracies in the figures given by Rawson.

E. Area and Population of the Parishes of Barbados, 1871

Parish	Area in Sq. Miles	% of Population
St. Philip	14.1	10.7
Christ Church	13.4	11.2
St. Michael (including Bridgetown)	9.0	30.4
St. George	10.2	8.8
St. Andrew	8.3	4.7
St. Lucy	8.2	5.5
St. Thomas	8.0	6.3
St. Peter	7.8	5.8
St. James	7.3	5.6
St. Joseph	5.6	5.0
St. John	8.1	6.0

F. Population Densities of the British West Indies, 1871

Colony	Density per Sq. Mile
Barbados	906
St. Kitts	412
Antigua	318
Grenada	284
St. Vincent	250
Tobago	175
St. Lucia	127
Dominica	93
Trinidad	62
British Guiana	25
Bahamas	9

SOURCE: Rawson to Kimberley, 22 August 1872, CO 28/216.

Appendix 8.   Governors of Barbados, 1821–85[a]

Sir Henry Warde, 1821–27
Sir James Lyon, 1828–33
Sir Lionel Smith, 1833–36
Sir Evan Murray MacGregor, 1836–41
Charles Henry Darling, Acting Governor, 1841
Sir Charles Edward Grey, 1841–46
William Reid, 1846–48
Sir William Colebrooke, 1848–51
K. G. Hamilton, 1851–52
Sir William Colebrooke, 1853–56
Francis Hincks, 1856–62
James Walker, 1862–68
Robert M. Mundy, Acting Governor, 1868–69
Rawson W. Rawson, 1869–75
Sandford Freeling, Acting Governor, 1875
John Pope Hennessy, 1875–76
Henry Dundas, Acting Governor, 1877
George G. Strahan, 1877–80
William Robinson, 1880–85

a. Knighthood indicated if applicable during the individual's term as governor of Barbados.

Bibliographical Essay

MUCH OF THE information in this book was derived from Colonial Office materials at the Public Record Office in London. The largest part of these manuscript sources are located in the CO 28 classification, which includes the dispatches of the governors of Barbados and other official reports and correspondence from the colony to the secretary of state for colonies. Barbadian governors wrote often and in great detail, and many of their dispatches contained enclosures written by other officials, such as local bishops, rectors, prison wardens, superintendents of emigration, justices of the peace, education inspectors, and harbor masters. The governors' communications likewise contained newspaper clippings and numerous letters from private individuals. The original correspondence in the CO 28 classification, encompassing the period 1689–1873, is important because virtually every dispatch and communication was endorsed in London with the minutes of such influential civil servants as Sir James Stephen and Sir Henry Taylor. Comments by the secretaries of state and the parliamentary under secretaries likewise frequently appear with the governors' dispatches. From these confidential observations, the researcher is able to obtain a picture of the behind-the-scene reactions in London and of the stages by which an exchange of opinions among high officials led to policy-making. With the correspondence in the CO 28 classification are the drafts of replies drawn up by the Colonial Office experts as the final version of the secretary's responses to the governors took shape. The evolution of the final draft, therefore, gives the researcher insight impossible to obtain by reading the printed versions that were sometimes produced in the *Parliamentary Papers.* The CO 29 classification, the official register of out-letters from the colonial office to the Barbadian governors, contains little more than the final drafts that were sent out over the signature of the secretary of state.

Other information is found in the circular dispatches sent from London to the governors in the West Indies. These papers are located in the CO 854 classification. The CO 30 documents provide copies of acts passed by the Barbadian legislature, but the notes on these documents do not always show clearly whether an act was confirmed or disallowed after reaching London. The CO 31 classification is helpful because it provides the debates and session papers of the council and assembly. From these materials, the researcher is able to discover attitudes of individual members of the legislature and to study the contents of the reports of numerous boards and committees. Such reports are particularly important because they encompass a wide range of problems—finance, taxation, public works, trade, agriculture, religion, education, health, military defense, and so forth. Other statistical details concerning exports, imports, births, deaths, food costs, expenditures, and revenues are located in the CO 33 classification under the title *Barbados Blue Books.*

In my search for information of an unofficial character, the *Minutes of the West India Planters* and the *Minutes of the West India Planters and Merchants* supplied an insight into the concerns of absentee planters and London sugar traders. Such materials are especially helpful for the period preceding emancipation, but they do not contribute much information on the period following the end of slavery. Similarly, an extensive investigation of such private manuscript sources as the Russell Papers did not disclose anything significantly different from what was learned from Colonial Office materials.

For the scholar interested in demographic and topographical data, there is an abundance of materials in Barbados. My needs for such information were filled by statistics found in the *Barbados Blue Books.* Some of the records of local government agencies, such as the Department of Education and the General Hospital, are found at the Barbados Department of Archives, which also possesses portions of the papers of the Barbadian legislature. Practically all of the latter are reproduced in the *Journals of the Barbados General Legislature,* which, as mentioned, are located in the CO 31 classification at the Public Record Office. Some of the most important private papers in Barbados consist of items gathered by Judge Nathanial Lucas in the period 1818–28. The Barbados Public Library, the Barbados Museum and Historical Society, and the island's Department of Archives possess materials that date back to the colony's early history. Many of these resources have been ably used by such scholars as Richard S. Dunn and Jerome S. Handler. But apart from numerous extracts from Barbadian newspapers and a few other helpful items that H.A. Vaughan supplied to me, the primary materials located in Barbados were not fully relevant to my interest in the period after 1834. Handler's *A Guide to Source Materials for the Study of Barbados History, 1627–1834* makes it clear that many records in Barbados are incomplete and poorly organized for research.

Second to St. Kitts as the oldest British colony in the Caribbean Sea, Barbados did not until recently attract the same interest of historians as did Jamaica. This does not mean that authoritative accounts of Barbados are altogether lacking, but the majority of such works have concentrated on the island's early years as a British possession or on very specialized topics. Among the important scholars who have shown an awareness of the early period are N. Darnell Davis, John Poyer, and Vincent Todd Harlow. Jerome Handler has also authored a study entitled *The Unappropriated People: Freedmen in the Slave Society of Barbados*, and more recently he joined Frederick W. Lange to produce an eminent work, *Plantation Slavery in Barbados: An Archaeological and Historical Investigation*. Otis P. Starkey's *The Economic Geography of Barbados* is another example of a study of a specialized nature, as are Bruce Hamilton's *Barbados and the Confederation Question, 1871–1885* and Sidney Greenfield's *English Rustics in Black Skin*. The only published work that can be cited as a general history of the island is Robert H. Schomburgk's *The History of Barbados*; it is a narrow statistical and topographical account and provides only a chronicle of the political and economic trends from early colonial times to 1846. My own investigation is also somewhat confined, but I hope that it may supply an adequate overview from 1833 to 1876.

1. PUBLIC RECORD OFFICE MANUSCRIPTS, CHANCERY LANE, LONDON
CO   7. Original correspondence concerning Antigua, 1702–1872.
CO   23. Original correspondence concerning the Bahamas, 1696–1919.
CO   28. Original correspondence concerning Barbados, 1689–1873, 1886–1912. For the years 1874–85, see CO 321.
CO   29. Entry books of correspondence from the Colonial Office to Barbados, 1627–1872.
CO   30. Barbados Acts, 1643–1919.
CO   31. Barbados sessional papers, including the *Journals of the Barbados General Assembly*, 1660–1919.
CO   33. Barbados miscellanea, including the *Barbados Blue Books*, 1678–1919.
CO   71. Original correspondence concerning Dominica, 1730–1872.
CO 101. Original correspondence concerning Grenada, 1747–1873.
CO 111. Original correspondence concerning British Guiana, 1781–1919.
CO 137. Original correspondence concerning Jamaica, 1689–1919.
CO 152. Original correspondence concerning the Leeward Islands, 1689–1919.
CO 253. Original correspondence concerning St. Lucia, 1709–1873.

CO 260. Original correspondence concerning St. Vincent, 1663–1873.
CO 285. Original correspondence concerning Tobago, 1700–1873.
CO 295. Original correspondence concerning Trinidad, 1783–1919.
CO 321. Original correspondence concerning the Windward Islands, 1874–1919, including correspondence pertaining to Barbados, 1874–85.
CO 854. Circular dispatches from the Colonial Office to the West India Colonies, 1808–73.

2. MANUSCRIPT SOURCES AT THE WEST INDIA COMMITTEE LIBRARY, 18 GROSVENOR STREET, LONDON

Minute Books of the West India Merchants, 1826–43.
Minute Books of the West India Planters and Merchants, 1826–43.
Minute Books of the West India Committee, 1843–80.

3. OFFICIAL PRINTED SOURCES

Great Britain House of Commons Sessional Papers, referred to as *Parliamentary Papers (PP)*, 1790–1898.
Great Britain Parliamentary Debates, referred to as Hansard, 1790–1890.
Great Britain, Papers Published by Command of the Crown, referred to as *Command Papers (C.)*, 1870–1900.

4. NEWSPAPERS (Dates indicate the years during which the newspaper contributed significant information.)

The Agricultural Reporter (Bridgetown), 1870–78.
The Barbadian (Bridgetown), 1822–58.
The Barbados Mercury (Bridgetown), 1833–47.
The Barbados Globe and Colonial Advocate (Bridgetown), 1830–36.
The Barbados Times (Bridgetown), 1870–76.
The Daily Globe (Toronto), 1876.
The Liberal (Bridgetown), 1837–59.
The Times (London), 1846.
The West Indian (Bridgetown), 1833–35.

5. SELECT LIST OF UNOFFICIAL PUBLISHED SOURCES RELATING TO THE BRITISH WEST INDIES

Adamson, Alan H. *Sugar without Slaves: The Political Economy of British Guiana, 1838–1904*. New Haven: Yale University Press, 1972.
Aspinall, Algernon. *Pocket Guide to the West Indies*. London: West India Committee, 1927.
Bennett, J.H., Jr. *Bondsmen and Bishops: Slavery and Apprenticeship on the Codrington Plantations of Barbados, 1710–1838*. Berkeley: University of California Press, 1958.
Boxer, C.R. *The Golden Age of Brazil, 1695–1750*. Berkeley: University of California Press, 1969.
Burn, William L. *Emancipation and Apprenticeship in the British West Indies*. London: Jonathan Cape, 1937.
Burns, Alan. *History of the British West Indies*. London: George Allen & Unwin, 1954.
Butcher, Thomas. *"Mordichim," or Recollections of Cholera in Barbados during the Middle of the Year 1854*. London, 1855.
Caldecott, Alfred. *The Church in the West Indies*. London, 1898.

Carmichael, A.C. (Mrs.). *Domestic Manners and Social Conditions of the White, Coloured, and Negro Population of the West Indies*. 2 vols. London, 1834.

Chandler, Michael J. *A Guide to Records in Barbados*. Oxford: Basil Blackwell, 1965.

Clarke, Charles P. *The Constitutional Crisis of 1876 in Barbados*. Bridgetown, Barbados, 1896.

Clarkson, Thomas. *The History of the Rise, Progress, and Accomplishment of the Abolition of the African Slave Trade*. 2 vols. London, 1808.

Coke, Thomas. *A History of the West Indies with an Account of the Missions*. 3 vols. London, 1810–11.

Coleridge, Henry N. *Six Months in the West Indies in 1825*. London, 1826.

Cowen, D.W., and Green, J.P., eds. *Neither Slave nor Free: The Role of the Free Black and the Free Mulatto in American Slave Societies*. Baltimore and London: Johns Hopkins University Press, 1972.

Curtin, Philip D. "The British Sugar Duties and West Indian Prosperity." *Journal of Economic History* 14 (1954): 157–64.

———. *Two Jamaicas: The Role of Ideas in a Tropical Colony*. Cambridge: Harvard University Press, 1955.

Davies, K.G. *The Royal Africa Company*. New York and London: Longmans, Green, 1957.

Davis, David B. *The Problem of Slavery in Western Culture*. Ithaca, N.Y.: Cornell University Press, 1968.

Davis, N. Darnell. *The Cavaliers and Roundheads of Barbados, 1650–1652, with Some Account of the Early History of Barbados*. Georgetown, British Guiana, 1887.

Davy, John. *The West Indies before and since Slave Emancipation*. London, 1854.

Deerr, Noel. *A History of Sugar*. 2 vols. London: Chapman & Hall, Ltd., 1949–50.

Degler, Carl. *Neither White nor Black*. New York: Macmillan Company, 1971.

Dunn, Richard. "The Barbados Census of 1680: Profile of the Richest Colony in English America." *William and Mary Quarterly*, 3d ser. 26 (1969): 3–30.

———. *Sugar and Slaves: The Rise of the Planter Class in the English West Indies, 1624–1713*. Chapel Hill: University of North Carolina Press, 1972.

Du Tertre, Jean B. *Histoire général des Antilles habitées par les François*. 4 vols. Paris, 1667–71.

Edwards, Bryan. *The History, Civil and Commercial of the British Colonies in the West Indies*. 2 vols. London, 1793.

Elkins, Stanley M. *Slavery: A Problem in American Institutional Life*. Chicago: University of Chicago Press, 1959.

Eltis, D. "Traffic in Slaves between the British West India Colonies, 1807–1833." *Economic History Review*, 2d ser. 25 (1972): 55–64.

Goveia, Elsa V. *Slave Societies in the British Leeward Islands at the End of the Eighteenth Century*. New Haven and London: Yale University Press, 1965.

———. "The West Indian Slave Laws of the Eighteenth Century." *Revista de Ciencias Sociales* 4 (1960): 75–105.

Green, William A. "The Apprenticeship in British Guiana, 1834–1838." *Caribbean Studies* 9 (1969): 44–66.

———. *British Slave Emancipation: The Sugar Colonies and the Great Experiment, 1830–1865*. Oxford: Clarendon Press, 1976.

———. "The Planter Class and British West Indian Sugar Production before and after Emancipation." *Economic History Review*, 2d ser. 26 (1973): 448–63.

Greenfield, Sidney M. *English Rustics in Black Skin*. New Haven: College & University Press, 1968.

Guillebaud, C.W. "The Crown Colonies, 1845–1870." In *The Cambridge History of the British Empire*, 2:473–524. Cambridge, England, 1940.

Hall, Douglas. *Five of the Leewards, 1834–1870: The Major Problems of the Post-Emancipation Period in Antigua, Barbados, Montserrat, Nevis, and St. Kitts*. St. Lawrence, Barbados: Caribbean Universities Press, 1971.

———. *Free Jamaica, 1838–1865: An Economic History*. New Haven: Yale University Press, 1959.

———. "Slaves and Slavery in the British West Indies." *Social and Economic Studies* 2 (1962); 305–18.

Hall, Gwendolyn. *Social Control in Slave Plantation Societies*. Baltimore and London: Johns Hopkins University Press, 1971.

Hall, Neville. "Law and Society in Barbados at the Turn of the Century." *Journal of Caribbean History*. 5 (1972): 20–45.

Hall, Richard, ed. *Acts Passed on the Island of Barbados from 1643 to 1762 Inclusive*. London, 1764.

———. *A General Account of the First Settlement and the Trade and Constitution of the Island of Barbados, Written in the Year 1755; with a Foreword by E.M. Shilston*. Bridgetown, Barbados, 1924.

[Hamden, Renn]. *A Report of a Select Committee of the Council of Barbados Appointed to Inquire into the Actual Condition of the Slaves of this Island*. London, 1824.

Hamilton, Bruce. *Barbados and the Confederation Question, 1871–1885*. London: Crown Agents for Overseas Governments and Administrations, 1956.

Hamshere, Cyril. *The British in the Caribbean*. Cambridge: Harvard University Press, 1972.

Handler, Jerome S. "The Amerindian Slave Population of Barbados in the Seventeenth and Early Eighteenth Centuries." *Caribbean Studies* 8 (1969): 38–64.

———. *A Guide to Source Materials for the Study of Barbados History, 1627–1834*. Carbondale and Edwardsville, Ill.: Southern Illinois University Press, 1971.

———. "Some Aspects of Work Organization on the Sugar Plantations of Barbados." *Ethnology* 4 (1965): 16–38.

———. *The Unappropriated People: Freedmen in the Slave Society of Barbados*. Baltimore and London: John Hopkins University Press, 1974.

Handler, Jerome S., and Frisbie, Charlotte J. "Aspects of Slave Life in Barbados: Music and its Cultural Context." *Caribbean Studies* 11 (1972): 5–46.

Handler, Jerome S., and Lange, Frederick W. *Plantation Slavery in Barbados: An Archaeological and Historical Investigation*. Cambridge: Harvard University Press, 1978.

Harlow, Vincent T. *A History of Barbados, 1625–1685*. Oxford: Clarendon Press, 1926.

———. *Christopher Codrington*. Oxford: Clarendon Press, 1928.

Harris, Marvin. *Patterns of Race in America*. New York: Walker and Company, 1964.

Herskovits, Melville J. *The Myth of the Negro Past*. New York: Harper and Brothers, 1941.

Higham, Charles S. *The Development of the Leeward Islands under the Restoration*. Cambridge: Cambridge University Press, 1921.

Hughes, Colin. "Experiments towards Closer Union in the British West Indies." *Journal of Negro History* 43 (1958): 85–104.

Jordan, G.W. *An Examination of the Principles of the Slave Registry Bill, and of the Means of Emancipation Proposed by the Authors of the Bill*. London, 1816.

Keith, A.B. *Constitutional History of the First British Empire*. Oxford: Clarendon Press, 1930.

Klineberg, F.G. *The Anti-Slavery Movement in England*. New Haven: Yale University Press, 1926.

Knaplund, Paul. *James Stephen and the British Colonial System, 1813–1847*. Madison: University of Wisconsin Press, 1953.

Knight, Franklin. *Slave Society in Cuba during the Nineteenth Century*. Madison: University of Wisconsin Press, 1970.

Labaree, Leonard. *Royal Government in America*. New York: Frederick Ungar Publishing Company, 1964.

Levy, Claude. "Barbados: The Last Years of Slavery, 1823–1833." *Journal of Negro History* 44 (1959): 308–45.

———. "Slavery and the Emancipation Movement in Barbados, 1650–1833." *Journal of Negro History* 55 (1970): 1–14.

Ligon, Richard. *A True and Exact History of the Island of Barbados*. London, 1657.

Lobdell, Richard A. "Patterns of Investment and Sources of Credit in the British West Indies Sugar Industry, 1838–97." *Journal of Caribbean History* 4 (1972): 31–53.

Long, Edward. *The History of Jamaica*. London, 1774.

McKinnen, Daniel. *A Tour of the British West Indies in the Years 1802–1803.* London, 1804.
McPherson, James M. "Was West Indian Emancipation a Success? The Abolitionist Argument during the American Civil War." *Caribbean Studies* 4 (1964): 28–34.
Marshall, Woodville K. "The Termination of the Apprenticeship System in Barbados and the Windward Islands: An Essay on Colonial Administration and Politics." *Journal of Caribbean History* 2 (1970): 112–28.
Mathew, W.M. "Peru and the British Guano Market, 1840–1870." *Economic History Review,* 2d ser. 23 (1970): 112–28.
Mathieson, W.L. *British Slave Emancipation, 1838–1849.* London: Longmans, Green, 1932.
———. *British Slavery and Its Abolition, 1828–1838.* London: Longmans, Green, 1926.
———. "The Emancipation of the Slaves, 1807–1838." In *The Cambridge History of the British Empire,* 2: 309–34. Cambridge: Cambridge University Press, 1940.
———. *The Sugar Colonies and Governor Eyre, 1848–1866.* London: Longmans, Green, 1936.
Mintz, Sidney. "The Question of Caribbean Peasantries: A Comment." *Caribbean Studies* 1 (1961): 31–34.
———. "Slavery and Slaves." *Caribbean Studies* 8 (1969): 65–70.
Moohr, Michael. "The Economic Impact of Slave Emancipation in British Guiana, 1832–1852." *Economic History Review,* 2d ser. 25 (1972): 588–607.
Morrell, W.P. *British Colonial Policy in the Age of Peel and Russell.* Oxford: Clarendon Press, 1930.
———. *British Colonial Policy in the Mid-Victorian Age.* Oxford: Clarendon Press, 1969.
Morris, Daniel. *Reports on the Economic Resources of the West Indies.* London, 1898.
Murray, D.J. *The West Indies and the Development of Colonial Government, 1801–1834.* Oxford: Clarendon Press, 1965.
Newton, Arthur P. *The European Nations in the West Indies, 1493–1688.* London: A. & C. Black, 1933.
Oldmixon, John. *The British Empire in America.* 2 vols. London, 1741.
Pares, Richard. *War and Trade in the West Indies, 1739–1763.* Oxford: Clarendon Press, 1936.
———. *A West India Fortune.* London: Longmans, Green, 1950.
Parry, J.H., and Sherlock, P.M. *A Short History of the West Indies.* London: Macmillan Company, 1957.
Penson, Lillian M. *The Colonial Agents of the British West Indies.* London: University of London Press, 1924.
Phillippo, James C. *Jamaica: Its Past and Present State.* London, 1843.
Phillips, U.B. *American Negro Slavery.* New York: D. Appleton, 1918.
———. *Life and Labor in the Old South.* Boston: Little, Brown and Company, 1929.
Pierson, Donald. *Negroes in Brazil.* Chicago: University of Chicago Press, 1942.
Pinckard, George. *Notes on the West Indies.* 2 vols. London, 1806.
Pitman, Frank W. *The Development of the British West Indies, 1700–1763.* New Haven: Yale University Press, 1917.
———. "Slavery on the British West India Plantations in the Eighteenth Century." *Journal of Negro History* 11 (1926): 584–688.
Poyer, John. *History of Barbados from the First Discovery of the Island in the Year 1605, till the Accession of Lord Seaforth, 1801.* London, 1808.
Ragatz, Lowell J. *The Fall of the Planter Class in the British Caribbean, 1763–1833.* New York: Century Co., 1928.
Reckford, Mary. "The Colonial Office and the Abolition of Slavery." *Historical Journal* 14 (1971): 723–34.
Reece, J.E., and Clark-Hunt, C.G., eds. *Barbados Diocesan History in Commemoration of the First Centenary of the Diocese, 1825–1925.* London: West India Committee, 1925.
Rice, C.D. "Humanity Sold for Sugar! The British Abolitionist Response to Free Trade in Slave Grown Sugar." *Historical Journal* 13 (1970): 402–18.
Roughly, Thomas. *The Jamaica Planter's Guide.* London, 1823.
Savage, Raymond. *Barbados, British West Indies.* London: Arthur Barker, 1936.
Schomburgk, Robert H. *The History of Barbados.* London, 1848.

Schutz, J.A. "Christopher Codrington's Will: Launching the S.P.G. into the Barbadian Sugar Business." *Pacific Historical Review* 15 (1946): 192–200.

Sewell, William G. *The Ordeal of Free Labor in the British West Indies*. New York, 1861.

Sheridan, Richard B. "The West India Sugar Crisis and British Slave Emancipation, 1830–1833." *Journal of Economic History* 21 (1961): 539–51.

Sires, Ronald V. "Negro Labor in Jamaica Following Emancipation." *Journal of Negro History* 25 (1940): 484–97.

Smith, M.G. *The Plural Society in the British West Indies*. Berkeley: University of California Press, 1965.

Spurdle, F.G. *Early West Indian Government*. Palmerston North, New Zealand: published by the author, n.d.

Stampp, Kenneth M. *The Peculiar Institution: Slavery in the Ante-Bellum South*. New York: Alfred A. Knopf, Inc., 1956.

Starkey, Otis P. *The Economic Geography of Barbados*. New York: Columbia University Press, 1939.

Sturge, Joseph, and Harvey, Thomas. *The West Indies in 1837*. London, 1838.

Tannenbaum, Frank. *Slave and Citizen: The Negro in the Americas*. New York: Alfred A. Knopf, Inc., 1947.

Thome, James A., and Kimball, J.H. *Emancipation in the West Indies: A Six Month's Tour in Antigua, Barbados, and Jamaica in the Year 1837*. New York, 1838.

Tree, Ronald. *A History of Barbados*. London: Hart-Davis, 1972.

Wesley, Charles H. "The Emancipation of the Free Colored Population of the British Empire." *Journal of Negro History* 19 (1934): 137–71.

Whitson, Agnes M. *The Constitutional Development of Jamaica*. Manchester: Manchester University Press, 1929.

Wood, Donald. *Trinidad in Transition: The Years after Slavery*. London and New York: Institute of Race Relations, 1968.

Wrong, Hume. *Government of the West Indies*. Oxford: Clarendon Press, 1923.

Index

158; on political reform, 144, 145; friction
with Kimberley, 145, 147; departure of,
148
Records, accuracy of, 2, 4, 41,43
"Red legs," 5
Reeves, William Conrad, 119
Refineries, 106, 158
Reform Act, 28
Registry bill, 20
Reid, William: appointed governor, 103; on
agricultural methods, 103-4; on sugar
tariffs, 105; resignation of, 105; on
indebtedness of planters, 110
Religion: influences treatment of slaves, 8;
effects of r. on inhabitants, 14, 15, 47, 130;
financial support of r. by Barbados
legislature, 15, 16, 90, 131, 158; differences
in West Indies compared, 131, 158. *See
also* Anglican Church; Baptists;
Methodists; Roman Catholic Church;
Quakers
Roads, 99-100. *See also* map, 34
Roman Catholic Church: influence on
treatment of slaves, 8; and Catholic
Emancipation Act, 25, 28; influence
on Trinidad, 47; financial support by
Barbados legislature, 131
Royal Africa Company, 3
Rum, 26, 88-89
Runaways, 37
Russell, Lord John: on Negroes' ownership
of land, 79; on emigration policy, 82-83;
on colonial laws, 83; on need for
eliminating Negroes' grievances, 85; on
courts of reconciliation, 86; on Anglican
clergy, 90; favorable attitude toward
planters, 101; interest in federation, 139

St. Johns (Antigua), 138
St. Kitts: amelioration in, 24; runaways in,
37; disorders in, 37, 58; slave emancipation in, 37, 70; number of Anglican
clergy in, 46; number of schools in, 48;
slave compensation paid to, 55; number
of laborers in, 56; apprenticeship in, 58,
70; contract law of, 72; soil fertility of,
93; West Indian Encumbered Estates
Court in, 107; sugar production in, 108;
wages in, 113. *See also* Leeward Islands
St. Lucia: amelioration in, 21; apprenticeship in, 43; available land in, 46;
number of schools in, 48; slave compensation paid to, 55; number of laborers in,
56; metayer system in, 108; sugar production in, 108; wages in, 113; disorders
in, 129; attitude on federation, 144. *See
also* Windward Islands
St. Michael Parish, 37
St. Paul's Meal Society, 93
St. Philip Parish, 20, 75
St. Vincent: amelioration in, 24; number of
Anglican clergy in, 46; number of

schools in, 48; slave compensation paid
to, 55; number of laborers in, 56; contract law of, 72; West Indian Encumbered Estates Court in, 107; sugar
production statistics in, 108; wages in,
113; disorders in, 129; executive committee in, 142; attitude on federation, 144.
See also Windward Islands
Savings bank, 21
Schomburgk, Robert: on Methodists, 16;
on Smith, 57; on the Barbados General
Hospital, 92; railroad project of, 100;
cites number of small landholders, 107;
cites number of estates, 172 n.9
Schools: early examples, 14, 16-20, 47-48;
influence on inhabitants, 14, 17, 37; Anglican, 15, 16, 19, 47-48, 91-92; for slaves,
16, 17, 19; Methodist and Moravian, 16,
17, 91; charity, 17, 19; whites favored by,
17, 19; blacks discriminated against, 17,
19, 48; teachers in, 17, 19, 91, 132; numbers of, 17, 48, 90, 118, 132; supported by
the legislature, 17, 92, 118, 132; curriculum of, 19, 91, 118, 132; supported by
imperial funds, 47-48, 91-92; enrollment
statistics of, 48, 92, 118, 132; Gladstone
on, 92; Governor Grey on, 92; secular
administration of, 92, 118; Earl Grey on,
118; Kay-Shuttleworth on, 118, 132. *See
also* Central schools; Codrington College; Colonial Charity School; Harrison's Free School; Lady Mico's Charity;
Legislature; Laws
Scoble, John, 61-62, 83
Seaforth, Francis, 5-6
Sealy, John, 147, 151
Searle, Daniel, 13
Semper, Hugh, 148
Sewell, W. G., 48, 108, 126, 136
Sharpe, Henry, 52
Sharpe, William, 76
Shrewsbury, William, 22
Silk, 122
Six Points, 149, 150, 151, 153. *See also* Hen-
nessy, John Pope
Slave emancipation: rumored, 20; sought
by the Anti-Slavery Society, 24; opposed
by Canning, 24; officially proposed,
32-33, 35; passed by Parliament, 35; ad-
versely affects free black children, 45;
overall beneficial results, 88. *See also*
Slaves
Slave protector, 23, 24, 25. *See also* Amelioration
Slave revolts, 7
Slaves: and British investors, 1; early numbers of, 1-2; work routine of, 1-5 *passim*,
10-11; American Indians as, 2; Africans
as, 2, 3, 9; best choice enjoyed by Barbados, 3; demand for, 3, 20; feared by
whites, 4, 7, 37, 41; hardships shared
with planters, 5; sexual relations with